Selections from Eliza Leslie

Legacies of Nineteenth-Century
American Women Writers

SERIES EDITOR
Sharon Harris, *University of Connecticut*

ADVISORY EDITOR
Karen Dandurand, *Indiana University of Pennsylvania*

BOARD OF EDITORS
Martha Cutter, *University of Connecticut-Storrs*
Frances Smith Foster, *Emory University*
Susan K. Harris, *University of Kansas*
Mary Kelley, *University of Michigan*
Venetria Patton, *Purdue University*
Karen Sanchez-Eppler, *Amherst College*
Elizabeth Young, *Mt. Holyoke College*

1. Eliza Leslie, as she was presented to readers of *Godey's Lady's Book* in January 1846. A portrait painted by Thomas Sully was the foundation for the engraving. Photo credit: The Library Company of Philadelphia.

Selections from Eliza Leslie

ELIZA LESLIE

Edited and with an introduction
by Etta M. Madden

University of Nebraska Press
Lincoln and London

© 2011 by the Board of Regents
of the University of Nebraska.
All rights reserved. Manufactured in
the United States of America.

LIBRARY OF CONGRESS
Cataloging-in-Publication Data
Leslie, Eliza, 1787–1858.
[Selections. 2011]
Selections from Eliza Leslie /
Eliza Leslie; edited and with an
introduction by Etta M. Madden.
p. cm.
Short stories and miscellaneous essays.
Includes bibliographical references.
ISBN 978-0-8032-3295-2 (pbk.: alk. paper)
1. Cooking, American. 2. Handicraft.
3. Etiquette for women.
I. Madden, Etta M., 1962– II. Title.
PS2244.L5A6 2011 818'.309—dc23
2011030431

Set in Adobe Caslon Pro by Bob Reitz.
Designed by A Shahan.

To my students past, present, and future

Contents

Acknowledgments

Research projects often have serendipitous beginnings. Such was the origin of my research for this volume. For the seeds of this project, many thanks go to the staff of the Library Company of Philadelphia, who, more than a decade ago, introduced me to the fascinating editor and author Eliza Leslie when I was on site for another project. A few years later, when I returned to the mental bookmark I had placed next to Leslie, Legacies of Nineteenth-Century American Women Writers series editor Sharon Harris helped germinate my interest in compiling this anthology. Throughout a period of several years, Harris, along with the series' coeditor, Karen Dandurand, its advisory editor, Cynthia Weinstein, as well as the anonymous readers for the University of Nebraska Press, provided insightful ideas regarding the volume's proposed content. Their suggestions, drawing from a wealth of knowledge of nineteenth-century American women writers and of the contemporary marketplace for literary studies, have contributed to what is now a much stronger collection of materials than it would have been otherwise. Kristen A. Elias Rowley of the University of Nebraska Press also ably assisted in many decisions in the later stages of taking the project from manuscript to print.

Members of the Society for the Study of American Women Writers and others provided feedback on several conference papers—presented at meetings of the Modern Language Association, Nineteenth Century Studies, American Literature Association, and the Transatlantic Women Conference, for example—on Eliza Leslie's writing. Some of those ideas have found their way into the volume's introduction.

For assistance in retrieval of print, electronic, and manuscript sources, I wish to acknowledge the graciousness of several archivists: Ann K. Barker at the University of Missouri; Erika Jean Dowell at Indiana University's Lilly Library; Janet H. Stuckey in the special collections at Miami University in Ohio; Wendy Woloson and James Green at the Library Company of Philadelphia; and the staffs of the Historical Society of Pennsylvania and the British Library. Closer to home, Shannon Conlon of Missouri State University's Meyer Library saw my numerous interlibrary loan requests as never beyond possibility. For her optimism and dedication, I thank her.

Most significant to this project's fruition, however, are numerous former students. In the years that have passed since this project's conception, I have learned as much from them in the process of our collaboration on Eliza Leslie as they have learned from me. Students in two sections of American Romantic Literature gave me insight into how advanced students of literature respond to Leslie's fiction. In addition, a handful endured the tedious labor of translating microform editions of Leslie's volumes into newer electronic formats, and they worked closely with me to compile the selective bibliographies included in this volume: Patrick S. Williams, Craig A. Meyer, Ingrid M. Bohnenkamp, Katherine Ellerbrake, and, most recently, Gordon C. Appleton Jr., and Brooksie Trout. The latter two had the added pleasure of assisting me with the final details of delivering this book to the press. The appreciation I extend to all of them is reiterated on this volume's dedication page.

Finally, to my generously supportive department head, W. D. Blackmon, and to the Graduate College at Missouri State University for a Faculty Research Fellowship that supported the project's final stages, I am indeed grateful.

Editor's Introduction

> "No writer of fiction in our country has ever had a wider, or more interested circle of readers [than Leslie]; and this is clearly proved by the increased circulation of all those publications in which her name has appeared as a regular contributor."
>
> JOHN S. HART,
> *Female Prose Writers of America*, 1852

By her own account, Eliza Leslie (1787–1858) "had begun to copy poetry before [she] was twelve years old—and to scribble it before . . . ten." Leslie was a seasoned writer and editor when she acknowledged these early "scribbl[ings]" as "foolish attempts" at poetry in a letter to her publisher, Henry Carey Baird. In the years intervening her first copying of verse and this letter, Leslie had become a composer of her own stories and essays as well as a regular contributor to and editor of periodical publications and gift annuals. Her literary ventures also included translating the prose tales and culinary works of others and eventually compiling her own. As publisher John S. Hart wrote of her at midcentury, "an interested circle of readers" looked for works that bore Leslie's name (26).[1]

Much sought after for advice about the literary marketplace, Leslie was visited by fans during approximately the last ten years of her life, when she lived at the United States Hotel in Philadelphia. Judging from her correspondence, she appears to have obliged her devotees. For example, during a week in

October 1847, a Mr. Pierce of New Orleans requested that she sit for the painting of a miniature. He paid the extravagant price of fifty dollars for the portrait, a gift for his daughters, plus at least twelve additional dollars for the frame, since he insisted on "one of the handsomest and newest style." Leslie indulged him, "though [she] could very ill spare the time" away from her writing, to sit for an hour each morning. The resulting image, according to Leslie, was "by no means so handsome as [Thomas] Sully's portrait of [her]," yet it was "a more correct likeness" (To Miss Gertrude Leslie).

Thomas Sully's portrait of Leslie, which appeared in *Godey's Lady's Book* in January 1846, also illustrates the height of Leslie's fame in this decade. Perhaps the foremost portrait painter of antebellum America, Sully was well known for his portraits of John Adams and Thomas Jefferson. As *Godey's* indicated in an accompanying article, "the writings of Miss Leslie are too well known to require description or enumeration" ("Our Contributors" 2).

By bringing together a sampling of Leslie's writings, as publishers often did in the 1840s, *Selections from Eliza Leslie* reflects the stature she held in the mid-nineteenth century. After Leslie's shorter works appeared in periodicals such as *Godey's*, they were often gathered and bound in volumes—an indication that publishers believed a market existed for volumes bearing her name. As *Godey's* points out in its essay on Leslie, for example, "The greater portion of her 'Pencil Sketches' originally appeared in our pages" ("Our Contributors" 2). While nineteenth-century publishers such as Carey and Hart of Philadelphia and Monroe and Francis of Boston attempted to use her name to turn a profit, this volume's goal is instead to introduce contemporary readers to this once-prominent writer and editor with a view more complete and nuanced than any single reprint story, scholarly article, or culinary volume could provide. Thus, this volume collects some of Leslie's tales for children, instructional essays for girls and women, popular culinary texts, and fictional pieces intended for adult females.

Relative to the sheer breadth of Leslie's oeuvre, the brevity of this collection prevents what might be called a fair, representative selection. A bibliography of Leslie's works is included to provide readers with a better sense of her pervasiveness in mid-nineteenth century print culture and also to indicate her near absence from twentieth-century literary reprint editions. The bibliography demonstrates the true range of Leslie's writings. Accompanied by the volume's reprinted literary works and the information provided in this introduction, it should prompt scholars of nineteenth-century writers to pursue further study of this fascinating literary figure.

The selections provide examples of themes, tones, and styles that frequently appeared in Leslie's works. While this introduction comments upon these aspects of Leslie's writings, it also builds upon late-twentieth-century scholarship, particularly from the last decade, that briefly introduced Leslie to readers interested in the recovery of nineteenth-century women writers. That is, *Selections from Eliza Leslie* extends the previous work of Nina Baym, Judith Fetterley, Patricia Okker, Etsuko Taketani, and Susan S. Williams, who have pointed to such facets of Leslie's writing as ideal womanhood among working-class women, insightful and poignant humor, oblique criticism of gendered and racial "separate spheres," and economic aspects of periodical and annual publications.[2]

In addition to building upon previous studies of Leslie's writing, this volume presents new information about her position in the literary marketplace, employing recent scholarship by Williams and a host of others on authorship, copyright laws, and reprint practices. Studies of nineteenth-century women writers such as Catharine Maria Sedgwick and Susan Warner provide lenses that clarify our vision of Leslie's stature. For example, these studies implicitly suggest analysis of the appearance of Leslie's name on the title and contents pages of her volumes as well as attention to reviews of and advertisements for her works. Leslie's first few publications did not include her name, while her later works employed the then well-known writer's name, apparently depending on it as a marketing technique. As Williams has explained, claims about the business of authorship must be highly individualized; they must "attend to the author's own self-understanding of . . . her profession and the host of external factors . . . that influence those self-understandings" as presented in her "letters, diaries, and published works," as well as in such works as "advertisements, reviews, sales records, and correspondence with readers, editors, and publishers." The result of such attention is the realization that "[m]ost mid-nineteenth-century literary authors were neither wholly divorced from the market nor wholly shaped by it. Instead, they balanced their authorial rights against the advantages afforded by an increasingly large and variegated literary market"(97).

Indeed, Leslie's correspondence confirms that she was fully immersed in the literary marketplace of her day, understanding not only economic aspects of the publishing industry but also issues associated with style. Thus, study of Leslie and her works broadens our understanding of women's varied roles in the "variegated" nineteenth-century literary culture.

A Literary Life and the Literary Marketplace

The life of a woman who scribbled verses by age ten and who continued to meet and correspond with publishers into her sixth decade certainly may be labeled literary. What prompted Leslie to devote her days and years to the literary marketplace? And how did she rise to a position of prominence in the mid-nineteenth century? Like so many of her contemporaries and those who preceded her, Leslie was motivated to put pen to page by at least two means: love of language and literature and financial necessity.

Being born in 1787 into a Philadelphia family that respected the arts and education was certainly an advantage. Leslie's father, Robert, a member of the American Philosophical Society and a friend of Benjamin Franklin and Thomas Jefferson, most likely encouraged her interest in and involvement with the latest ideas circulating in print and in conversation. According to her autobiographical "Letter to Mrs. Alice B. Neal," Robert noticed his daughter's keen memory and decided to have her educated at home in languages and the fine arts. Domestic arts, of course, were also part of her later training. In Eliza's early years the family moved to London, where two of her brothers were born, and in 1799 they all returned to Philadelphia. The death of Eliza's father in 1803 forced the family into a financial situation that necessitated creativity combined with practicality—Eliza's mother ran a boarding house in which Eliza assisted, most likely learning about cooking as well as about the diverse types of clients that demanded service and about financial and domestic management.[3] Leslie's first published volume was *Seventy-Five Receipts for Pastry, Cakes, and Sweetmeats* in 1827, the success of which brought her into the realm of fiction writing and editing, as Boston publishers Munroe and Francis encouraged her to try her hand at other genres.

Leslie's original juvenile fiction soon poured from the press, with *The Mirror* in 1828, *The Young Americans* in 1829, *American Girl's Book* in 1831, and *Atlantic Tales, or Pictures of Youth* in 1833. Munroe and Francis also published Leslie's 1828 translation of the French tale "Eugene and Lolotte," written by Stéphanie-Félicité de Genlis, and by May of 1830 Leslie also had translated the children's tale "Alphonsine" from the French.[4] Leslie continued to publish juvenile works with Munroe and Francis, often in their popular *Parley's Magazine*, throughout the 1830s. In 1832 Leslie submitted "Mrs. Washington Potts" to a *Godey's* fiction contest, for which she received the prize. As a result, she was ushered into her role as a regular contributor to *Godey's* and author of fiction for adult females. Her works for adults also appeared in *Graham's Lady's and Gentleman's Magazine* in the 1840s.

Leslie learned more about the marketplace while she served as editor for *The Violet* and *The Gift*, annuals published by Carey and Hart in the 1830s; as Sarah Josepha Hale's assistant editor for *Godey's*; and, in 1843, as the editor of the short-lived *Miss Leslie's Magazine*. After 1848 most of Leslie's involvement with texts appears to have been with reprint editions of her own works. Correspondence from her final decade consistently refers to such contractual agreements, financial needs, and fatigue.[5]

Although Leslie advises the public in "Conduct to Literary Women" that they should not ask about the truthfulness or sources of literature, "or if they were mere invention," it is impossible not to notice the degree to which Leslie's life experiences influenced her writing (272). She acknowledges in the same essay that "the intellect of a good writer . . . is always brightened by . . . taking in and laying up ideas" and that she "*has* painted from life" (272).

Leslie's early travels, as well as her observations in the boarding house in Philadelphia, undoubtedly influenced her writing; living abroad and then returning to the States not only enriched her perspective of diverse cultures, but also fostered her love of home. In addition to these experiences, however, Eliza's social and family relationships had an impact that becomes apparent in her works. In particular, her brothers Thomas and Charles, and her ongoing relationship with a childhood friend, Abigail "Abbe" Bailey, who moved west with her family to Cincinnati, appear to have significantly influenced Leslie's writings about places and customs. Due to Thomas's military career and the tradition of unmarried women living with family, Leslie stayed for a time with her brother at West Point and observed American military life, about which she wrote from a social and cultural perspective. Her beloved brother Charles Robert, one of the two children born abroad, lived only briefly in America, married into the English family of Harriet Stone, was inducted into England's Royal Academy for his accomplishments as a painter, and considered himself more English than American.[6] Eliza's emotional engagement with Charles and his wife, revealed in the siblings' correspondence, undoubtedly emerged in her fiction, as she wrote about the complicated and often manipulative relationships between husbands and wives and the differences in tastes and manners between Americans and the English. Many of her works for children even detail what she sees as differences between the two cultures. Introductory comments in *The Mirror*, for example, explain:

> There are many striking points of dissimilarity between the habits and manners of the children of America and those of England, to which country we have hitherto been indebted for nearly all our juvenile books of amusement. These books, excellent as most of them are, abound in allusions and localities which are often unintelligible to their young readers on this side of the Atlantic. The writer of the subsequent pages has endeavoured to compose a work essentially American . . . with reference to the ideas of American children and to the manners in which they are educated. (iii–iv)

Charles also seems to have been responsible for two aspects of his sister's development as a writer. First, he was involved in her first publication in London, "The Travelling Tin-Man," for which he prepared an illustration. The degree to which he was involved in the British publications that followed is difficult to determine. Second, in his letters to Eliza he advised her on stylistic matters, commenting upon didacticism and realism. He advised against the former and in favor of the latter, citing writers such as his acquaintances Sir Walter Scott and Washington Irving as exemplary for their style (290). Eliza seems to have adhered to her brother's advice. While her fiction for youth conveys moralistic messages, the fiction for more mature audiences, written later in her career, reflects the development of a more complex style. By comparing popular and often reprinted children's stories, such as "The Tale-Tell" or "The Boarding School Feast," with those written for adults, such as "Nothing Morally Wrong," readers will see the development of the realism Charles advocated.

Abbe Bailey also influenced her childhood friend Eliza's writing in two ways. The Bailey family's move to the western frontier likely prompted Eliza's interest in that region, and it may have provided specific accounts that fed the writer's creative juices. In addition, the act of letter writing gave Eliza practice in writing for an imagined audience. Thus, we see in Leslie's stories for youth such accounts as "The Settlers," that provide insights into frontier life, a marked contrast to her educational *Cards of Boston* (1832), which emphasizes the city's history.

Another important family relationship that influenced Eliza's literary life was that of her brother-in-law, Henry C. Carey, a prominent Philadelphia publisher. As Leslie explained in an 1838 letter, because of this relationship, "I have of course an opportunity of knowing many things connected with publishing and book-selling that the world is not aware of" (To Miss A. H. Woodbridge). This family connection undoubtedly contributed to Leslie's entrée into the literary world and helped to sustain it, as the next generation of Carey family members continued to be involved in Leslie's literary career.

An important perspective of Leslie's relationship with Carey, however, emerges through consideration of the larger context of the claim Leslie makes to Miss A. H. Woodbridge. This comment is embedded in a larger exposé on the market value of poetry relative to prose. Woodbridge has inquired of Leslie the possibility of publishing a collection of "juvenile poetry." Leslie provides a candid response:

> Since the receipt of your letter I have been making enquiries of our principal publishers . . . . I am sorry to say that no one offers the least encouragement, poetry being (as they express it) an absolute drug in the market. Since the days of Scott and Byron the publication of poetry, even in England, has not indemnified the proprieties of the work for the expense of the paper, with the exception perhaps of that of Mrs. Hemans, and even she is more praised than read.[7]

Leslie does not stop with this painful truth, however, but continues with discourses on two related topics. She provides her aesthetic views of popular poetry and includes specific details regarding the financial value of prose. Noting her "duty as editor [is] confined to the reading, selecting and arranging the literary matter," she states she "believe[s] the publishers allow two dollars for each printed page of the Gift, and one dollar and a half for each page of the Violet." With regard to *Godey's Lady's Book*, for which she regularly wrote at that time, "Mr. Godey . . . pays from one to two dollars a page (octavo, printed in columns) for amusing prose—for verse, he gives nothing—having always . . . more [poetry] gratuitously than he can possibly make use of" (To Miss A. H. Woodbridge). We come to understand Leslie's attention to the octavo page format, as she notes that Monroe and Francis, to whom she also regularly contributes works that usually appear in *Parley's Magazine*, pay the same per printed page as *Godey's*. Because the print in *Parley's* was larger there was less material per page, and thus Leslie earned more money for the same amount of literary labor.

Stylistically, Leslie's complaint about contemporary poetry is not only "that it is too gloomy, and too much tinctured with fanaticism," but also that too many poets have adopted "an affectation of Mrs. Hemans in her greatest fault"—namely, "a strange, harsh, and irregular measure." Notably, Leslie concludes the letter, which might have stated simply that no publishers are interested in verses for children, with the encouragement that Miss Woodbridge submit a piece to *The Violet* or *The Gift*.[8] As in the earlier correspondence between Leslie and her brother Charles Robert, other letters reveal Leslie's savvy understanding and support of the literary marketplace, underscoring her successful self-positioning within it.[9]

A Variety of Venues, A Medley of Messages

In addition to what Leslie's correspondence reveals of her knowledge of and beliefs about literature and the literary marketplace, the author's skillful movement among genres and publishing houses in the first three decades of her career signifies her skill as a writer and businesswoman. She was in tune not only with her audiences and the marketplace but also with ideas she wished to express and the particular forms in which to express them. By her own account and those of others, Leslie's "books on domestic economy . . . were her greatest source of income" and "deservedly bestsellers" (Letter to Mrs. Alice B. Neal 32; Wilson 392). As Patrick Dunne and Charles L. Mackie have claimed of Leslie and her successful cookery texts, her "genius lay in filling a need and creating a market" (72). Dunne and Mackie's statement should be extended to include Leslie's work as a writer of fiction and other genres that equally exhibited her genius. Approximately twenty-five years following the first appearance of *Seventy-Five Receipts,* for example, John S. Hart prominently featured Leslie in his 1852 collection *Female Prose Writers of America* and praised her fiction.

Leslie's movement across genres may be labeled a trajectory of development and maturation: she began by copying other people's writing, then moved to translating, to compiling culinary collections, to sketching stories and essays for youth, and finally, to writing fiction for adult women. Yet rather than suggesting a neat and progressive movement through a hierarchy of genres, Leslie's publications in fact indicate that she continued to write, edit, and negotiate revisions and reprints of various genres as the inspiration and need struck her and her publishers. She continued to submit children's stories to Munroe and Francis, even as she wrote for *Godey's* and edited *The Gift* and *The Violet* for Carey and Hart.

Leslie's involvement with some of the reprinting is apparent in her correspondence, but other reprinting was beyond her control or that of her initial publishers. The "Editors' Book Table" from *Godey's*, for example, noted that both "Mrs. Washington Potts" and "Mr. Smith" had been reprinted in newspapers with no credit given to the sources (251). Other works appear in imprints issued from British publishing houses infamous for pirating materials from American presses, such as *Parley's Magazine.*[10]

In addition to the cachet associated with Leslie's name, the desire to publish and reprint her works must also be attributed to their content. That content is, according to *Godey's* "Our Contributors" column, "the manners of social and domestic life" (1) with the "aim to make improvements in the style of housekeeping and reforms in the manners" (2). More recent commentary concludes that Leslie's works present moralistic messages to children and bourgeois, middle-class ideals of womanhood to adult readers.[11] Rather than a monolithic mantra reiterated in each work, however, these messages are mixed and multiple, providing a medley of ideas for contemplation.

Often the tales are told with reality-based humor, for which Leslie was also known.[12] Leslie distinguishes herself from other humor writers with a style that exceeds theirs in its realism. While Irving's Rip Van Winkle and Ichabod Crane come to life in part due to the author's use of exaggeration, Leslie's humor is such that it causes us to laugh by remembering similar social situations we have observed. Among the situations she clearly depicts are those in which people assert themselves as being better than those around them—in learning, in taste, in conversation.

The humor within Leslie's writing allows readers to maintain a safe distance from the poignant truths it contains. Stories such as "Mrs. Washington Potts," "Nothing Morally Wrong," and "Alina Derlay" could be mistakenly read as defenses of bourgeois domesticity, separate spheres, and national identity. Critical readers will notice, however, that these tales also provide insight into the problems associated with simplistic views of patriotism and material success, pointing to the constructed nature of such ideals and the inhumane treatment of some of the individuals that undergird them.[13]

Indeed, much of Leslie's overtly moralistic writing underscores the constructed nature of gendered, racial, national, and class-based identities by pointing to the tensions and ironies surrounding the characters and their counterpoints and parallels in Leslie's nonfiction works and her own life experiences. To present these complexities and the several messages offered through Leslie's writing, this collection begins with fictional works, appearing in chronological order according to earliest known publication date. Next, the nonfiction pieces for children and adults, also presented in order of publication date, reflect more simplistic visions of socially acceptable and ideal behaviors.

The nonfiction selections here, in spite of their didacticism, may be distinguished from those of Leslie's contemporaries in a number of ways. For example, *Seventy-Five Receipts* avoids the directness of her contemporary Lydia Maria Child's *The American Frugal Housewife*. Attention to thrift is as important to Leslie as it is to Child, but not at the cost of "meanness" in appearances or in hospitality, as illustrated in the story "Mr. and Mrs. Woodbridge." In fact, in *Domestic French Cookery* Leslie offers ways in which cooks can reproduce popular French cuisine with American resources and without unnecessary and excessive expenses.

The pieces written for youth, such as "A Basket Pincushion" and "The Elephant," together reinforce the context for the American literary marketplace at the time Leslie was actively writing. With an emphasis on the domestic and the foreign, these two early works provide readers with a glimpse of an American literary culture much broader than what they might imagine if only introduced to writings for children by Child or Nathaniel Hawthorne, or even to Leslie's award-winning "Mrs. Washington Potts," which was published in close chronological proximity to these shorter works for children.

Unlike the seemingly straightforward nonfiction essays and "receipts," Leslie's works of adult fiction, such as "Nothing Morally Wrong," comically present female characters whose behavior defies the socially acceptable. Miss Jonathina Judd is "careless, unmannered, unbeautiful, uncouth . . . ill-dressed" and "under no government but her own" (223, 225). Yet as Leslie comments through the title and repeats in the story's conclusion after Jonathina marries a man who finds her "fascinating," no inherent immoral quality lies within her; as the narrator concludes, "truly, in her whole heterogeneous composition, there is nothing morally wrong" (227). Jonathina must change her behavior slightly, though, before she is married at the tale's end. Alongside other works by Leslie and her contemporaries, this tale demonstrates that the acquired aspects of female social codes have nothing to do with morality and that they do not necessarily produce the desired results. That is, they demonstrate the complexity of choices available to women—including women writers—and they suggest that the consequences vary. Jonathina changes some of her behavior but not all; nonetheless, she receives and accepts a marriage proposal from a man who appears to be attracted to her distinctive behavior. The couple is happily married at the narrative's conclusion. With Leslie's experiences as a single woman in view, readers may wonder why Leslie recognizes the behavioral codes as disaffiliated from morality, why she had the character reform only some aspects of her behavior, and why Jonathina receives and accepts a marriage proposal. Finally, what is Jonathina's relationship to women such as Margaret Fuller, who also willingly moved against the nap of the social fabric?

Many of Leslie's fictional works may be labeled idealized courtship tales, even though they provide not only comments on morality and gender roles, but also ideas about popular genres, such as the romance, and observations on literary conventions. Eliza Farnham, in the tale of the same name, attracts her husband because of the consistency between her letter writing and her internal sense of self, rather than exhibiting an inward emptiness in her personality and intellect by imitating the flowery rhetoric of some popular romances.[14] In contrast, in "The Beaux," the Denning sisters believe that "reading girls never take" or have beaux, because men abhor women who can think. The heroine, Sabina, however, prefers reading to shopping and loves Jane Austen. Her conversation with the dandy art critic and writer Jackaway Jempson includes such topics as American publishers, international copyright laws, the mistreatment of American artists, and the nonexistence of original American art. "Mr. and Mrs. Woodbridge" includes conversations on fashionable literature and the gothic (the longer *Leonilla Lynmore* connects the gothic to racial and ethnic stereotypes). Additionally, through its plot it provides some revisions of typical temperance and reform literature, where often an ideal wife wrestles with an inebriate or profligate husband, even as it comments on consumer culture. Such messages are exhibited in descriptions of and conversations about architecture and the use of domestic space, the decorative arts, and entertainment.

Even when Leslie's overt attention focuses on excessive consumerism, her works belie the cultural support of consumerism by means of slavery and the laboring classes. While Leslie's works may be compared readily to those of Harriet Beecher Stowe and Susan Warner in their concern with consumerism and domesticity, they differ significantly. Stowe and Warner infuse Christian spirituality into women's work in the domestic sphere, the denial of excessive and conspicuous consumption of material goods, and other social reforms such as temperance; Leslie, however, writing in the preemancipation era, noticeably eschews Christian morality or a reward in an ethereal afterlife as she critiques consumer culture and materialism.

In "The Travelling Tin-Man," for example, Leslie emphasizes a frugal Quaker family's "appropriate" treatment of African American servants as well as its consumption only of necessities. The family's honesty and thrift contrast with the dishonesty and greed of the Yankee peddler. Complicating the tale for contemporary readers, however, is the ending, which emphasizes a second generation of householders who are applauded for being not quite as thrifty as their parents were. Religious or spiritual bases for these ethical decisions are notably absent. Similarly, a conflict and resolution regarding consumerism appears in "Mr. and Mrs. Woodbridge." The new bride, Mrs. Charlotte Woodbridge, obsessively focuses on appearances of gentility, yet, more important, she possesses the fault of being too "mean" to offer her guests an ample meal or to let her husband take his meals in a comfortable environment. Is there an acceptable and appropriate middle ground, in Leslie's eyes? And if it is not a ground measured by a religious moral standard, by what means may this middle ground be determined? Because these questions are not answered overtly in the narrative, readers are left with the challenge of developing their own interpretations.

Perhaps the most troubling questions arising today from Leslie's writing are those associated with race and class. Throughout her works Leslie does not present race as a socially constructed category. Instead she followed the pattern of the nation's founding fathers, with whom her biological father associated, and she employed racial stereotypes that suggested these types reflected "natural" reality. "The Travelling Tin-Man," for example, provides insights into Leslie's position on issues associated with race that inform examinations of the servant class and immigrants in her later works. Appearing first in London in 1831, it was published in America by 1833, the same year as Child's *An Appeal in Favor of that Class of Americans Called Africans* and just after Maria Stewart's lectures and essays began to circulate.[15] In "The Travelling Tin-Man" Leslie appears to have responded to abolition with her own version of social reform. The tale asserts that "improvement" of African Americans is possible and recommended. Although it does not overtly decry the colonization movement that Child and Stewart vehemently opposed and Stowe later supported, the tale presents as a model of social improvement an orphaned free black child being raised by white Quakers until she is released at age eighteen, ready for successful independence.[16] Leslie's approach echoes the views of national leaders such as Thomas Jefferson, Benjamin Franklin, and Benjamin Rush, who saw Africans as inferior but advocated for their "improvement" through "adoption" by whites. Promoting conservative views about race in yet another way, Leslie's tale includes an older African servant who remains dedicated to the white family with whom she lives and works. Not unlike the servants in Catharine Maria Sedgwick's 1835 novel *The Linwoods* and Leslie's "The Settlers," the servants remain grateful and dedicated to their beneficent masters and mistresses.

While African American servants in Leslie's fiction tend to be dedicated, they are also superstitious and silly. Similarly stereotyped, the Irish in Leslie's stories have unkempt hair and a tendency to drink. In "Mr. and Mrs. Woodbridge," the Irish servant drinks too much; in other tales the black servants are superstitious. These reflections of Leslie's beliefs—and perhaps her prejudices—are confirmed by her niece Emma Leslie and Eliza's brother Thomas in letters detailing the family's struggles with how to care for "Aunt Eliza" late in her life, when she lived alone at the United States Hotel. Such comments about race and ethnicity in Leslie's writing must have been included to meet the needs of some readers, and they reflect attitudes toward immigrants in the 1840s that Monique Dull describes in her analysis of Leslie's *Amelia* as an adoption tale. In this period "twenty percent of the American male population" fought "for the exclusive enfranchisement of those born on American soil" (164–65). Serving and laboring characters in Leslie's fiction, Patricia Okker has explained, remind us that "only in a racially [and ethnically] divided society "can some thrive in "the middle-class privilege of a gendered separatism." Thus, Leslie's writing includes "economic realities" that critique a vision of separate spheres as natural, even as it demonstrates the ethnic and national separatism that divides and distinguishes females by social class (36).

Leslie's complicated attitude toward nationalism emerges in several of her works. In the fiction, for example, Leslie's heavy use of French phrases (usually without translation) raises questions about her patriotism and exudes a Francophilia demonstrated in her other writings. Letters from her brother Charles, written after Napoleon's death, remark upon Eliza's former fascination with the leader before his fall from prominence (318–19). Her translations of *Alphonsine* and *Domestic French Cookery* demonstrate her facility with the language and her love of at least the culture's food, if not the culture itself.

In *Miss Leslie's Behavior Book*, the author advises writers not to use too many French phrases for the sake of appearance: "Unless you know that your correspondent is well versed in French, refrain from interlarding your letters with Gallic words or phrases" (266). Yet she includes what appears to be an excessive amount in her fiction. Such contradictions invite an in-depth analysis of her cultural commentary: which characters use what French phrases, and to what end? The lack of translation, of course, suggests that she assumes her readers will know French, and those who do not, should. To complicate matters, these phrases are sometimes voiced by characters who exhibit too profoundly an aping of European culture. Thus, it appears to be "the imitating of foreign values" (Fetterley 73)—in the absence of an inwardly developed good taste—that Leslie abhors.

How does this attitude translate to Leslie's approach to things American? According to *Godey's*, many readers "thought [her] an Englishwoman," most likely because "while exposing . . . follies and faults of her young countrywomen," they "imagined that she was seeking for subjects of censure, with the feelings of a foreigner" ("Our Contributors" 1). Yet Leslie's works offer an overwhelming support for the nation, often even asserting the prominence of American life and manners over those of the English. "Country Houses of America" and "The Settlers," both early works, exude a love of country, although Leslie's juvenile works from the same period also support travel abroad and knowledge of other cultures. The adoption tales *Amelia* and "The Travelling Tin-Man" are not alone in introducing American culture as one that encourages new beginnings. "The Show Girl," a tale of transatlantic kidnapping and forced performance, implicitly upholds America over England as it explicitly reminds children to obey their parents. "The Beaux" clearly asserts Leslie's belief in the value of American art. In this regard, the writings included in this collection are no exception. A reading of these works in light of Leslie's life and the breadth of her publications underscores the writer's complex attitudes toward nationalism and international relations. She desired to contribute to and further the development of American literature, but she by no means believed her country to have the exclusive right to reputable and noteworthy art and ideas.

When considered within the context of Leslie's life as a writer, editor, and antebellum American citizen, the works in this volume also demonstrate changes in her attitudes through the years. As a single woman with a prominent family heritage in Philadelphia and connections both east across the Atlantic and west to the frontier, Leslie and her perceived identity, of course, shifted as she matured. Yet Leslie consistently used writing to maintain a sense of identity as well as financial sustenance. The works emerging from her fluid and dynamic vision of self, mission, and audience sit squarely in the middle of contemporary discussions of nineteenth-century American literary culture. They invite readers to consider multiple messages conveyed through a variety of genres in the antebellum marketplace. As these works invite readers to consider messages of the past, they encourage us also to contemplate the mixed modes of communication in our contemporary culture.

Notes

1. Hart's *Female Prose Writers of America* includes Leslie as the second author in the volume, following Catharine Maria Sedgwick. Since the sections on each author are neither alphabetical by last name nor chronological by birth date, the order of appearance suggests prestige or popularity. Materials comprising the section dedicated to Leslie include a biographical sketch (26), Leslie's autobiographical "Letter to Mrs. Alice B. Neal" (27–32), and her short story "Mrs. Derrington's Reception Day"(32–48).
2. For details regarding the criticism by each of these scholars, see notes 11–13.
3. In addition to Leslie's autobiographical "Letter to Mrs. Alice B. Neal," general information about her life and writing may be found in works by Susan Coultrap-McQuin, Patrick Dunne and Charles L. Mackie, John S. Hart, Ophia D. Smith, Frank L. Mott, and Mary Tolford Wilson. Brief references to Leslie's writing and editing career are included in volumes by Bayard Taylor (404–7), Patricia Okker (35–37, 197), Carolyn Karcher (93), Susan S. Williams (96), Susan Belasco (265), Alice M. Jordan (52), and Aleta Feinsod Cane and Susan Alves (3).
4. The title page of "Eugene and Lolotte" reads only, "By a Lady of Philadelphia." However, the title page of Leslie's *The Young Americans* notes that the volume is written by the same author who translated "Eugene and Lolotte." Charles Leslie notes the translation of "Alphonsine" in a letter to Eliza. He attempted to secure a London publisher for it, but was refused because of its length and because it was a translation (*Autobiographical Recollections* 290).

5. On fatigue, see Leslie's letter to Miss Gertrude Leslie. On financial needs and contracts, see several letters to Henry Carey Baird: 17 Dec. 1850, 10 Mar. 1851, 27 Mar. 1855, 23 Feb. 1854, and 26 Sept. 1854. In the last of these, Leslie expresses disappointment that he thinks her cookery book is no longer profitable due to competition. She complains that it is his fault—she tried before to get him to let her improve it by substituting new and better receipts for older ones. And while the print is too small (the fault of Baird's uncle Edward, according to Leslie), Baird has argued consistently that replacing the plates with larger fonts or revisions in recipes would be cost prohibitive. Then she gives the terms on which "Mr. Peterson will take it" if Baird "wish[es] to get rid of it": Peterson will weigh the plates and break them up, then pay Baird for the lead within them, create new plates, and give Baird the first thousand bound copies. Until they are delivered, he "will not put to press another edition." Leslie requests that Baird "not decide hastily against" this proposal but "discuss it next with Mr. Peterson," as she has "no more say" on the matter.
6. Ophia D. Smith has written two essays on Leslie that draw from Charles's *Autobiographical Recollections* and from Eliza's letters to the Bailey family in Cincinnati. The original Abbe-Eliza correspondence, cited as being among the John H. James Family papers, appears to be no longer a part of this collection (although a conversation with Eliza in Philadelphia is referenced in a letter of Ellen Bailey).
7. The British poet Felicia Dorothea Browne Hemans (1793–1835) published verse beginning in 1808, some volumes of which were issued by the reputable printer John Murray. She gained the attention of Percy Bysshe Shelley and William Wordsworth and was well known in both England and America.
8. Bayard Taylor also records his memory of Leslie being supportive of his literary efforts and negative toward Mrs. Hemans's style (405–6).
9. See, for example, Leslie's letter to Erastus Perry; letter to Sarah Josepha Hale; letter to A. Hart; and letters to Mrs. Carey and Hart, 30 Dec. 1839 and 10 Feb. 1840. Also see Alfred B. Street's

letter to Eliza Leslie and Emma C. Embury; and his letter to Eliza Leslie.

10. For example, Thomas Tegg, who was known for pirating from *Parley's* (Darton 224–26), printed *The Girl's Book of Diversions, or Occupations for Play Hours*, in several editions; it includes excerpts from Leslie's *American Girl's Book*. Edward Lacey, well known for buying remainders of juvenile fiction (Darton 226), sold at least one volume that is entitled *Miss Leslie's Nursery Stories*. It is uncertain whether Leslie was the author of these stories, as they have not been located elsewhere. The *American Miscellany*, a British periodical, published "Frank Finlay" and "The Ladies' Ball" in 1840. The house of Darton, known for sound business practices (Darton 203), reprinted "The Quilting," and "The Show Girl" in 1835. As the bibliography illustrates, numerous other works were republished in England.
11. Early in the recovery of nineteenth-century women writers, Nina Baym encouraged interest in Leslie's fiction even as she asserted that Leslie used *Amelia* to espouse ideal womanhood through her working-class heroine (84–85). Similarly, Etsuko Taketani's discussion of the children's sailor tale "Billy Bedlow," explains how the work advocates sexual "heteronormativity" (363–64, 368).
12. On Leslie's humor, see Judith Fetterley (73–74). For the larger context of antebellum humor, see Karen Kilcup's special issue of *Studies in American Humor*.
13. Taketani argues, for example, that while overtly supporting heteronormativity, "Billy Bedlow" implicitly points to the socially-constructed nature of gender-containing categories. Patricia Okker comments upon similar racial and class divisions that emerge in "The Batson College" (35–37).
14. Leslie's choice of title character is remarkable, since the works of the New York activist and writer Eliza Farnham (1815–64) were most likely known by Leslie.
15. The tale was announced in the "New Books" column of the March-April 1832 issue of *Juvenile Miscellany* (108) as appearing in Franklin Edmand's *Lilliputian Quarto*, no. 2. An early edition of Edmand's work has not been located.

16. It is possible that Leslie wrote the work in response to the life and work of Stewart, who was orphaned at age five, raised by a white minister until age fifteen, and thereafter supported herself as a domestic servant until she married and moved to Boston.

Works Cited

Bailey, Ellen. Letter to Gertrude P. James. 23 Mar. 1848. James Papers. Box 7, folder 20. Walter Havighurst Special Collections. Miami University, Oxford OH.

Baym, Nina. *Woman's Fiction: A Guide to Novels by and about Women in America, 1820–70*. 2nd ed. Urbana: University of Illinois Press, 1993. Print.

Belasco, Susan. "The Cultural Work of National Magazines." In Casper, Groves, Nissenbaum, and Winship. 258–69.

Cane, Aleta Feinsod, and Susan Alves, eds. *"The Only Efficient Instrument": American Women Writers and the Periodical, 1837–1916*. Iowa City: University of Iowa Press, 2001. Print.

Casper, Scott E., and Jeffrey D. Groves, Stephen W. Nissenbaum, and Michael Winship. *The Industrial Book, 1840–1880*. Chapel Hill: University of North Carolina Press, 2007. Print. Vol. 3 of *A History of the Book in America*. 5 vols. 2007–10.

Coultrap-McQuinn, Susan. "Eliza Leslie." In *American Women Writers*, edited by Lina Mainiero. Vol. 2. New York: Frederick Ungar, 1980. 558–61. Print.

Darton, F. J. Harvey. *Children's Books in England: Five Centuries of Social Life*. 3rd ed. Rev. by Brian Alderson. Cambridge: Cambridge University Press, 1982. Print.

Dull, Monique. "Kinship and Nation in *Amelia* (1848)." In *The Rhetoric of Canadian Writing*, edited by Conny Steenman-Marcusse. Amsterdam: Rodopi, 2002. 161–78. Print.

Dunne, Patrick, and Charles L. Mackie. "Philadelphia Story: In the Benevolent, Prolific Eliza Leslie We Found the Mother of American Cookery." *Historic Preservation* 46.4 (1994): 72, 74–75, 103. Print.

"Editors' Book Table." *Godey's Lady's Book* (Oct. 1848): 249–52. *American Periodical Series Online*. Web. July 20, 2006.

Embury, Emma C. Letter to Eliza Leslie. January 20, 1839. ALS 6/29. Historical Society of Pennsylvania, Philadelphia.

Fetterley, Judith. *Provisions: A Reader from 19th-Century American Women.* Bloomington: Indiana University Press, 1985. Print.

Hall, Anna Maria S. C. *The Juvenile Forget-Me-Not: A Christmas and New Year's Gift or Birth-day Present.* London: R. Ackerman, 1833. Print.

Hart, John S. *Female Prose Writers of America.* Philadelphia: E. H. Butler, 1855. Print.

Jackson, Leon. *The Business of Letters: Authorial Economies in Antebellum America.* Stanford CA: Stanford University Press, 2008. Print.

Jordan, Alice M. "The Juvenile Miscellany and Its Literary Ladies." *From Rollo to Tom Sawyer and Other Papers.* Boston: Horn Book, 1948. 46–60. Print.

Karcher, Carolyn L. "Lydia Maria Child and the Juvenile Miscellany: The Creation of an American Children's Literature." In Price and Belasco Smith, 90–114.

Kilcup, Karen, ed. *Early and Antebellum American Humor.* Special issue of *Studies in American Humor* 3.11 (2004): 1–72. Print.

Leslie, Charles Robert. *Autobiographical Recollections with Selections from His Letters.* Edited by Tom Taylor. London: John Murray, 1860. Print.

Leslie, Eliza. Letter to A. Hart. August 19, 1839. ALS 6/32. Historical Society of Pennsylvania, Philadelphia.

———. Letter to Erastus Perry. June 21, 1836. 6/6 ALS Historical Society of Pennsylvania.

———. Letter to Henry Carey Baird. December 17, 1850. Henry Carey Baird Papers, Baird Section. Series 1A, box 2, folder 5. Historical Society of Pennsylvania.

———. Letter to Henry Carey Baird. March 10, 1851. Dreer Collection, American Prose Writers. 6/12 ALS Historical Society of Pennsylvania.

———. Letter to Henry Carey Baird. February 23, 1854. Edward Carey Gardiner Collection. Series 1A, box 2, folder 5. Historical Society of Pennsylvania.

———. Letter to Henry Carey Baird. September 26, 1854. Edward Carey Gardiner Collection. Series 1A, box 2, folder 5. Historical Society of Pennsylvania.

———. Letter to Henry Carey Baird. March 27, 1855. Edward Carey Gardiner Collection. Series 1A, box 2, folder 5. Historical Society of Pennsylvania.

———. Letter to Henry Carey Baird. June 17, 1856. Edward Carey Gardiner Collection. Series 1A, box 2, folder 5. Historical Society of Pennsylvania.

———. Letter to Miss A. H. Woodbridge. 1833. ALS 6/32. Historical Society of Pennsylvania.

———. Letter to Miss Gertrude Leslie. October 10, 1847. Connaroe Papers. Vol. 6: 45. Historical Society of Pennsylvania.

———. "Letter to Mrs. Alice B. Neal." In Hart 27–32.

———. Letter to Mrs. Carey and Hart. December 30, 1839. ALS6/32. Historical Society of Pennsylvania.

———. Letter to Mrs. Carey and Hart. February 10, 1840. ALS 6/23. Historical Society of Pennsylvania.

———. Letter to Sarah Josepha Hale. October 31, 1836. ALS Library Company, ABC. Historical Society of Pennsylvania.

Leslie, Emma. Letter to Henry C. Carey. March 14, 1855. Edward Carey Gardiner Collection. Henry C. Carey Papers. Section 5B, box 15. Historical Society of Pennsylvania.

Leslie, Thomas J. Letter to Henry C. Carey. April 30, 1857. Edward Carey Gardiner Collection. Henry C. Carey Papers. Section 5B, box 15. Historical Society of Pennsylvania.

Mott, Frank L. *A History of American Magazines*. Vol. 1. Cambridge: Harvard University Press, 1930. 409–12. Print.

Okker, Patricia. *Our Sister Editors: Sarah J. Hale and the Tradition of Nineteenth-Century American Women Editors*. Athens: University of Georgia Press, 1995. Print.

"New Books." *Juvenile Miscellany* (Mar.-Apr. 1832): 107–8. *American Periodical Series Online*. Web. July 20, 2006.

"Our Contributors: Miss Eliza Leslie." *Godey's Magazine and Lady's Book* Jan. 1846: 1–2. *American Periodical Series Online*. Web. July 19, 2006.

Price, Kenneth M., and Susan Belasco Smith, eds. *Periodical Literature in Nineteenth-Century America*. Charlottesville: University Press of Virginia, 1995. Print.

Smith, Ophia D. "Charles and Eliza Leslie." *Pennsylvania Magazine of History and Biography* 74.4 (1950): 512–27. Print.

———. "Eliza Leslie's Impressions of New York and West Point." *New-York Historical Society Quarterly* 35.1 (1951): 344–53. Print.

Street, Alfred B. Letter to Eliza Leslie. May 22, 1840. ALS 6/36. Historical Society of Pennsylvania.

Taketani, Etsuko. "Spectacular Child Bodies: The Sexual Politics of Cross-Dressing and Calisthenics in the Writings of Eliza Leslie and Catharine Beecher." *Lion and the Unicorn: A Critical Journal of Children's Literature* 23.3 (1999): 355–72. Print.

Taylor, Bayard. *Prose Writings of Bayard Taylor: At Home and Abroad.* Rev. ed. 2nd series. New York: G. P. Putnam, 1862. Print.

Williams, Susan S. "Authors and Literary Authorship." In Casper, Groves, Nissenbaum, and Winship, 90–116.

Wilson, Mary Tolford. "Eliza Leslie." *Notable American Women, 1607–1950: A Biographical Dictionary*. Edited by Edward T. James. 3 Vols. Cambridge: Harvard University Press, 1971.

A Note on the Text

In an attempt to maintain nineteenth-century style, the selections included here are presented in a format as close as possible to that of the earliest located published versions of the works. (The bibliography and the chronological index of Leslie's works provide publication information.) Although I have not updated nineteenth-century conventions of spelling (e.g., Shakspeare, colour, neighbour, visiter, waggon), I have chosen to silently correct obvious typographical errors and some nineteenth-century publishers' conventions of punctuation (such as spaces before colons and the use of commas and quotation marks with dialogue). The few footnotes that appeared in the original texts have been maintained as notes, indicated as "note in original." They are included within the contemporary explanatory notations that follow the selections.

Regarding the selections published serially in *Godey's*: material that appeared at the opening of each installment after the first (such as the story title and author's name) has been omitted to avoid redundancy; headings such as "Part the First" and "Part the Second" have been retained to indicate where issue installments began. The bibliography at the end of this volume cites the issues in which the segments appeared.

Leslie's excessive use of non-English phrases merits some translation. Decisions about providing the translations were made on a case-by-case basis, depending upon the richness an understanding of the non-English phrase contributes to Leslie's messages.

Of course, reading Leslie's works as they appeared in the nineteenth century is ideal. The format of periodical publications, the visual enhancements of various reprintings of culinary works, and the acknowledged borrowings from previous publications enhance a reader's understanding of the literary marketplace. Nonetheless, this twenty-first-century edition provides insights into Leslie's creativity and skills as a writer—worthy elements that are not lost with changes in format.

Selections from Eliza Leslie

FICTION

The Travelling Tin-Man

"And, indeed sir, there are cozeners abroad;
therefore it behoves men to be wary."

SHAKSPEARE,
The Winter's Tale, act 4, scene 4, lines 2140–41

Micajah Warner was owner and cultivator of a small farm in one of the oldest, most fertile, and most beautiful counties of the State of Pennsylvania, not far from the Maryland line. Micajah was a plain Quaker,[1] and a man of quiet and primitive habits. He was totally devoid of all ambitious cravings after tracts of ten thousand acres, and he aspired not to the honour and glory of having his name given to a town in the western wilderness, (though *Warnerville* would not have sounded badly,) neither was he possessed of an unconquerable desire of becoming a judge, or of going to Congress. Therefore, he had always been able to resist the persuasions and example of those of his neighbours, who left the home of their fathers, and the comforts of an old settlement, to seek a less tedious road to wealth and consequence, on the other side of the Alleghany. He was satisfied with the possession of two hundred acres, one half of which he had lent (not given) to his son Israel, who expected shortly to be married to a very pretty and very notable young woman in the neighbourhood, who was, however, no heiress.

Upon this event, Israel was to be established in an old frame house that had long since been abandoned by his father in favour of the substantial stone dwelling which the family occupied at the period of our story. The house had been taken up and transplanted to that part of the farm now allotted to Israel, and he very prudently deferred repairing it till he saw whether it survived its progress across the domain. But as it did not fall asunder during the journey, it was judged worthy of a new front door, new windowpanes, and new shingles to cover the vast chasms of the roof; all which improvements were made by Israel's own hands. This house was deposited in the vicinity of the upper branch of the creek, and conveniently near to a saw-mill which had been built by Israel in person.

Like most of her sect, whether in town or country, Bulah, the wife of Micajah Warner, was a woman of even temper, untiring industry, and great skill in housewifery. Her daughters, commonly called Amy and Orphy, were neat pretty little quaker girls, extremely alert, and accustomed from their earliest childhood, to assist in the work of the house. As her daughters were so handy and industrious, and only went half the year to school, Mrs. Warner did not think it necessary to keep any other *help* than an indentured Negro girl, named Cloe.

Except the marriage of Israel, which was now in prospect; a flood in the neighbouring creek, which had raised the water so high as to wash away the brick oven from the side of the house; a tornado that carried off the roof of the old stable, and landed it whole in an adjoining clover field; and a visit from a family of beggars, (an extraordinary phenomenon in the country,) nothing occurred among the Warners for a long succession of years that had occasioned more than a month's talk of the mother, and a month's listening of the children. "They kept the even tenor of their way." The occupations of Israel and his father (assisted occasionally by a few hired men) were, of course, those of the farm, except when Israel took a day, now and then, to attend his saw-mill.

With regard to domestic arrangements, everything connected with household affairs went on in the same course year after year, except that, as the daughters of the family improved in capability of work, Cloe, the black girl, retrograded. They washed on Monday, (with the assistance of a woman, hired for the day,) ironed on Tuesday, performed what they called "the little baking," on Wednesday, and "the big baking," on Friday; cleaned the house on Saturday, and clear-starched their book-muslin collars; rode on horseback to Friends' meeting on Sunday morning, and visited their neighbours on Sunday afternoon.

It was the day after the one on which Israel and his bride-elect had passed Meeting,[2] and consequently, a month before the one fixed for the wedding, that something like an adventure fell among the Warner family.

It was a beautiful evening at the close of August. The father and son had been all day in the meadows, mowing the second crop of grass; Mrs. Warner was darning stockings in the porch, with her two daughters knitting on the bench beside her; Amy being then fourteen, and Orphy about twelve. Cloe was absent, having been borrowed by a relation, about five miles off, to do the general work of the house, while the family were engaged in preparing for a quilting frolic.

"Come, girls," said Mrs. Warner, to her daughters, "it's just sun-down. The geese are coming home, and daddy and Israel will soon be here. Amy, do thee go down to the spring-house and bring up the milk and butter; and Orphy, thee can set the table."

The two girls put up their knitting, (not, however, till they had knit to the middle of the needle,) and, in a short time, Amy was seen coming back from the spring-house, with a large pitcher of milk and a plate of butter. In the meantime, Orphy had drawn out the ponderous claw-footed walnut table that stood all summer in the porch, and spreading over it a brown linen cloth, placed in regular order their every-day supper-equipage of pewter plates, earthen porringers, and iron spoons.

The viands consisted of an immense round loaf of bread, nearly as large as a grindstone, and made of wheat and Indian meal, the half of a huge cheese, a piece of cold pork, a peach pie, and an apple pie; and, as it had been baking-day, there was the customary addition of a rice-pudding, in an earthen pan of stupendous size. The last finish to the decorations of the table was a large bowl of cool water, placed near the seat occupied by the father of the family, who never could begin any of his meals without a copious draught of the pure element.

In a few minutes, the farmer and his son made their appearance as they turned the angle of the peach- orchard fence, preceded by the geese, their usual avant-couriers, who went out every morning to feed in an old field beyond the meadows.

As soon as Micajah and Israel had hung up their scythes, and washed themselves at the pump, they sat down to table; the farmer in his own blue-painted, high-backed, high-armed chair, and Israel taking the seat always allotted to him, a low chair, the rushes of which having long since deserted the bottom, had been replaced by cross pieces of cloth listing, ingeniously interwoven with each other; and this being, according to the general opinion, the worst seat in the house, always fell to the share of the young man, who was usually passive on all occasions, and never seemed to consider himself entitled to the same accommodation as the rest of the family.

Suddenly, the shrill blast of a tin trumpet resounded through the woods that covered the hill in front of the house, to the great disturbance of the geese, who had settled themselves quietly for the night in their usual bivouac around the ruins of an old waggon. The Warners ceased their supper to listen and look; and they saw emerging from the woods, and rattling down the hill at a brisk trot, the cart of one of those itinerant tin merchants, who originate in New England, and travel from one end of the Union to the other, avoiding the cities, and seeking customers among the country people; who, besides buying their ware, always invite them to a meal and a bed.

The tin-man came blowing his horn to the steps of the porch, and there stopping his cart, addressed the farmer's wife in the true nasal twang that characterizes the lower class of New Englanders, and enquired "if she had any notion of a bargain." She replied that "she believed that she had no occasion for anything"; her customary answers to all such questions. But Israel, who looked into futurity, and entertained views towards his own housekeeping, stepped forward to the tin-cart, and began to take down and examine various mugs, pans, kettles, and coffee-pots—the latter particularly, as he had a passion for coffee, which he secretly determined to indulge both morning and evening as soon as he was settled in his domicile.

"Mother," said Amy, "I do wish thee would buy a new coffee-pot, for ours has been leaking all summer, and I have to stop it every morning with rye meal. Thee knows we can give the old one to Israel."

"To be sure," replied Mrs. Warner, "it will do well enough for young beginners. But I cannot say I feel quite free to buy a new coffee-pot at this time. I must consider about it."

"And there's the cullender," said Orphy, "it has such a big crack at the bottom, that when I am smashing the squashes for dinner, not only the water, but the squashes themselves drip through. Better give it to Israel, and get a new one for ourselves."

"What's this?" she continued, taking up a tin water dipper.

"That's for dipping water out of the bucket," replied the tin-man.

"Oh, yes!" cried Amy, "I've seen such a one at Rachel Johnson's. What a clever thing it is! with a good long handle, so that there's no danger of splashing the water on our clothes. Do buy it mother. Thee knows that Israel can have the big calabash[3]: I patched it myself, yesterday, where it was broken, and bound the edge with new tape, and it's now as good as ever."

"I don't know," said the farmer, "that we want anything but a new lantern, for ours had the socket burnt out long before these moonlight nights, and its dangerous work taking a candle into the stable."

The tin-man knowing that our plain old farmers, though extremely liberal of everything that is produced on their plantations, are frequently very tenacious of coin, and much averse to parting with actual money, recommended his wares more on account of their cheapness, than their goodness; and, in fact, the price of most of the articles was two or three cents lower than they could be purchased for at the stores.

Old Micajah thought there was no absolute necessity for anything except the lantern; but his daughters were so importunate for the coffee-pot, the cullender, and the water-dipper, that, finally, all three were purchased and paid for. The tin-man in vain endeavoured to prevail on Mrs. Warner to buy some large patty pans, which the girls looked at with longing eyes; and he reminded them how pretty their pumpkin pies would look at their next quilting, baked in scollop-edged tin. But this purchase was premptorily refused by the good quaker woman; alleging that scollop-edged pies were all pride and vanity, and that if properly made, they were quite good enough baked in round plates.

The travelling merchant then produced divers boxes and phials of quack medicines, prepared at a celebrated manufactory of those articles, and duly sealed with the maker's own seal, and inscribed with his name in his own handwriting. Among these, he said, "there were certain cures for every complaint in natur; draps for the agur, the tooth-ache, and the rheumatiz; salves for the ring-worms, corns, frost-bitten heels, and sore eyes, and pills for consumption and fall fevers; beside that most valuable of all physic, Swaim's Wormifuge."

The young people exclaimed with one accord against the purchase of any of the medicines; and, business being over, the tin-man was invited by the farmer to sit down and take supper with the family—an invitation as freely accepted as given.

The twilight was now closing, but the full moon had risen, and afforded sufficient light for the supper-table in the porch. The tin-man took a seat, and before Mrs. Warner had finished her usual invitation of "stranger reach to, and help thyself; we are poor hands at inviting, but thee's welcome to it, such as it is"—he had already cut himself a huge piece of the cold pork, and an enormous slice of bread. He next poured out a porringer of milk, to which he afterwards added one-third of the peach-pie, and several plates full of rice-pudding. He then said, "I suppose you haven't got no cider about the house"; and Israel at his father's desire, immediately brought up a pitcher of that liquor from the cellar.

During supper, the tin-man entertained his entertainers with anecdotes of the roguery of his own countrymen, or rather, as he called them, his "statesmen." In his opinion of their general dishonesty, Mrs. Warner most cordially joined. She related a story of an itinerant Yankee, who persuaded her to empty some of her pillows and bolsters, under colour of exchanging with him old feathers for new—a thing which she acknowledged had puzzled her not a little, as she thought it strange that any man should bargain so badly for himself. He produced from his cart a bag of feathers which he declared were quite new; but after his departure she found that he had given her such short measure that she had not half enough to fill her ticking, and most of the feathers were proved upon examination, to have belonged to chickens, rather than to geese—nearly a whole cock's tail having been found amongst them.

The farmer pointed into the open door of the house, and showed the tin-man a large wooden clock, put up without a case between two windows, the pendulum and the weights being "exposed and bare." This clock he had bought for ten dollars, of a travelling Yankee who had set out to supply the country with these machines. It had only kept tolerable time for about two months, and had ever since been getting faster and faster, though it was still faithfully wound up every week. The hands were now going merrily round at the rate of ten miles an hour, and it never struck less than twelve.

The Yankee tin-man, with a candour that excited the admiration of the whole family, acknowledged that his statesmen were the greatest rogues "on the face of the yearth"; and recounted instances of their trickery that would have startled the belief of any, but the inexperienced and credulous people who were now listening to him. He told, for example, of sausages being brought to market in the eastern towns, that when purchased and prepared for frying, were found to be filled with chopped turnip and shreds of red flannel.

For once, thought the Warners, we have found an honest Yankee.

They sat a long while at the table, and though the tin-man seemed to talk all the time he was eating, the quantity of victuals that he caused to disappear surprised even Mrs. Warner, accustomed as she was to the appetite of Israel.

When the Yankee had at last completed his supper, the farmer invited him to stay all night; but he replied, "that it was a moonshiny, and fine cool travellin after a warm day, he preferred putting on toward Maryland as soon as his creatur was rested, and had a feed."

He then without more ceremony led his horse and cart into the barn-yard and stopping near the stable door, fed the animal by the light of the moon, and carried him a bucket of water from the pump.

The girls being reminded by their mother that it was late, and that the cows had long since come home, they took their pails and went out to milk, while she washed up the supper things. While they were milking, the subsequent dialogue took place between them.

ORPHY. I know it's not right to notice strangers, and to be sure the man's welcome, but Amy, did thee ever see any body take victuals like this Yankee?

AMY. Yes, but he didn't eat all he took, for I saw him slip a great chunk of bread and cheese into his pocket, and then a big piece of pie, while he was talking and making us laugh.

ORPHY. Well, I think a man must be very badly off to do such a thing. I wonder he did not ask for victuals to take away with him. He need not have been afraid. He must know that victuals is no object. And then he has travelled the road long enough to be sure that he can get a meal for nothing at any house he stops at, as all the tin-men do. He must have seen us looking at his eating so much, and may-be his pride is hurt, and so he's made up his mind, all of a sudden, to take his meals no more at people's houses.

AMY. Then why can't he stop at a tavern, and pay for his victuals?

ORPHY. May-be he don't want to spend his money in that trifling way. Who knows but he is saving it up to help an old mother, or to buy back land, or something of that sort? I'll be bound he calculates upon eating nothing to-morrow but what he slipped off from our table.

AMY. All he took will not last him a day. It's a pity of him, any how.

ORPHY. I wish he had not been too bashful to ask for victuals to take with him.

AMY. And still he did not strike me at all as a bashful man.

ORPHY. Suppose we were just in a private way to put some

victuals into his cart for him, without letting him know any thing about it? Let's hide it among the tins, and how glad he'll be when he finds it to-morrow!

AMY. So we will; that's an excellent notion! I never pitied any body so much since the day the beggars came, which was five years ago last harvest, for I have kept count ever since; and I remember it as well as if it was yesterday.

ORPHY. We don't know what a hard thing it is to want victuals, as the Irish schoolmaster used to tell us, when he saw us emptying pans of milk into the pig-trough, and turning the cows into the orchard to eat the heaps of apples laying under the trees.

AMY. Yes, and it must be much worse for an American to want victuals, than for people from the old countries who are used to it.

After they had finished their milking, and strained and put away the milk, the kind-hearted little girls proceeded to accomplish their benevolent purpose. They took from the large wire-safe in the cellar, a pie, half a loaf of bread, and a great piece of cheese; and putting them into a basket, they went to the barn-yard, intending to tell their mother as soon as the tin-man was gone, and not for a moment doubting her approval, since in the house of an American farmer, victuals, as Orphy just observed, is no object.

As they approached the barn-yard, they saw, by the light of the moon, the Yankee coming away from his cart and returning to the house. The girls crouched down behind the garden-fence till he had passed, and then cautiously proceeded on their errand. They went to the back of the cart, intending to deposit their provisions, when they were startled at seeing something evidently alive, moving behind the round opening of the cover; and in a moment the head of a little black child peeped out of the hole.

The girls were so surprised that they stopped short and could not utter a word, and the young Negro, evidently afraid of being seen, immediately popped down its head among the tins.

"Amy, did thee see that?"—asked Orphy, in a low voice.

"Yes I did so," replied Amy; "what can the Yankee be doing with that little neger, and why does he hide it? Let's go and ask the child."

"No, no!" exclaimed Orphy, "the tin-man will be angry."

"And who cares if he is?" said Amy; "he has done something he is ashamed of, and we need not be afraid of him."

They then went quite close to the back of the cart, and Amy said, "Here, little snow-ball shew thyself and speak; and do not be afraid, for nobody's going to hurt thee."

"How did thee come into this cart?" asked Orphy; "and why does the Yankee hide thee? Tell us all about it, and be sure not to speak above thy breath."

The black child again peeped out of the hole, and looking cautiously round, said, "Are you quite sure the naughty man won't hear us?"

"Quite sure," answered Amy, "but is thee boy or girl?"

"I'm a little gal," replied the child; and with the characteristic volubility of her race she continued, "and my name's Dinah, and I'm five year old, and my daddy and mammy are free coloured people, and they lives a big piece off, and daddy works out, and mammy sells gingerbread and molasses-beer, and we have a sign over the door with a bottle and cake on it."

AMY. But how did this man get hold of thee, if thy father and mother are free people? Thee can't be bound to him, or he need not hide thee.

DINAH. O, I know I an't bounded to him—I expect he stole me.

AMY. Stole thee! What here in the free state of Pennsylvany?

DINAH. I was out picking huckleberries in the woods up the

road, and I strayed off a big piece from home. Then the tin-man comed along, driving his cart, and I run close to the road-side to look, as I always does when any body goes by. So he told me to come into his cart, and he would give me a tin mug to put my huckleberries in, and I might choose it myself, and it would hold them a heap better than my old Indian basket. So I was very glad, and he lifted me up into the cart, and I choosed the very best and biggest tin mug he had, and emptied my huckleberries into it. And then he told me he'd give me a ride in his cart, and then he set me far back on a box, and he whipped his creatur and druv and druv, and jolted me so that I tumbled all down among the tins. And then he picked me up, and tied me fast with his handkercher to one of the back posts of the cart to keep me steady he said. And, then, for all I was steady, I couldn't help crying, and I wanted him to take me home to daddy and mammy. But he only sniggered at me, and said he wouldn't, and bid me hush; and then he got mad, and because I couldn't hush up just in a minute, he whipped me quite smart.

ORPHY. Poor little thing!

DINAH. And then I got frightened, for he put on a wicked look, and said he'd kill me dead if I cried any more or made the least bit of noise. And so he has been carrying me along in his cart for two days and two nights, and he makes me hide away all the time, and he won't let nobody see me. And I hate him, and yesterday, when I know'd he didn't see me, I spit on the crown of his hat.

AMY. Hush!—thee must never say thee hates any body.

DINAH. At night I sleeps upon the bag of feathers; and when he stops any where to eat, he comes sneaking to the back of the cart and pokes in victuals, (he has just now brung me some,) and he tells me he wants me to be fat and good-looking. I was afeard he was going to sell me to the butcher, as Nace Willet did his fat calf, and I thought I'd ax him about it, and he laughed and told me he was going to sell me sure enough, but not to a butcher. And I'm almost all the time very sorry, only sometimes I'm not, and then I should like to play with the tins, only he won't let me. I don't dare to cry out loud, for fear the naughty man would whip me; but I always moan when we're going through woods, and there's nobody in sight to hear me. He never lets me look out of the back of the cart, only when there's nobody to see me, and he won't let me sing even when I want to. And I moan most when I think of my daddy and mammy, and how they are wondering what has become of me; and I think moaning does me good, only he stops me short.

AMY. Now, Orphy, what's to be done? The tin-man has, of course, kidnapped this black child to take her into Maryland, where he can sell her for a good price; as she is a fat, healthy-looking thing, and that is a slave state. Does thee think we ought to let him take her off?

ORPHY. No, indeed! I think I could feel free to fight for her myself—that is, if fighting was not forbidden by Friends. Yonder's Israel coming to turn the cows into the clover-field. Little girl, lay quiet and don't offer to show thyself.

Israel now advanced—"Well, girls," said he, "what's thee doing at the tin-man's cart? Not meddling among his tins, I hope? Oh! the curiosity of women-folks!"

"Israel," said Amy, "step softly—we have something to show thee."

The girls then lifted up the corner of the cart cover, and displayed the little negro girl, crouched upon the bag of feathers—a part of his merchandize which the Yankee had not thought it expedient to produce, after hearing Mrs. Warner's anecdote of one of his predecessors.

The young man was much amazed, and his two sisters began both at once to relate to him the story of the black child. Israel looked almost indignant. His sisters said to him, "To be sure we won't let the Yankee carry this child off with him."

"I judge we won't," answered Israel.

"Then," said Amy, "let us take her out of the cart, and hide her in the barn or somewhere, till he has gone."

"No," replied Israel, "I can't say I feel free to do that. It would be too much like stealing her over again; and I've no notion of evening myself to a Yankee in any of his ways. Put her down in the cart and let her alone. I'll have no underhanded work about her. Let's all go back to the house; mother has got down all the broken crockery from the top shelf in the corner cupboard, and the Yankee's mending it with a sort of stuff like sticks of sealing-wax, that he carries about with him; and I dare say he'll get her to pay more for it than the things are worth. But say nothing."

The girls cautioned Dinah not to let the tin-man know that they had discovered her, and to keep herself perfectly quiet; and they then accompanied their brother to the house, feeling very fidgetty and uneasy.

They found the table covered with old bowls, old tea-pots, old sugar-dishes, and old pitchers; whose fractures the Yankee was cementing together, while Mrs. Warner held the candle, and her husband viewed the operation with great curiosity.

"Israel," said his mother, as he entered, "this friend is making the china as good as new, only that we can't help seeing the join; and we are going to give all the mended things to thee."

The Yankee, having finished his work and been paid for it, said it was high time for him to be about starting, and he must go and look after his cart. He accordingly left the house for that purpose; and Israel, looking out at the end window, exclaimed, "I see he's not coming round to the house again, but he's going to try the short cut into the back road. I'll go and see that he puts up the bars after him."

Israel went out, and his sisters followed him to see the tin-man off.

The Yankee came to the bars, leading his horse with the cart, and found Israel there before him.

"Are you going to let down the bars for me?" said the tin-man.

"No," replied Israel, "I'm not going to be so polite; but I intend to see that thee carries off nothing more than belongs to thee."

"What do you mean?" exclaimed the Yankee, changing colour.

"I expect I can show thee," answered Israel. Then stepping up to the back of the cart and putting in his hands, he pulled out the black child and held her up before him, saying, "Now, if thee offers to touch this girl, I think we shall be apt to differ."

The tin-man then advanced towards Israel, and with a menacing look raised his whip; but the fearless young Quaker (having consigned the little girl to his sisters, who held her between them) immediately broke a stick from a tree that grew near, and stood on the defensive with a most steadfast look of calm resolution.

The Yankee went close up to him, brandishing his whip; but before he had time to strike, Israel with the utmost coolness, and with great strength and dexterity, seized him by the collar, and swinging him round to some distance, flung him to the ground with such force as to stun him, saying, "Mind, I don't call myself a fighting character, but if thee offers to get up I shall feel free to keep thee down."

The tin-man began to move, and the girls ran shrieking to the house for their father, dragging with them the little black girl, whose screams (as is usual with all of her colour) were the loudest of the loud.

In an instant the stout old farmer was at the side of his son, and notwithstanding the struggles of the Yankee, they succeeded by main force in conveying him to the stable, into which they fastened him for the night.

Early next morning, Israel and his father went to the nearest magistrate for a warrant and a constable, and were followed home by half the township. The county court was then in session; the tin-man was tried, and convicted of having kidnapped a free black child, with the design of selling her as a slave in one of the southern states; and he was punished by fine and imprisonment.

The Warner family would have felt more compassionate for him than they did, only that all the mended china fell apart again the next day, and his tins were so badly soldered that all their bottoms came out before the end of the month.

Mrs. Warner declared that she had done with Yankee tin-men for ever, and in short with all other Yankees. But the store-keeper, Philip Thompson, who was the most sensible man of the neighbourhood, and took two Philadelphia newspapers, convinced her that some of the best and greatest men America can boast of, were natives of the New England states. And he even asserted that in the course of his life (and his age did not exceed sixty-seven) he had met with no less than five *perfectly* honest Yankee tin-men; and besides being honest, two of them were not in the least impudent. Among the latter, however, he did not, of course, include a very handsome fellow, that a few years since made the tour of the United States with his tin-cart, calling himself the Boston Beauty, and wearing his own miniature round his neck.

To conclude—an advertisement having been inserted in several of the papers, to designate where Dinah the little black girl was to be found, and the tin-man's trial having also been noticed in the public prints, in about a fortnight her father and mother (two very decent free negroes) arrived to claim her; having walked all the way from their cottage at the extremity of the next county. They immediately identified her, and the meeting was most joyful to them and to her. They told at full length every particular of their anxious search after their child, which was ended by a gentleman bringing a newspaper to their house, containing the welcome intelligence that she was safe at Micajah Warner's.

Amy and Orphy were desirous of retaining little Dinah in the family, and as the child's parents seemed very willing, the girls urged their mother to keep her instead of Cloe, who they said could very easily be made over to Israel. But, to the astonishment of the whole family, Israel on this occasion proved refractory, declaring that he would not allow his wife to be plagued with such an imp as Cloe, and that he chose to have little Dinah himself, if her parents would bind her to him till she was eighteen. This affair was soon satisfactorily arranged.

Israel was married at the appointed time, and took possession of the house near the saw-mill. He prospered; and in a few years was able to buy a farm of his own, and to build a stone house on it. Dinah turned out extremely well, and the Warner family still talk of the night when she was discovered in the cart of the travelling tin-man.

Mrs. Washington Potts

Bromley Cheston, an officer in the United States navy, had just returned from a three years' cruize in the Mediterranean. His ship came into New York; and after he had spent a week with a sister that was married in Boston, he could not resist his inclination to pay a visit to his maternal aunt, who had resided since her widowhood at one of the small towns on the banks of the Delaware.

The husband of Mrs. Marsden had not lived long enough to make his fortune, and it was his last injunction that she should retire with her daughter to the country, or at least to a country town. He feared that if she remained in Philadelphia she would have too many temptations to exercise her taste for unnecessary expense: and that, in consequence, the very moderate income, which was all he was able to leave her, would soon be found insufficient to supply her with comforts.

We will not venture to say that duty to his aunt Marsden was the young lieutenant's only incentive to this visit: as she had a beautiful daughter about eighteen, for whom, since her earliest childhood, Bromley Cheston had felt something a little more vivid than the usual degree of regard that boys think sufficient for their cousins. His family had formerly lived in Philadelphia, and till he went into the navy Bromley and Albina were in habits of daily intercourse. Afterwards, on returning from sea, he always as soon as he set his foot on American ground began to devise means of seeing his pretty cousin, however short the time and however great the distance. And it was in meditation on Albina's beauty and sprightliness that he had often "while sailing on the midnight deep," beguiled the long hours of the watch, and thus rendered more tolerable the dreariest part of a seaman's duty.

On arriving at the village, Lieutenant Cheston immediately established his quarters at the hotel, fearing that to become an inmate of his aunt's house might cause her some inconvenience. Though he had performed the whole journey in a steamboat, he could not refrain from changing his waistcoat, brushing his coat sleeves, brushing his hat, brushing his hair, and altering the tie of his cravat. Though he had "never told his love," it cannot be said that concealment had "preyed on his damask cheek"; the only change in that damask having been effected by the sun and wind of the ocean.

Mrs. Marsden lived in a small modest-looking white house, with a green door and green venetian shutters. In early summer the porch was canopied and perfumed with honeysuckle, and the windows with roses. In front was a flower garden, redolent of sweetness and beauty; behind was a well-stored potager, and a flourishing little orchard. The windows were amply shaded by the light and graceful foliage of some beautiful locust-trees.

"What a lovely spot," exclaimed Cheston—and innocence—modesty—candour—contentment—peace—simple pleasures—intellectual enjoyments—and various other delightful ideas chased each other rapidly through his mind.

When he knocked at the door, it was opened by a black girl named Drusa, who had been brought up in the family, and whose delight on seeing him was so great that she could scarcely find it in her heart to tell him that "the ladies were both out, or at least partly out." Cheston, however, more than suspected that they were wholly at home, for he saw his aunt peeping over the bannisters, and had a glimpse of his cousin flitting into the back parlour; and besides, the whole domicile was evidently in some great commotion, strongly resembling that horror of all men, a house-cleaning. The carpets had been removed, and the hall was filled with the parlour-chairs: half of them being turned bottom upwards on the others, with looking-glasses and pictures leaning against them; and he knew that, on such occasions, the ladies of a family in middle life are never among the missing.

"Go and give Lieutenant Cheston's compliments to your ladies," said he, "and let them know that he is waiting to see them."

Mrs. Marsden now ran down stairs in a wrapper and morning cap, and gave her nephew a very cordial reception. "Our house is just now in such confusion," said she, "that I have no place to invite you to sit down in except the back porch."—and there they accordingly took their seats.

"Do not suppose," continued Mrs. Marsden, "that we are cleaning house: but we are going to have a party to-night, and therefore you are most fortunate in your arrival, for I think I can promise you a very pleasant evening. We have sent invitations to all the most genteel families within seven miles, and I can assure you there was a great deal of trouble in getting the notes conveyed. We have also asked a number of strangers from the city, who happen to be boarding in the village; we called on them for that purpose. If all that are invited were to come, we should have a complete squeeze; but unluckily we have received an unusual number of regrets, and some have as yet returned no answers at all. However, we are sure of Mrs. Washington Potts."

"I see," said Cheston, "you are having your parlours papered."—"Yes," replied Mrs. Marsden, "we could not possibly have a party with that old-fashioned paper on the walls, and we sent to the city a week ago for a man to come and bring with him some of the newest patterns, but he never made his appearance till last night after we had entirely given him up, and after we had had the rooms put in complete order in other respects. But he says, as the parlours are very small, he can easily put on the new paper before evening, so we thought it better to take up the carpets, and take down the curtains, and undo all that we did yesterday, rather than the walls should look old-fashioned. I *did* intend having them painted, which would of course be much better, only that there was no time to get *that* done before the party, so we must defer the painting now for three or four years till this new paper has grown old."

"But where is Albina?" asked Cheston.

"The truth is," answered Mrs. Marsden, "she is very busy making cakes; as in this place we can buy none that are fit for a party. Luckily Albina is very clever at all such things, having been a pupil of Mrs. Goodfellow.[1] But there is certainly a great deal of trouble in getting up a party in the country."

Just then the black girl, Drusa, made her appearance, and said to Mrs. Marsden, "I've been for that there bean you call wanilla, and Mr. Brown says he never heard of such a thing."

"A man that keeps so large a store has no right to be so ignorant," remarked Mrs. Marsden.—"Then, Drusa, we must flavour the ice-cream with lemon."

"There a'n't no more lemons to be had," said the girl, "and we've just barely enough for the lemonade."

"Then the lemons must be taken for the ice-cream," replied Mrs. Marsden, "and we must make out the lemonade with cream of tartar."

"I forgot to tell you," said Drusa, "that Mrs. Jones says she can't spare no more cream, upon no account."

"How vexatious!" exclaimed Mrs. Marsden, "I wish we had two cows of our own—one is not sufficient when we are about giving a party. Drusa we must make out the ice-cream by thickening some milk with eggs."

"Eggs are scace," replied the girl, "Miss Albinar used up so many for the cakes."

"She must spare some eggs from the cakes," said Mrs. Marsden, "and make out the cakes by adding a little pearl-ash.[2] Go directly and tell her so."

Cheston, though by no means *au fait* to the mysteries of confectionary, could not help smiling at all this making out—"Really," said his aunt, "these things are very annoying. And as this party is given to Mrs. Washington Potts, it is extremely desirable that nothing should fail. There is no such thing now as having company, unless we can receive and entertain them in a certain style."

"I perfectly remember," said Cheston, "the last party at which I was present in your house. I was then a midshipman, and it was just before I sailed on my first cruize in the Pacific. I spent a delightful evening."

"Yes, I recollect that night," replied Mrs. Marsden. "In those days it was not necessary for us to support a certain style, and parties were then very simple things, except among people of the first rank. It was thought sufficient to have two or three baskets of substantial cakes at tea, some almonds, raisins, apples, and oranges handed round afterwards, with wine and cordial, and then a large-sized pound-cake at the last. The company assembled at seven o'clock, and generally walked; for the ladies' dresses were only plain white muslin. We invited but as many as could be accommodated with seats. The young people played at forfeits, and sung English and Scotch songs, and at the close of the evening danced to the piano. How Mrs. Washington Potts would be shocked if she was to find herself at one of those obsolete parties!"

"The calf-jelly won't be clear," said the black girl, again making her appearance. "Aunt Katy has strained it five times over through the flannen-bag."

"Go then and tell her to strain it five- and-twenty times," said Mrs. Marsden, angrily—"It must and shall be clear. Nothing is more vulgar than cloudy jelly; Mrs. Washington Potts will not touch it unless it is transparent as amber."

"What Nong tong paw again," said Cheston. "Now do tell me who *is* Mrs. Washington Potts?"

"Is it possible you have not heard of her!" exclaimed Mrs. Marsden.

"Indeed I have not," replied Cheston. "You forget that for several years I have been cruising on classic ground, and I can assure you that the name of Washington Potts has not yet reached the shores of the Mediterranean."

"She is wife to a gentleman that has made a fortune in New Orleans," pursued Mrs. Marsden. "They came last winter to live in Philadelphia, having first visited London and Paris. During the warm weather they took lodgings in this village, and we have become quite intimate. So we have concluded to give them a party, previous to their return to Philadelphia, which is to take place immediately. She is a charming woman, though she certainly makes strange mistakes in talking. You have no idea how sociable she is, at least since she returned our call; which, to be sure, was not till the end of a week; and Albina and I had sat up in full dress to receive her for no less than five days: that is, from twelve o'clock till three. At last she came, and it would have surprised you to see how affably she behaved to us."

"Not at all," said Cheston, "I should not have expected that she would have treated you rudely."

"She really," continued Mrs. Marsden, "grew quite intimate before her visit was over, and took our hands at parting. And as she went out through the garden, she stopped to admire Albina's moss-roses: so we could do no less than give her all that were blown. From that day she has always sent to us when she wants flowers."

"No doubt of it," said Cheston.

"You cannot imagine," pursued Mrs. Marsden, "on what a familiar footing we are. She has a high opinion of Albina's taste, and often gets her to make up caps and do other little things for her. When any of her children are sick, she never sends any where else for currant jelly or preserves. Albina makes gingerbread for them every Saturday. During the holidays she frequently sent her three boys to spend the day with us. There is the very place in the railing where Randolph broke out a stick to whip Jefferson with, because Jefferson had thrown in his face a hot baked apple which the mischievous little rogue had stolen out of old Katy's oven."

In the mean time, Albina had taken off the brown holland bib apron which she had worn all day in the kitchen, and telling the cook to watch carefully the plumb-cake that was baking, she hastened to her room by a back staircase, and proceeded to take the pins out of her hair; for where is the young lady that on any emergency whatever, would appear before a young gentleman with her hair pinned up. Though, just now, the opening out of her curls was a considerable inconvenience to Albina, as she had bestowed much time and pains on putting them up for the evening.

Finally she came down "in prime array," and Cheston who had left her a school-girl, found her now grown to womanhood and more beautiful than ever. Still he could not forbear reproving her for treating him so much as a stranger, and not coming to him at once in her morning-dress.

"Mrs. Washington Potts," said Albina, "is of opinion that a young lady should never be seen in dishabille by a gentleman."

Cheston now found it difficult to hear the name of Mrs. Potts with patience.—"Albina," thought he, "is bewitched as well as her mother."

He spoke of his cruize in the Mediterranean, and Albina told him that she had seen a beautiful view of the Bay of Naples in a souvenir belonging to Mrs. Washington Potts.

"I have brought with me some sketches of Mediterranean scenery," pursued Cheston.—"You know I draw a little. I promise myself great pleasure in showing and explaining them to you."

"Oh! do send them this afternoon," exclaimed Albina. "They will be the very things for the centre table. I dare say the Montagues will recognize some of the places they have seen in Italy, for they have travelled all over the south of Europe."

"And who are the Montagues?" enquired Cheston.

"They are a very elegant English family," answered Mrs. Marsden, "cousins in some way to several noblemen."

"Perhaps so," said Cheston.

"Albina met with them at the lodgings of Mrs. Washington Potts," pursued Mrs. Marsden—"where they have been staying a week for the benefit of country air; and so she inclosed her card, and sent them invitations to her party. They have as yet returned no answer; but that is no proof they will not come, for perhaps it may be the newest fashion in England not to answer notes."

"You know the English are a very peculiar people," remarked Albina.

"And what other lions have you provided?" said Cheston.

"Oh! no others except a poet," replied Albina. "Have you never heard of Bewley Garvin Gandy."[3]

"Never!" answered Cheston—"Is that all one man?"

"Nonsense," replied Albina; "you know that poets generally have three names. B.G.G. was formerly Mr. Gandy's signature, when he wrote only for the newspapers, but now since he has come out in the magazines, and annuals, and published his great poem of the World of Sorrow, he gives his name at full length. He has tried law, physics, and divinity, has resigned all for the Muses. He is a great favourite with Mrs. Washington Potts."

"And now, Albina," said Cheston, "as I know you can have but little leisure to-day, I will only detain you while you indulge me with 'Auld lang syne'—I see the piano has been moved out into the porch."

"Yes," said Mrs. Marsden, "on account of the parlour papering."

"Oh! Bromley Cheston," exclaimed Albina, "do not ask me to play any of those antediluvian Scotch songs. Mrs. Washington Potts cannot tolerate any thing but Italian."

Cheston who had no taste for Italian, immediately took his hat, and apologizing for the length of his stay, was going away with the thought that Albina had much deteriorated in growing up.

"We shall see you this evening without the ceremony of a further invitation," said Albina.

"Of course," replied Cheston.

"I quite long to introduce you to Mrs. Washington Potts," said Mrs. Marsden.

"What simpletons these women are," thought Cheston, as he hastily turned to depart.

"The big plumb-cake's burnt to a coal," said Drusa, putting her head out of the kitchen door.

Both the ladies were off in an instant to the scene of disaster. And Chaston returned to his hotel, thinking of Mrs. Potts, (whom he had made up his mind to dislike) of the old adage that "evil communication corrupts good manners," and of the almost irresistible contagion of folly and vanity. "I am disappointed in Albina," said he, "in future I will regard her only as my mother's niece, and more than a cousin she shall never be to me."

Albina having assisted Mrs. Marsden in lamenting over the burnt cake, took of her silk frock, again pinned up her hair, and joined assiduously in preparing another plumb-cake to replace the first one. A fatality seemed to attend nearly all the confections, as is often the case when particular importance is attached to their success. The jelly obstinately refused to clarify, and the blanc-mange was equally unwilling to congeal. The maccaroons having run in baking, had neither shape nor feature, the kisses declined rising, and the sponge-cake contradicted its name. Some of the things succeeded, but most were complete failures: probably because (as old Katy insisted) "there was a spell upon them." In a city these disasters could easily have been remedied (even at the eleventh hour) by sending to a confectioner's shop, but in the country there is no alternative. Some of these mischances might perhaps have been attributed to the volunteered assistance of a mantua-maker that had been sent for from the city to make new dresses for the occasion, and who on this busy day, being "one of the best creatures in the world," had declared her willingness to turn her hand to anything.

It was late in the afternoon before the papering was over, and then great indeed was the bustle in clearing away the litter, cleaning the floors, putting down the carpets, and replacing the furniture. In the midst of the confusion, and while the ladies were earnestly engaged in fixing the ornaments, Drusa came in to say that Dixon, the waiter that had been hired for the evening, had just arrived, and falling to work immediately he had poured all the blanc-mange down the sink mistaking it for bonny-clabby.[4] This intelligence was almost too much to bear, and Mrs. Marsden could scarcely speak for vexation.

"Drusa," said Albina, "you are a raven that has done nothing all day but croak of disaster. Away and show your face no more, let what will happen."

Drusa departed, but in a few minutes she again put in her head at the parlour door and said, "Ma'am may I jist speak one time more."

"What now," exclaimed Mrs. Marsden.

"Oh! there's nothing else spiled or flung down the sink, jist now," said Drusa, "but something's at hand a heap worse than all. Missus's old Aunt Quimby has jist landed from the boat, and is coming up the road with baggage enough to last all summer."

"Aunt Quimby!" exclaimed Albina, "this indeed caps the climax!"

"Was there ever any thing more provoking," said Mrs. Marsden. "When I lived in town she annoyed me sufficiently by coming every week to spend a day with me, and now she does not spend days but *weeks*. I would go to Alabama to get rid of her."

"And then," said Albina, "she would come and spend *months* with us. However, to do her justice she is a very respectable woman."

"All bores are respectable people," replied Mrs. Marsden, "if they were otherwise, it would not be in their power to bore us, for we would cut them and cast them off at once. How very unlucky. What will Mrs. Washington Potts think of her—and the Montagues too, if they *should* come? Still we must not affront her, as you know she is rich."

"What can her riches signify to us," said Albina, "she has a married daughter."

"True," replied Mrs. Marsden, "but you know riches should always command a certain degree of respect, and there are such things as legacies."

"After all, according to the common saying, ''tis an ill wind that blows no good,' the parlours having been freshly papered, we can easily persuade Aunt Quimby that they are too damp for her to sit in, and so we can make her stay up stairs all evening."

At this moment the old lady's voice was heard at the door,

discharging the porter who had brought her baggage on his wheelbarrow; and the next minute she was in the front parlour. Mrs. Marsden and Albina were also properly astonished, and properly delighted at seeing her; but each, after a pause of recollection, suddenly seized the old lady by the arms and conveyed her into the entry, exclaiming, "Oh! Aunt Quimby, Aunt Quimby! This is no place for you."

"What's the meaning of all this," cried Mrs. Quimby, "why won't you let me stay in the parlour."

"You'll get your death," answered Mrs. Marsden, "you'll get the rheumatism. Both parlours have been newly papered to-day, and the walls are quite wet."

"That's a bad thing," said Mrs. Quimby—"a very bad thing—I wish you had put off your papering till next spring. Who'd have thought of your doing it this day of all days."

"Oh! Aunt Quimby," said Albina, "why did you not let us know that you were coming?"

"Why, I wanted to give you an agreeable surprise," replied the old lady. "But tell me why the rooms are so decked out, with flowers hanging about the looking-glasses and lamps, and why the candles are drest with cut paper, or something that looks like it."

"We are going to have a party to-night," said Albina.—"A party—I'm glad of it. Then I'm just come in the nick of time."

"I thought you had long since given up parties," said Mrs. Marsden, turning pale.

"No, indeed—why should I—I always go when I am asked—to be sure I can't make much figure at parties now, being in my seventy-fifth year. But Mrs. Howks and Mrs. Himes, and several other of my old friends, always invite me to their daughters' parties, along with Mary; and I like to sit there and look about me and see people's new ways. Mary had a party herself last winter, and it went off very well, only that both the children came out that night with the measles; and one of the lamps leaked, and the oil ran all over the side-board and streamed down on the carpet; and, it being the first time we ever had ice-cream in the house, Peter, the stupid black boy, not only brought saucers to eat it in, but cups and saucers both."

The old lady was now hurried up stairs, and she showed much dissatisfaction on being told that as the damp parlours would not certainly give her her death, there was no alternative but for her to remain all evening in the chamber allotted to her. This chamber, (the best furnished in the house) was also to be 'the ladies' room,' and Albina somewhat consoled Mrs. Quimby by telling her that as the ladies would come up there to take off their hoods and arrange their hair, she would have an opportunity of seeing them all before they went down stairs. And Mrs. Marsden promised to give orders that a portion of all the refreshments, should be carried up to her, and that Miss Matson, the mantua-maker, should sit with her a great part of the evening.

It was now time for Albina and her mother to commence dressing, but Mrs. Marsden went down stairs again with 'more last words,' to the servants, and Albina to make some change in the arrangement of the centre-table.[5]

She was in a loose gown, her curls were pinned up and to keep them close and safe she tied over her head an old gauze handkerchief. While bending over the centre-table and marking with rose-leaves some of the most beautiful of Mrs. Hemans' poems, and opening two or three souvenirs at their finest plates, a knock was suddenly heard at the door, which proved to be the baker with the second plumb-cake, it having been consigned to *his* oven. Albina desired him to bring it to her, and putting it on the silver waiter, she determined to divide it herself into slices, being afraid to trust that business to any one else, lest it should be awkwardly cut or broken to pieces; it being quite warm.

The baker went out leaving the front-door open, and Albina intent on her task of cutting the cake, did not look up till she heard the sound of footsteps in the parlour, and then what was her dismay on perceiving Mr. and Mrs. Montague and their daughter.

Albina's first impulse was to run away, but she saw that it was now too late; and pale with confusion and vexation she tried to summon sufficient self-command to enable her to pass off this *contre-temps* with something like address.[6]

It was not yet dusk, the sun being scarcely down, and of all the persons invited to the party, it was natural to suppose that the English family would have come to the latest.

Mr. Montague was a long-bodied short-legged man, with round grey eyes, that looked as if they had been put on the outside of his face, the sockets having no apparent concavity: a sort of eye that is rarely seen in an American. He had a long nose, and a large heavy mouth with projecting under teeth, and altogether an unusual quantity of face; which face was bordered round with whiskers, and began at his eyes and met under his chin, and resembled in texture the coarse wiry fur of a black bear. He kept his hat under his arm, and his whole dress seemed as if modelled from one of the caricature prints of a London dandy.

Mrs. Montague (evidently some years older than her husband) was a gigantic woman, with features that looked as if seen through a magnifying glass. She had heavy piles of yellowish curls, and a crimson velvet tocque.[7] Her daughter was a tall hard-faced girl of seventeen, meant for a child by her parents, but not meaning herself as such. She was drest in a white muslin frock and trowsers, and had a mass of black hair curling on her neck and shoulders.

They all fixed their large eyes directly upon her, and it was no wonder that Albina quailed beneath their glance or rather their stare, particularly when Mrs. Montague surveyed her through her eye-glass. Mr. Montague spoke first. "Your note did not specify the hour—Miss—Miss Martin," said he, "and as you Americans are early people, we thought we were only complying with the simplicity of republican manners by coming before dark. We suppose that in general you adhere to the primitive maxim of 'early to bed and early to rise.'[8] I forget the remainder of the rhyme, but *you* know it undoubtedly."

Albina at that moment wished for the presence of Bromley Cheston. She saw from the significant looks that passed between the Montagues, that the unseasonable earliness of this visit did not arise from their ignorance of the customs of American society, but from premeditated impertinence. And she regretted still more having invited them, when Mr. Montague with impudent familiarity walked up to the cake (which she had nicely cut into slices without altering its form) and took one of them out.—"Miss Martin," said he, "your cake looks so inviting that I cannot refrain from helping myself to a piece. Mrs. Montague give me leave to present one to you. Miss Montague will you try a slice?"

They sat down on the sofa, each with a piece of cake, and Albina saw that they could scarcely refrain from laughing openly, not only at her dishabille, but at her disconcerted countenance.

Just at this moment Drusa appeared at the door, and called out, "Miss Albinar, the presarved squinches are all working.[9] Missus found 'em so when she opened the jar." Albina could bear no more, but hastily darting out of the room, she ran up stairs almost crying with vexation.

Old Mrs. Quimby was loud in her invectives against Mr. Montague for spoiling the symmetry of the cake, and helping himself and his family so unceremoniously. "You may rely upon it," said she, "a man that will do such a thing in a strange house is no gentleman."

"On the contrary," observed Mrs. Marsden, "I have no doubt that in England these free and easy proceedings are high ton. Albina have not you read some such things in *Vivian Grey*?"[10]

"I do not believe," said Mrs. Quimby, "that if this Englishman was in his own country, he would dare to go and take other people's cake without leave or license. But he thinks any sort of behaviour good enough for the Yankees, as they call us."

"I care not for the cake," said Albina, "although the pieces must now be put into baskets, I only think of the Montagues walking in without knocking, and catching me in complete dishabille: after I had kept poor Bromley Cheston waiting half an hour this morning rather than he should see me in my pink gingham gown and with my hair in pins."

"As sure as sixpence," remarked Mrs. Quimby, "this last shame has come upon you as a punishment for your pride to your own cousin."

Mrs. Marsden having gone into the adjoining room to dress, Albina remained in this, and placed herself before the glass for the same purpose. "Heigho!" said she, "how pale and jaded I look. What a fatiguing day I have had! I have been on my feet since five o'clock this morning, and I feel now more fit to go to bed than to add to my weariness by the task of dressing, and then playing the agreeable for four or five hours. I begin to think that parties (at least such parties as are now in vogue) should only be given by persons who have large houses, large purses, conveniences of every description, and servants enough to do all that is necessary."

"Albina is talking quite sensibly," said Aunt Quimby to Mrs. Marsden, who came in to see if her daughter required her assistance in dressing.

"Pho," said Mrs. Marsden, "think of the eclat of giving a party to Mrs. Washington Potts, and of having the Montagues among the guests. We shall find the advantage of it when we visit the city again."

"Albina," said Aunt Quimby, "now we are about dressing, just quit for a few moments and help me on with my long stays and my new black silk gown, and let me have the glass awhile; I am going to wear my lace cap with the white satin riband. This dark calico gown and plain muslin cap won't do at all to sit here in, before all the ladies that are coming up."

"Oh! no matter," replied Albina, who was unwilling to relinquish the glass or to occupy any of her time by assisting her aunt in dressing, (which was always a troublesome and tedious business with the old lady) and her mother had now gone down to be ready for the reception of the company, and to pay her compliments to the Montagues. "Oh! no matter," said Albina, "your present dress looks perfectly well, and the ladies will be too much engaged with themselves and their own dresses to remark any thing else. No one will observe whether your gown is calico or silk, and whether your cap is muslin or lace. Elderly ladies are always privileged to wear what is most convenient to them."

Albina put on the new dress that the mantua-maker had made for her. When she had tried it on the preceding evening Miss Matson declared that "it fitted like wax." She now found that it was scarcely possible to get it on at all, and that one side of the forebody was larger than the other. Miss Matson was called up, and by dint of the pulling, stretching, and smoothing well known to mantua-makers, and still more by means of her pertinacious assurances that the dress had no fault whatever, Albina was obliged to acknowledge that she *could* wear it, and the redundancy of the large side was pinned down and pinned over. In sticking in her comb she broke it in half, and it was long before she could arrange her hair to her satisfaction without it. Before she had completed her toilette, several of the ladies arrived and came into the room, and Albina was obliged to snatch up her paraphernalia and make her escape into the next apartment.

At last she was drest—she went down stairs. The company arrived fast, and the party began.

Bromley Cheston had come early to assist in doing the honours, and as he led Albina to a seat, he saw that in spite of her smiles she looked weary and out of spirits, and he pitied her.—"After all," thought he, "there is much that is interesting about Albina Marsden."

The party was *very* select, consisting of the elite of the village and its neighbourhood; but still, as is often the case, those whose presence was most desirable had sent excuses, and those who were not wanted had taken care to come. And Miss Boreham, (a young lady who having nothing else to recommend her, had been invited solely on account of the usual elegance of her attire, and whose dress was expected to add prodigiously to the effect of the rooms.) came most unaccountably in an old faded frock of last year's fashion, with her hair quite plain and tucked behind her ears with two side-combs. Could she have had a suspicion of the reason for which she was generally invited, and have therefore perversely determined on a reaction?

The Montagues sat together in a corner, putting up their eye-glasses at every one that entered the room, and criticising the company in loud whispers to each other; poor Mrs. Marsden endeavouring to catch opportunities of paying her court to them.

About nine o'clock, appeared an immense cap of blond lace, gauze riband, and flowers; and under the cap was Mrs. Washington Potts, a little thin trifling looking woman with a whitish freckled face, small sharp features, and flaxen hair. She leaned on the arm of Mr. Washington Potts, who was nothing in company or any where else; and she led by the hand a little boy in a suit of scarlet, braided and frogged with blue: a pale rat-looking child whose name she pronounced Laughy-yet, meaning La Fayette; and who being the youngest scion of the house of Potts, always went to parties with his mother, because he would not stay at home.

Bromley Cheston, on being introduced to Mrs. Washington Potts was surprised at the insignificance of her figure and face. He had imagined her tall in stature, large in feature, loud in voice, and in short the very counterpart to Mrs. Montague. He found her, however, as he had supposed, replete with vanity, pride, ignorance and folly: to which she added a sickening affectation of sweetness and amiability, and a flimsy pretension to extraordinary powers of conversation founded on a confused assemblage of incorrect and superficial ideas, which she mistook for a general knowledge of every thing in the world.

Mrs. Potts was delighted with the handsome face and figure, and the very genteel appearance of the young lieutenant, and she bestowed upon him a large portion of her talk.

"I hear, sir," said she, "you have been in the Mediterranean Sea. A sweet pretty place is it not?"

"Its shores," replied Cheston, "are certainly very beautiful."

"Yes, I should admire its chalky cliffs vastly," resumed Mrs. Potts, "they are quite poetical you know. Pray, sir, which do you prefer, Byron or Bonaparte. I doat upon Byron; and considering what sweet verses he wrote, 'tis a pity he was a corsair, and a vampyre pirate, and all such horrid things. As for Bonaparte, I never could endure him after I found that he had cut off poor old King George's head. Now, when we talk of great men, my husband is altogether for Washington. I laugh, and tell Mr. Potts it's because he and Washington are namesakes. How do you like La Fayette,"—(pronouncing the name *a la canaille*.)[11]

"The man or the name?" enquired Cheston.

"Oh! both to be sure. You see we have called our youngest blossom after him. Come here La Fayette, stand forward my dear, hold up your head, and make a bow to the gentleman."

"I won't," screamed La Fayette. "I'll never make a bow when you tell me."

"Something of the spirit of his ancestors," said Mrs. Potts, affectedly smiling to Cheston, and patting the urchin on the head.

"His ancestors!" thought Cheston. "Who could they have possibly have been?"

"Perhaps the dear fellow may be a little, a very little spoiled," pursued Mrs. Potts. "But to make a comparison in the marine line, (quite in your way, you know,) it is natural for a mother's heart to turn to her youngest darling as it is for the needle to point out the longitude. Now we talk of longitude have you read Cooper's last novel by the author of the Spy? It's a sweet book—Cooper is one of my pets. I saw him in dear delightful Paris. Are you musical Mr. Cheston?—But of course you are. Our whole aristocracy is musical now. How do you like Paganini?[12] You must have learned him in Europe. It's a very expensive thing to hear Paganini.—Poor man! He is quite ghastly with his own playing. Well; as you have been in the Mediterranean, which do you prefer, the Greeks or the Poles?"

"The Poles, decidedly," answered Cheston, "from what I have heard of *them*, and seen of the Greeks."

"Well, for my part," resumed Mrs. Potts, "I confess I like the Greeks, as I have always been rather classical. They are so Grecian. Think of their beautiful statues and paintings by Rubens and Reynolds.[13] Are you fond of paintings? At my house in the city, I can show you some very fine ones."

"By what artists?" asked Cheston.

"Oh! by my daughter Harriet. She did them at drawing-school with theorems. They are beautiful flower-pieces, all framed and hung up; they are almost worthy of Sir Benjamin West."[14]

In this manner Mrs. Potts ran on till the entrance of tea, and Cheston took that opportunity of escaping from her; while she imagined him deeply imbued with admiration of her fluency, vivacity and variety of information. But in reality, he was thinking of the strange depravity of taste that is sometimes found even in intelligent minds; for in no other way could he account for Albina's predilection for Mrs. Washington Potts. "And yet," thought he, "is a young and inexperienced girl more blameable for her blindness in friendship, (or what she imagines to be friendship) than an acute, sensible, talented man for the blindness in love. The master-spirits of the earth have almost proverbially married women of weak intellect, and almost as proverbially the children of such marriages resemble the mother rather than the father. A just punishment for choosing so absurdly. Albina I must know you better."

The party went on, much as parties generally do where there are four or five guests that are supposed to rank all the others. The patricians evidently despised the plebeians, and the plebeians were offended at being despised; for in no American assemblage is any real inferiority of rank ever felt or acknowledged. There was a general dullness, and a general restraint. Little was done, and little was said. La Fayette wandered about in every body's way; having been kept wide awake all the evening by two cups of strong coffee, which his mother allowed him to take because he would have them.

There was always a group round the centre table, listlessly turning over the souvenirs, albums, &c. and picking at the flowers; and La Fayette ate plumb-cake over Cheston's beautiful drawings.

Albina played an Italian song extremely well, but the Montagues exchanged glances at her music; and Mrs. Potts, to follow suit, hid her face behind her fan and simpered; though in truth she did not in reality know Italian from French, or a semibreve from a semiquaver. All this was a great annoyance to Cheston. At Albina's request, he led Miss Montague to the piano. She ran her fingers over the instrument as if to try it; gave a shudder, and declared it most shockingly out of tune, and then rose in horror from the music stool. This much surprised Mrs. Marsden, as a musician had been brought from the city only the day before for the express purpose of tuning this very instrument.

"No," whispered Miss Montague, as she resumed her seat beside her mother, "I will not condescend to play before people who are incapable of understanding my style."

At this juncture (to the great consternation of Mrs. Marsden and her daughter) who should make her appearance but Aunt Quimby in the calico gown which Albina now regretted having persuaded her to keep on. The old lady was wrapped in a small shawl and two large ones, and her head was secured from cold by a black silk handkerchief tied over her cap and under her chin. She smiled and nodded all round to the company, and said—"How do you do, good people; I hope you are all enjoying yourselves. I thought I *must* come down and have a peep at you. For after I had seen all the ladies take off their hoods, and had my tea, I found it pretty dull work sitting up stairs with the mantua-maker, who had no more manners than to fall asleep while I was talking."

Mrs. Marsden, much discomfited, led Aunt Quimby to a chair between two matrons who were among "the unavoidably invited," and whose pretensions to refinement were not very palpable. But the old lady had no idea of remaining stationary all the evening between Mrs. Johnson and Mrs. Jackson. She wisely thought "she could see more of the party," if she frequently changed her place, and being of what is called a sociable disposition, she never hesitated to talk to any one that was near her, however high or however low.

"Dear mother," said Albina in an under voice, "what can be the reason that every one in tasting the ice-cream, immediately sets it aside as if it was not fit to eat. I am sure every thing is in it that ought to be."

"And something more than ought to be," replied Mrs. Marsden, after trying a spoonful—"the salt that was laid round the freezer has got into the cream, (I suppose by Dixon's carelessness) and it is *not* fit to eat."

"And now," said Albina starting, "I will show you a far worse mortification than the failure of the ice-cream. Only look—there sits Aunt Quimby between Mr. Montague and Mrs. Washington Potts."

"How in the world did she get there?" exclaimed Mrs. Marsden. "I dare say she walked up, and asked them to make room for her between them. There is nothing now to be done but to pass her off as well as we can, and to make the best of her. I will manage to get as near as possible, that I may hear what she is talking about, and take an opportunity of persuading her away."

As Mrs. Marsden approached within hearing distance, Mr. Montague was leaning across Aunt Quimby, and giving Mrs. Potts an account of something that had been said or done during a splendid entertainment at Devonshire House.—"Just at that moment," said he, "I was lounging into the room with Lady Augusta Fitzhenry on my arm (unquestionably the finest woman in England) and Mrs. Montague was a few steps in advance, leaning on my friend the Marquis of Elvington."

"Pray, sir," said Mrs. Quimby, "as you are from England, do you know any thing of Betsey Dempsey's husband?"

"I have not the honour of being acquainted with that person," replied Mr. Montague, after a withering stare.

"Well that's strange," pursued Aunt Quimby, "considering that he has been living in London at least eighteen years—or perhaps it is only seventeen. And yet I think it must be near eighteen, if not quite. Maybe seventeen and a half. Well, it's best to be on the safe side, so I'll say seventeen. Betsey Dempsey's mother was an old school-mate of mine. Her father kept the Black Horse tavern. She was the only acquaintance I ever had that married an Englishman. He was a grocer, and in very good business; but he never liked America, and was always finding fault with it, and so he went home, and was to send for Betsey. But he never sent for her at all; for a very good reason; which was that he had another wife in England, as most of them have—no disparagement to you, sir."

Mrs. Marsden now came up, and informed Mrs. Potts in a whisper that the good old lady beside her, was a distant relation or rather connexion of *Mr.* Marsden's, and that, though a little primitive in appearance and manner, she had considerable property in bank-stock. To Mrs. Marsden's proposal that she should exchange her seat for a very pleasant one in the other room next to her old friend Mrs. Willis, Aunt Quimby replied nothing but "Thank you, I'm doing very well here."

Mrs. and Miss Montague, apparently heeding no one else, had talked nearly the whole evening to each other, but loudly enough to be heard by all around them. The young lady, though dressed as a child, talked like a woman, and she and her mother were now engaged in an argument whether the flirtation of the Duke of Risingham with Lady Georgiana Melbury would end seriously or not. "To my certain knowledge," said Miss Montague, "his Grace has never yet declared himself to Lady Georgiana, or to any one else."—"I'll lay you two to one," said Mrs. Montague, "that he is married to her before we return to England."—"No," replied the daughter, "like all others of his sex he delights in keeping the ladies in suspense."

"What you say, Miss, is very true," said Aunt Quimby, leaning in her turn across Mr. Montague, "and considering how young you are you talk very sensibly. Men certainly have a way of keeping women in suspense, and an unwillingness to answer questions even when we ask them. There's my son-in-law, Bill Fairfowl, that I live with. He married my daughter Mary eleven years ago, the 23d of last April. He's as good a man as ever breathed, and an excellent provider too. He always goes to market himself; and sometimes I can't help blaming him a little for his extravagance. But his greatest fault is his being so unsatisfactory. As far back as last March, as I was sitting at my knitting in the little front parlour with the door open, (for it was quite warm weather for the time of year) Billy Fairfowl came home carrying in his hand a good-sized shad; and I called out to him to ask what he gave for it, for it was the very beginning of shad season; but he made not a word of answer; he just passed on, and left the shad in the kitchen, and then went to his store. At dinner we had the fish, and a very nice one it was; and I asked him again how much he gave for it, but he still avoided answering, and began to talk of something else; so I thought I'd let it rest awhile. A week or two after, I again asked him; so then he actually said he had forgotten all about it. And to this day I don't know the price of that shad."

The Montagues looked at each other—almost laughed aloud, and drew back their chairs as far from Aunt Quimby as possible. So also did Mrs. Potts. Mrs. Marsden came up in an agony of vexation, and reminded her aunt in a low voice of the risk of renewing her rheumatism by staying so long between the damp newly-papered walls. The old lady answered aloud—"Oh! you need not fear, I am well wrapped up on purpose. And indeed considering that the parlours were only papered to-day, I think the walls have dried wonderfully, (putting her hand on the paper)—I am sure nobody could find out the damp if they were not told."

"What!" exclaimed the Montagues; "only papered to-day—starting up and testifying all that prudent fear of taking cold, so characteristic of the English. How barbarous to inveigle us into such a place!"

"I thought I felt strangely chilly all the evening," said Mrs. Potts, whose fan had scarcely been at rest five minutes.

The Montagues proposed going away immediately, and Mrs. Potts declared she was *most* apprehensive for poor little La Fayette. Mrs. Marsden who could not endure the idea of their departing till all the refreshments had been handed round, (the best thing yet to come) took great pains to persuade them that there was no real cause for alarm, as she had had large fires all the afternoon. They held a whispered consultation, in which they agreed to stay for the oysters and chicken salad, and Mrs. Marsden went out to send them their shawls, with one for La Fayette.

By this time the secret of the newly-papered walls had spread round both rooms; the conversation now turned entirely on colds and rheumatisms; there was much shivering and considerable coughing, and the demand for shawls increased. However nobody actually went home in consequence.

"Papa," said Miss Montague, "let us all take French leave as soon as the oysters and chicken-salad have gone round."

Albina now came up to Aunt Quimby (gladly perceiving that the old lady looked tired,) and proposed that she should return to her chamber, assuring her that the waiters should be punctually sent up to her—"I do not feel quite ready to go yet," replied Mrs. Quimby. "I am very well here. But you need not mind *me.* Go back to your company, and talk a little to those three poor girls in the yellow frocks that nobody has spoken to yet, except Bromley Cheston. When I am ready to go I shall take French leave, as these English people call it."

But Aunt Quimby's idea of French leave was very different from the usual acceptation of the term; for having always heard that the French were a very polite people, she concluded that their manner of taking leave must be particularly respectful and ceremonious. Therefore, having paid her parting compliments to Mrs. Potts and the Montagues, she walked all round the room, curtseying to every body and shaking hands, and telling them she had come to take French leave. To put an end to this ridiculous scene, Bromley Cheston (who had been on assiduous duty all the evening) now came forward and taking the old lady's arm in his, offered to escort her up stairs. Aunt Quimby was much flattered by this unexpected civility from the finest looking young man in the room, and she smilingly departed with him, complimenting him on his politeness, and assuring him that he was a real gentleman; trying also to make out the degree of relationship that existed between them.

"So much for Buckingham," said Cheston, as he ran down stairs after depositing the old lady at the door of her room. "Fools of all ranks and of all ages are to me equally intolerable. I never can marry into such a family."

The party went on.

"In the name of heaven, Mrs. Potts," said Mrs. Montague, "what induces you to patronize these people?"

"Why, they are the only tolerable persons in the neighbourhood," answered Mrs. Potts, "and very kind and obliging in their way. I really think Albina a very sweet girl, very sweet indeed: and Mrs. Marsden is rather amiable too, quite amiable. And they are so grateful for any little notice I take of them, that it is really quite affecting. Poor things! how much trouble they have given themselves in getting up this party. They look as if they had had a hard day's work; and I have no doubt they will be obliged, in consequence, to pinch themselves for months to come; for I can assure you their means are very small, very small indeed. As to this intolerable old aunt, I never saw her before, and as there is something rather genteel about Mrs. Marsden and her daughter; rather so at least about Albina; I did not suppose they had any such relations belonging to them. I think, in future, I must confine myself entirely to the aristocracy."

"We deliberated to the last moment," said Mrs. Montague, "whether we would come. But as Mr. Montague is going to write his tour when we return to England,[15] he thinks it expedient to make some sacrifices, for the sake of seeing the varieties of American society."

"Oh! these people are not in society," exclaimed Mrs. Potts eagerly. "I can assure you these Marsdens have not the slightest pretensions to society. Oh! no—I beg of you not to suppose that Mrs. Marsden and her daughter are at all in society."

This conversation was overheard by Bromley Cheston, and it gave him more pain than he was willing to acknowledge, even to himself.

At length all the refreshments had gone their rounds, and the Montagues had taken real French leave; but Mrs. Washington Potts preferred a conspicuous departure, and therefore made her adieux with a view of producing great effect. This was the signal for the company to break up, and Mrs. Marsden gladly smiled them out, while Albina could have said with Gray's Prophetess—

"Now my weary lips I close,
Leave me, leave me to repose."[16]

But, according to Mrs. Marsden, the worst of all was the poet, the professedly eccentric Bewley Garvin Gandy, author of the World of Sorrow, Elegy on a Broken Heart, Lines on a Suppressed Sigh, Sonnet to a Hidden Tear, Stanzas to Faded Hopes, &c. &c. and who was just now engaged in a tale called "The Bewildered," and an Ode to the Waning Moon, which set him to wandering about the country, and "kept him out o'nights." The poet, not being a man of this world, did not make his appearance at the party till the moment of the bustle occasioned by the exit of Mrs. Washington Potts. He then darted suddenly into the room, and looked wild.

We will not insinuate that he bore any resemblance to Sandy Clark. He certainly wore no chapeau, and his coat was not in the least *a la militaire*, for it was a dusky brown frock. His collar was open, in the fashion attributed to Byron, and much affected by scribblers who are incapable of imitating the noble bard in any thing but his follies. His hair looked as if he had just been tearing it, and his eyes seemed "in a fine frenzy rolling." He was on his return from one of his moonlight rambles on the banks of the river, and his pantaloons and coat-skirt showed evident marks of having been deep among the cat-tails and splatter-docks that grew in the mud of its margin.

Being a man that took no note of time, he wandered into Mrs. Marsden's house between eleven and twelve o'clock, and remained an hour after the company had gone; reclining at full length on a sofa, and discussing Barry Cornwall and Thomas Haynes Bayley, L.E.L. and Mrs. Cornwall Baron Wilson. After which he gradually became classical, and poured into the sleepy cars of Mrs. Marsden and Albina a parallel between Tibullus and Propertius, a dissertation of Alcæus and another on Menander.

Bromley Cheston who had been escorting home two sets of young ladies that lived "far as the poles asunder," passed Mrs. Marsden's house on returning to his hotel, and seeing the lights still gleaming, he went in to see what was the matter, and kindly relieved his aunt and cousin by reminding the poet of the lateness of the hour, and "fairly carrying him off."

Aunt Quimby had long since been asleep. But before Mrs. Marsden and Albina could forget themselves in "tir'd nature's sweet restorer," they lay awake for an hour, discussing the fatigues and vexations of the day, and the mortifications of the evening. "After all," said Albina, "this party has cost us five times as much as it was worth, both in trouble and expense, and I really cannot tell what pleasure we have derived from it."

"No one expects pleasure at their own party," replied Mrs. Marsden. "But you may depend on it, this little compliment to Mrs. Washington Potts will prove highly advantageous to us hereafter. And then it is *something* to be the only family in the neighbourhood that could presume to do such a thing."

Next morning, Bromley Cheston received a letter which required his immediate presence in New York on business of importance. When he went to take leave of his aunt and cousin, he found them busily engaged in the troublesome task of clearing away and putting in order; a task which is nearly equal to that of making the preparations for a party. They looked pale and spiritless, and Mrs. Washington Potts had just sent her three boys to spend the day with them.

When Cheston took Albina's hand at parting, he felt it tremble, and her eyes looked as if they were filling with tears. "After all," thought he, "she is a charming girl, and has both sense and sensibility."—"I am very nervous to-day," said Albina, "the party has been too much for me; and I have in prospect for to-morrow the pain of taking leave of Mrs. Washington Potts, who returns with all her family to Philadelphia."

"Strange infatuation," thought Cheston, as he dropped Albina's hand, and made his parting bow. "I must see more of this girl, before I can resolve to trust my happiness to her keeping; I cannot share her heart with Mrs. Washington Potts. When I return from New York I will talk to her seriously about the ridiculous woman, and I will also remonstrate with her mother on the folly of straining every nerve in the pursuit of what she calls a certain style."

In the afternoon, Mrs. Potts did Albina the honour to send for her to assist in the preparations for to-morrow's removal to town; and in the evening the three boys were all taken home sick, in consequence of having laid violent hands on the fragments of the feast: which fragments they had continued during the day to devour almost without intermission. Also Randolph had thrown Jefferson down stairs, and raised two green bumps on his forehead, and Jefferson had pinched La Fayette's fingers in the door till the blood came; not to mention various minor squabbles and hurts.

At parting, Mrs. Potts went so far as to kiss Albina, and made her promise to let her know immediately, whenever she or her mother came to the city.

In about two weeks, Aunt Quimby finished her visitation: and the day after her departure Mrs. Marsden and Albina went to town to make their purchases for the season, and also with a view towards a party which they knew Mrs. Potts had in contemplation. This time they did not as usual stay with their relations, but they took lodgings at a fashionable boarding-house where they could receive their "great woman," *comme il faut*.[17]

On the morning after their arrival Mrs. Marsden and her daughter, in their most costly dresses, went to visit Mrs. Potts that she might be apprised of their arrival; and they found her in a spacious house, expensively and ostentatiously furnished. After they had waited till even *their* patience was nearly exhausted, Mrs. Potts came down stairs to them, but there was evidently a great abatement in her affability. She seemed uneasy, looking frequently towards the door, got up several times and went to the window, and appeared fidgetty when the bell rung. At last there came in two very flaunting ladies, whom Mrs. Potts received as if she considered them people of consequence. They were not introduced to the Marsdens, who after the entrance of these new visiters sat awhile in the pitiable situation of cyphers, and then took their leave. "Strange," said Mrs. Marsden, "that she did not say a word of her party."

Three days after their visit, Mrs. Washington Potts left cards for Mrs. and Miss Marsden, without enquiring if they were at home. And they heard from report that her party was fixed for the week after next, and that it was expected to be very splendid, as it was to introduce her daughter who had just quitted boarding-school. The Marsdens had seen this young lady, who had spent the August holidays with her parents. She was as silly as her mother, and as dull as her father in the eyes of all who were not blindly determined to think her otherwise, or who did not consider it particularly expedient to uphold all of the name of Potts.

At length they heard that the invitations were going out for Mrs. Potts's party, and that though very large it was not to be general; which meant that only one or two of the members were to be selected from each family with whom Mrs. Potts thought proper to acknowledge an acquaintance. From this moment Mrs. Marsden, who at the best of times had never really been treated with much respect by Mrs. Potts, gave up all hope of an invitation for herself; but she counted certainly on one for Albina, and every ring at the door was expected to bring it. There were many rings but no invitation, and poor Albina and her mother took turns in watching at the window.

At last Bogle was seen to come up the steps with a handful of notes; and Albina, regardless of all rule, ran to the front-door herself. They were cards for a party, but not Mrs. Potts's, and were intended for two other ladies that lodged in the house.

Every time that Albina went out and came home, she enquired anxiously of all the servants if no note had been left for her. Still there was none. And her mother still insisted that the note *must* have come, but had been mislaid afterwards, or that Bogle had lost it in the street.

Wednesday, Thursday, Friday, and Saturday passed over, and still no invitation. Mrs. Marsden talked much of the carelessness of servants, and had no doubt of the habitual negligence of Messrs. Bogle, Shepherd, and other "fashionable party-men." Albina was almost sick with "hope deferred." At last, when she came home on Monday morning from Second street, her mother met her at the door with a delighted face, and showed her the long-desired note, which had just been brought by Mrs.

Potts's own man. The party was to take place in two days: and so great was now Albina's happiness, that she scarcely felt the fatigue of searching the shops for articles of attire that were very elegant and yet not *too* expensive; and shopping with a limited purse is certainly no trifling exercise both of mind and body; so also is the task of going round among fashionable mantua-makers in the hope of coaxing one of them to undertake a dress at a short notice.

Next morning, Mrs. Potts sent for Albina immediately after breakfast, and told her that as she knew her to be very clever at all sorts of things, she wanted her to stay that day and assist in the preparations for the next. Mrs. Potts, like many other people who live in showy houses and dress extravagantly, was very economical in servants. She gave such low wages that none would come to her who could get places any where else, and she kept them on such limited allowance that none would stay with her who were worth having.

Fools, are seldom consistent in their expenditures. They generally (to use a homely expression) strain at gnats and swallow camels.

About noon Albina having occasion to consult Mrs. Potts concerning something that was to be done, found her in the front parlour with Mrs. and Miss Montague. After Albina had left the room, Mrs. Montague said to Mrs. Potts—"Is not that the girl that lives with her mother at the place on the river, I forget what you call it?—I mean the niece of the aunt."

"That is Albina Marsden," replied Mrs. Potts.

"Yes," pursued Mrs. Montague, "the people that made so great an exertion to give you a sort of party, and honoured Mr. and Miss Montague and myself with invitations."

"She's not to be here to-morrow night, I hope!" exclaimed Miss Montague.

"Really," replied Mrs. Potts, "I could do no less than ask

her. The poor thing did her very best to be civil to us all last summer."

"Oh!" said Mrs. Montague, "in the country one is willing sometimes to take up with such company as we should be very sorry to acknowledge in town. You assured me that your party to-morrow night would be extremely *recherchee*. And as it is so early in the season, you know that it is necessary to be more particular now than at the close of the campaign, when every one is tired of parties and unwilling to get new evening dresses lest they should be out of fashion before they are wanted again. Excuse me, I speak only from what I have heard of American customs."

"I am always particular about my parties," said Mrs. Potts.

"A word in your ear," continued Mrs. Montague. "Is it not impolitic, or rather are you not afraid to bring forward so beautiful a girl as this Miss Martin on the very night of your own daughter's debut."

Mrs. Potts looked alarmed for a moment, and then recovering herself said—"I have no fear of Miss Harriet Angelina Potts being thrown in the shade by a little country girl like this. Albina Marsden is pretty enough, to be sure—at least, rather pretty—but then there is a certain style—a certain air which she of course—in short, a certain style—"

"As to what you call a certain style," said Mrs. Montague, "I do not know exactly what you mean. If it signified the air and manner of a lady, this Miss Martin has as much of it as any other American girl. To me they are all nearly alike. I cannot distinguish those minute shades of difference that you all make such a point of. In my unpractised eyes the daughters of your mechanics and shopkeepers look as well and behave as well as the daughters of your lawyers and doctors, for I find your nobility is chiefly made up of these two professions, with the addition of a few merchants; and you call every one a merchant that does not sell his commodities by the single yard or the single quart."

"Mamma," whispered Miss Montague, "if that girl is to be here I don't wish to come. I can't endure her."

"Take my advice," continued Mrs. Montague to Mrs. Potts, "and put off this Miss Martin. If she was not so strikingly handsome, she might pass unnoticed in the crowd. But her beauty will attract general observation, and you will be obliged to tell exactly who she is, where you picked her up, and to give or to hear an account of her family and all her connexions; and from the specimen we have had in the old aunt, I doubt if they will bear a very minute scrutiny. So if she *is* invited, endeavour to uninvite her."

"I am sure I would willingly do that," replied Mrs. Potts, "but I can really think of no excuse."

"Oh! send her a note to-morrow," answered Mrs. Montague, carelessly, and rising to depart, "any thing or nothing, so that you only signify to her that she is not to come."

All day Mrs. Potts was revolving in her mind the most feasible means of preventing Albina from appearing at her party; and her conscience smote her when she saw the unsuspecting girl so indefatigable in assisting her with the preparations. Before Albina went home, Mrs. Potts had come to the conclusion to follow Mrs. Montague's advice, but she shrunk from the task of telling her so in person. She determined to send her, next morning, a concise note, politely requesting her not to come; and she intended afterwards to call on her and apologize, on the plea of her party being by no means general, but still so large that every inch of room was an object of importance; also that the selection consisted entirely of persons well known to each other and accustomed to meet in company, and that there was every reason to fear that her gentle and modest friend Albina would have been unable to enjoy herself among so many strangers, &c. &c. These excuses, she knew were very flimsy, but she trusted to Albina's good nature, and she thought she could smooth off all by inviting both her and her mother to a sociable tea.

Next morning, Mrs. Potts who was on no occasion very ready with her pen, considering that she professed to be *au fait* to every thing, employed near an hour in manufacturing the following note to Albina.

"Mrs. Washington Potts's compliments to Miss Marsden, and she regrets being under the necessity of dispensing with Miss M.'s company to join the social circle at her mansion-house this evening. Mrs. W.P. will explain hereafter, hoping Mrs. and Miss M. are both well. Mr. W.P. requests his respects to both ladies, as well as Miss Potts, and their favourite little La Fayette desires his best love."

This billet arrived while Albina had gone to her mantua-maker to have her new dress fitted on for the last time. Her mother opened the note and read it; a liberty which no parent should take with the correspondence of a grown-up daughter. Mrs. Marsden was shocked at its contents, and at a loss to guess the motive of so strange an interdiction. At first her only emotion was resentment against Mrs. Potts. Then she thought of the disappointment and mortification of poor Albina, whom she pictured to herself passing a forlorn evening at home, perhaps crying in her own room. Next, she recollected the elegant new dress in which Albina would have looked so beautifully, and which would now be useless.

"Oh!" soliloquized Mrs. Marsden, "what a pity this unaccountable note was not dropped and lost in the street. But then, of course some one would have found and read it, and that would have been worse than all. How could Mrs. Potts be guilty of such abominable rudeness, as to desire poor Albina not to come, after she had been invited. But great people think they may do any thing. I wish the note had fallen into the fire before it came into my hands; then Albina would have known nothing of it; she would have gone to the party, looking more charmingly than ever she did in her life; and she would be seen there, and admired, and make new acquaintances, and Mrs. Potts could do no otherwise than behave to her politely in her own house. Nobody would know of this vile billet, which perhaps after all is only a joke, and Mrs. Potts would suppose that of course Albina had not received it; besides I have no doubt that Mrs. Potts will send for her to-morrow, and make a satisfactory explanation. But then, to-night, if Albina could only get there to-night. What harm can possibly arrive from my not showing her the note till to-morrow. Why should the dear girl be deprived of all the pleasure she anticipated this evening. And even if she expected no enjoyment whatever, still how great will be the advantage of having her seen at Mrs. Washington Potts's select party; it will at once get her on in the world. Of course Mrs. Potts will conclude that the note miscarried, and will treat her as if it had never been sent. I am really most strongly tempted to suppress it, and let Albina go."

The more Mrs. Marsden thought of this project the less objectionable it appeared to her. When she saw Albina come home delighted with her new dress which fitted her exactly, and when she heard her impatiently wishing that evening was come, this weak and ill-judging mother could not resolve (as she afterwards said) to dash all her pleasant anticipations to the ground and demolish her castles in the air. "My daughter shall be happy to-night," thought she, "whatever may be the event of to-morrow." She hastily concealed the note, and kept her resolution of not mentioning it to Albina.

Evening came, and Albina's beautiful hair was arranged and decorated by a fashionable French barber. She was drest, and looked charmingly.

Albina knew that Mrs. Potts had sent an invitation to the United States Hotel for Lieutenant Cheston,[18] who was daily expected but had not yet returned from New York, and she regretted much that she could not go to the party under his escort. She knew no one else of the company, and she had no alternative but to send for a carriage and proceeded thither by herself, after her mother had dispatched repeated messages to the hotel to know if Mr. Cheston had yet arrived, for he was certainly expected back that evening.

As Albina drove to the house, she felt all the terrors of diffidence coming upon her, and already repented that she had ventured on this enterprize alone. On arriving, she did not go into the ladies' room but gave her hood and cloak at once to a servant, and tremulously requested another attendant to inform Mr. Potts that a lady wished to see him. Mr. Potts accordingly came out into the hall, and looked surprized at finding Albina there, for he had heard his wife and daughter talking of the note of interdiction. But concluding, as he often did, that it was in vain for him to try to comprehend the proceedings of women, he thought it best to say nothing.

On Albina requesting him to accompany her on her entrance, he gave her his arm in silence, and with a very perplexed face escorted her into the principal room. As he led her up to his wife, his countenance gradually changed from perplexity to something like fright. Albina paid her compliments to Mrs. Potts, who received her with evident amazement, and without replying. Mrs. Montague, who sat next to the lady of the mansion, opened still wider her immense eyes, and then "to make assurance doubly sure" applied her opera-glass. Miss Montague first stared, and then laughed.

Albina, much disconcerted, turned to look for a seat; Mr. Potts having withdrawn his arm. As she retired to the only vacant chair, she heard a half whisper running along the line of ladies, and though she could not distinguish the words so as to make any connected sense of them, she felt that they alluded to her.

"Can I believe my eyes?" said Mrs. Potts.

"The assurance of American girls is astonishing," said Mrs. Montague.

"She was forbidden to come," said Miss Montague to a young lady beside her. "Mrs. Potts herself forbade her to come."

"She was actually prohibited," resumed Mrs. Montague leaning over to Mrs. Jones.

"I sent her myself a note of prohibition," said Mrs. Potts leaning over to Mrs. Smith. "I had serious objections to having her here."

"I never saw such downright impudence," pursued Mrs. Montague. "This I suppose is one of the consequences of the liberty, and freedom and independence that you Americans are always talking about. I must tell Mr. Montague for really this is too good to lose."

And beckoning her husband to come to her—"My dear," said she, "put down in your memorandum-book, that when American married ladies invite young ladies to parties, they on second thoughts forbid them to come, and that the said American young ladies boldly persist in coming, in spite of the forbiddance."

And she then related to him the whole affair, at full length, and with numerous embellishments, looking all the time at poor Albina.

The whole story soon circulated round the room in whispers and murmurs, and no one had candour or kindness to suggest the possibility of Miss Marsden's having never received the note.

Albina soon perceived herself to be an object of remark and animadversion, and she was sadly at a loss to divine the cause.

The two ladies that were nearest to her rose up and left their seats, while two others edged their chairs farther off. She knew no one, she was introduced to no one, but she saw that every one was looking at her as she sat by herself, alone, conspicuous, and abashed. Tea was waiting for a lady that came always last, and the whole company seemed to have leisure to gaze on poor Albina and to whisper about her.

Her situation now became intolerable. She felt that there was nothing left for her but to go home. Unluckily she had ordered the carriage at eleven o'clock. At last she resolved on making a great effort, and on plea of a violent headache (a plea which by this time was literally true) to ask Mrs. Potts if she would allow a servant to bring a coach for her.

After several attempts, she rose for this purpose; but she saw at the same moment that all eyes were turned upon her. She tremblingly and with downcast looks advanced till she got into the middle of the room, and then all her courage deserted her at once, when she heard some one say "I wonder what she is going to do next."

She stopped suddenly, and stood motionless, and she saw Miss Potts giggle, and heard her say to a school-girl near her—"I suppose she is going to speak a speech." She turned very pale, and felt as if she could gladly sink into the floor, when suddenly some one took her hand, and the voice of Bromley Cheston said to her—"Albina—Miss Marsden—I will conduct you wherever you wish to go"—and then lowering his tone, he asked her—"Why this agitation—what has happened to distress you?"

Cheston had just arrived from New York, having been detained on the way by an accident that happened to one of the boats, and finding that Mrs. Marsden was in town, and had that day sent several messages for him, he repaired immediately to her lodgings. He had intended declining the invitation of Mrs.

Potts, but when he found that Albina had gone thither, he hastily changed his dress and went to the party. When he entered, what was his amazement to see her standing alone in the centre of the room, and the company whispering and gazing at her.

Albina on hearing the voice of a friend, the voice of Bromley Cheston, was completely overcome, and she covered her face and burst into tears. "Albina," said Cheston, "I will not now ask an explanation; I see that, whatever may have happened, you had best go home."—"Oh! most gladly, most thankfully," she exclaimed in a voice almost inarticulate with sobs. Cheston drew her arm within his and bowing to Mrs. Potts, he led Albina out of the apartment, and conducted her to the staircase, whence she went to the ladies' room to compose herself a little, and prepare for her depature.

Cheston then sent one servant for a carriage, and another to tell Mr. Potts that he desired to speak with him in the hall. Potts came out with a pale frightened face, and said—"Indeed, sir—indeed, I had nothing to do with it; ask the women. It was all them entirely. It was the women that laughed at Miss Albina and whispered about her."

"For what?" demanded the lieutenant. "I insist on knowing for what cause."

"Why sir," replied Potts, "she came here to my wife's party, after Mrs. Potts had sent her a note desiring her to stay away; which was certainly an odd thing for a young lady to do."

"There is some mistake," exclaimed Cheston, "I'll stake my life that she never saw the note. And now, for what reason did Mrs. Potts write such a note? How did she dare—"

"Oh!" replied Potts stammering and hesitating, "women will have their notions; men are not half so particular about their company. Somehow, after Mrs. Potts had invited Miss Albina, she thought on farther consideration that poor Miss Albina was not quite genteel enough for her party. You know all the women now make a great point of being genteel. But, indeed, sir, (observing the storm that was gathering on Cheston's brow) indeed, sir—*I* was not in the least to blame. It was altogether the fault of my wife."

The indignation of the lieutenant was so highly excited, that nothing could have checked it but the recollection that Potts was in his own house. At this moment Albina came down stairs, and Cheston took her hand and said to her—"Albina did you receive a note from Mrs. Potts interdicting your presence at the party."—"Oh! no, indeed!" exclaimed Albina, amazed at the question. "Surely she did not send me such a note."—"Yes, she did though," said Potts quickly.—"Is it then necessary for me to say," said Albina indignantly, "that under those circumstances nothing could have induced me to enter this house, now or ever. I saw or heard nothing of this note. And is this the reason that I have been treated so rudely—so cruelly—"

Upon this Mr. Potts made his escape, and Cheston having put Albina into the carriage, desired the coachman to wait a few moments. He then returned to the drawing-room, and approached Mrs. Potts who was standing with half the company collected round her, and explaining with great volubility the whole history of Albina Marsden. On the appearance of Cheston she stopped short, and all her auditors looked foolish.

The young officer advanced into the centre of the circle, and first addressing Mrs. Potts, he said to her—"In justice to Miss Marsden, I have returned madam, to inform you that your note of interdiction, with which you have so kindly made all the company acquainted, was till this moment unknown to that young lady. But even had she come wilfully, and in the full knowledge of your prohibition, no circumstances whatever could justify the rudeness with which I find she has been treated. I have now only to say that if any gentleman presumes either here or hereafter to cast a reflection on the conduct of

Miss Albina Marsden, in this or in any other instance, he must answer to me for the consequences. And if I find that any lady has invidiously misrepresented this occurrence, I shall insist on an atonement from her husband, her brother or her admirer."

He then bowed and departed, and the company looked still more foolish.

"This lesson," thought Cheston, "will have the salutary effect of curing Albina of her predominant follies. She is a lovely girl after all, and when withdrawn from the influence of her mother will make a charming woman and excellent wife."

Before the carriage stopped at the residence of Mrs. Marsden, Cheston had made Albina an offer of his heart and hand, and the offer was not refused.

Mrs. Marsden was scarcely surprised at the earliness of Albina's return from the party, for she had a secret misgiving that all was not right, that the suppression of the note would not eventuate well, and she bitterly regretted having done it. When her daughter related to her the story of the evening, Mrs. Marsden was overwhelmed with compunction, and though Cheston was present, she could not refrain from acknowledging at once her culpability, for it certainly deserved no softer name. Cheston and Albina were shocked at this disclosure, but in compassion to Mrs. Marsden they forbore to add to her distress by a single comment. Cheston shortly after took his leave, saying to Albina as he departed—"I hope you are done for ever with Mrs. Washington Potts."

Next morning, Cheston seriously but kindly expostulated with Albina and her mother on the folly and absurdity of sacrificing their comfort, their time, their money, and indeed their self-respect to the paltry distinction of being capriciously noticed by a few vain silly heartless people, inferior to themselves in every thing but in wealth and in a slight tincture of soi-disant fashion; and who, after all, only took them on or threw them off as it suited their own convenience.

"What you say is very true, Bromley," replied Mrs. Marsden. "I begin to view these things in their proper light, and as Albina remarks, we ought to profit by this last lesson. To tell the exact truth, I have heard since I came to town that Mrs. Washington Potts is, after all, by no means in the first circle, and it is whispered that she and her husband are both of very low origin."

"No matter for her circle or her origin," said Cheston, "in our country the only acknowledged distinction should be that which is denoted by superiority of mind and manners."

Next day Lieutenant Cheston escorted Mrs. Marsden and Albina back to their own home—and a week afterwards he was sent unexpectedly on a cruize in the West Indies.

He returned in the spring, and found Mrs. Marsden more rational than he had ever known her, and Albina highly improved by a judicious course of reading which he had marked out for her, and still more by her intimacy with a truly genteel, highly talented, and very amiable family from the eastward, who had recently bought a house in the village, and in whose society she often wondered at the infatuation which had led her to fancy such a woman as Mrs. Washington Potts, with whom, of course, she never had any farther communication.

A recent and very large bequest to Bromley Cheston from a distant relation made it no longer necessary that the young lieutenant should wait for promotion before he married Albina; and accordingly their union took place immediately on his return.

Before the Montagues left Philadelphia to prosecute their journey to the south, there arrived an acquaintance of theirs from England, who injudiciously "told the secrets of his prison-house," and made known in whispers "not loud but deep," that Mr. Dudley Montague, of Normancourt Park, Hants, (alias Mr. John Wilkins of Lamb's Conduit street, Clerkenwell,) had long been well-known in London as a reporter for a newspaper: that he had recently married a widow, the ci-devant governess of a Somers Town Boarding-school,[19] who had drawn her ideas of fashionable life from the columns of the Morning Post, and who famished her pupils so much to her own profit that she had been able to retire on a sort of fortune. With the assistance of this fund, she and her daughter (the young lady was in reality the offspring of her mother's first marriage) had accompanied Mr. Wilkins across the Atlantic: all three assuming the lordly name of Montague, as one well calculated to strike the republicans with proper awe. The truth was, that for a suitable consideration proffered by a tory publisher, the soi-disant Mr. Montague had undertaken to add another octavo to the numerous volumes of gross misrepresentation and real ignorance that profess to contain an impartial account of the United States of America.[20]

The Settlers

A DIALOGUE

Ellen–Maria

MARIA. Now, Ellen, let us move the sofa closer to the hearth, and let us put our feet on the fender, and talk by fire-light, till we are called into the back-parlour to tea;—but, first, I will let down the window-curtains.

ELLEN. How comfortable and pleasant your house always seems! It is so large and so handsome, and has so many conveniences!

MARIA. You could not have said so, had you visited us ten years since. Our house was then a log-cabin.

ELLEN. A log-cabin?

MARIA. Yes, indeed. My father was the first settler in this place, which was then a wilderness, and is now a thriving village.

ELLEN. And did you ever live in a log-cabin? Why, your father is now in Congress, and is considered one of the most wealthy men in the country; and your brothers are at college, and you have been at boarding-school.

MARIA. True: our circumstances are now very prosperous, and we have every thing that we desire; but you can have no idea of all the privations we endured when we first emigrated from Pennsylvania. My grandfather was a wealthy farmer, but he had nine children, and at his death, when his property was equally divided, the portion that fell to each child was not very great. My father and my uncle Robert determined to improve their condition, by selling the small farms allotted to them and buying a large tract in one of the new states, where land was cheap, with the intention of removing thither and settling on it.

ELLEN. I wonder your mother consented to go to a place, which, at that time, was certainly the backwoods.

MARIA. Her love for my father, and her devotion to his interest, would have induced her to accompany him even beyond the rocky mountains, had he judged it expedient to remove thither; and she had excellent health and spirits, and a disposition to make the best of every thing. She was certainly very sorry to part from her friends, and to leave the neighbourhood in which she had lived from her infancy; but, then, the objects of her warmest affection, her husband and her four children, were still with her.

ELLEN. Have you any recollection of the journey?

MARIA. I remember it perfectly—I have a very good memory, and I often hear my parents and my uncle talk of our little adventures on the road, and the manner in which we lived for some time after our emigration.

ELLEN. I suppose you travelled in the stages and steam-boats, as our family did when we came hither, a few weeks since?

MARIA. No: on the route *we* took, there were then neither stages nor steam-boats.

ELLEN. Then you came in your own carriage?

MARIA. Our own carriage was our own waggon.

ELLEN. How dreadful it must have been to travel several hundred miles in a waggon!

MARIA. On the contrary, we enjoyed the journey. My two brothers were fine healthy boys, my sister Fanny was one of the happiest little things in the world, my father and mother are both naturally cheerful, and, I believe, we were all disposed to think as lightly as possible of the inconveniences which we knew to be unavoidable. We were accompanied by my uncle Robert, who had bought some land adjoining to my father's new tract, and who had a waggon of his own. We all loved our uncle very much, as he was the sort of person that children are always fond of—my brothers, in particular, were his warm friends and favourites.

ELLEN. But how could you be comfortable in the waggon?

MARIA. We thought ourselves very comfortable—the canvass cover sheltered us from the sun; the bottom of the waggon was covered thickly with straw; we sat or reclined upon the beds we were bringing with us; and for tables we used the tops of chests and boxes. Though the waggons were heavily laden, we had a sufficient number of horses to draw them without difficulty. The boys generally rode in my uncle's waggon, and my mother, my sister, and myself, sat in my father's, with Phillis, the faithful black woman whom we brought with us from Pennsylvania, and who is now our cook.

ELLEN. And who were the drivers?

MARIA. My father and my uncle Robert, each riding one of the horses of his own team.

ELLEN. And did they continue to dress like gentlemen?

MARIA. To tell the truth, their clothes had *never* been of a very fashionable cut; but, during the journey, they wore gray jackets and brown linen trousers faced with black leather. My mother, my sister, and myself, had dark gingham dresses, with sun-bonnets of the same, and gray cloth cloaks. The boys were in full suits of homespun.

ELLEN. What a contrast to your present manner of dressing!

Your father and uncle now look like gentlemen,—and, indeed, all the family make as good an appearance as if you lived in a city. I wish I could have seen you all on the road.

MARIA. Can you not imagine those waggons—one painted blue, the other red, with their feeding-troughs behind, and a half-bushel measure lying in each; a pot of grease swinging below, for the benefit of the wheels, and a mastiff walking underneath; though my brothers generally managed to keep the dogs so much in *their* vehicle, that the animals rode more than they walked. I think I see that waggon now, with sometimes a boy's face and sometimes a dog's face peeping out of the aperture at the back part of the cover.

ELLEN. Did you always find stopping-places, where you could eat and sleep?

MARIA. Not always; and the farther we proceeded the fewer they became. These stopping-places were generally log-huts, called taverns. Some of them were so open that the light shone through between the logs; and they were scarcely better in appearance than large corn-cribs. At many of these taverns they had nothing to set before the travellers but Indian cakes, bacon, and whisky. In the yard of one of them we saw a girl preparing green apples for pies; she laid them, without paring or coring, on a broad flat stone, and chopped them in pieces with an axe. Her mother, at a table under a tree, was preparing the paste, which she rolled with a black bottle instead of a rolling-pin. This pie-crust was made of rye-meal, mixed with fat skimmed from the bacon-pot; and, instead of sugar, the apples were sweetened with a little wild honey.

ELLEN. What horrid pies! Surely you did not taste them?

MARIA. Yes, we did—our appetites were not fastidious; and I can assure you we were quite impatient till they came out of the oven. My mother afterwards reminded me of a naughty tantrum I had at about four years old, when I threw a nice piece of cranberry tart on the floor, and stamped on it, because I did not think it sufficiently sweet; and now I was glad to eat the coarsest of coarse pies.

ELLEN. And did you always find beds in these taverns?

MARIA. No; we generally depended on those we brought with us, which we took out of the waggons, and spread on the floor, the fatigues of the day causing us to sleep soundly. On arriving one night at a tavern, we preferred sleeping in the waggons, as in the only room of the house a ball was going on.

ELLEN. A ball?

MARIA. Yes: we saw something of it, as we looked out the waggon. The room was lighted with pine slips stuck in potatoes, in which a hole had been cut for the purpose. An old negro sat on a stone in the capacious chimney-place, playing on the banjo, which you know is a hollow gourd, with strings stretched across it; and the dancers (among whom we saw no females) were men of the roughest appearance. They wore blanket coats, and danced with their hats on their heads, and segars in their mouths. Their shuffling and stamping, as they seemed to beat the tune into the earthen floor, my brothers then thought most excellent dancing; and they stood at the door and looked in at them, while our dogs barked in chorus with astonishment.

ELLEN. What would Monsieur Pirouette say upon such an occasion? He would shut his eyes, stop his ears, and run away in horror.[1]

MARIA. We once passed the night in the cabin of a hunter, which we discerned at a great distance, illuminated by the fire on the hearth, which shone most brilliantly through the openings between the logs that formed the walls, and through the loose boards that covered the roof. This hut had no other door than a curtain of buffalo-hide, and no other furniture than two bedsteads of rough logs, with boards laid over them (the bedding being of bear-skins), a sort of table, and a bench of the same description, a large iron pot, and a shelf, with a few tin cups and earthen plates. A rifle stood in one corner, and an axe in the other. The wife and daughter of the hunter had buck-skin gowns, and the man himself was also drest in skins. We found them cooking venison, which was cut into steaks, and stuck on long forked sticks; and thus they held it to the fire, and roasted, or rather toasted it. On inquiring if we could have supper and lodging, they readily assented, and the daughter began to set the table, wiping the dust from the plates with a handful of leaves pulled from a tree, whose branches came almost in at the door. After supper the hunter related various adventures he had met with in the course of his profession, to which my brothers listened with a deep interest and almost breathless attention. The mother then told the daughter to go out and feed the bear. We children all followed the girl, and found a young pet bear chained to a tree behind the house: he had appeared to be very tame, and played with her just like a dog, as she said, though I never saw a dog play in so rough and clumsy a manner. My brothers immediately became familiar with him; but Fanny and I were afraid to go very near, and preferred patting the hunter's fine hound. At bed-time the family would have given up their beds to us, but we chose rather to spread our mattresses on the floor; and as we looked up, we saw the stars through the broken roof above our heads.

ELLEN. What could you do when you found no house to stop at?

MARIA. We depended then on the provisions we always kept in the waggon in case of emergencies, such as biscuits, cheese, dried venison, and gingerbread; and we had tin cups, with which, when we were thirsty, we dipped water from the springs and brooks. Sometimes, when we stopped to rest in the shade, we made a fire and cooked a wild turkey, or some squirrels, or wild pigeons, which had been shot by my uncle, who had his gun with him, or by one of the boys with my father's gun. We found a great deal of wild fruit in the woods, such as papaws, mandrakes, mulberries, fox-grapes, blackberries, and huckleberries.

ELLEN. Were you not afraid of snakes and wild beasts?

MARIA. The boys killed several snakes; among them a copper-head, which they found charming a bird, by fixing his eyes steadily upon it, and by some unknown power of attraction compelling the poor little thing to fly nearer and nearer, till it would have fallen into his open mouth, if Harry had not despatched him by a well-aimed stone, directed at his head. As soon as the snake fell, the bird (who had been chirping all the time in the most terrified manner) was released from this incomprehensible fascination, and flew joyfully away.

ELLEN. Did you meet any bears or panthers?

MARIA. We saw a bear at a distance, turning over some decayed logs in search of worms, and another rolling about in the long grass; but before we came up, they had gone into the thicket. We got to a place where a tornado had, at some former period, torn up hundreds of trees by the roots, and they were now lying prostrate, covering the ground almost as far as we could see. We were obliged to take a considerable circuit round, as it was impossible to pass through them. They looked as if they might shelter vast numbers of wild animals; and as we approached, we actually saw the eyes of a panther glaring upon us from under the fallen branches.

ELLEN. How dreadful!

MARIA. One day we saw a deer start out from amidst the trees a little before us; and as he went bounding along the road, a woman who was spinning at her door ran into the cabin, and bringing out a rifle, pointed it at the animal, and immediately shot him dead. When we came up, she told us it was not the first time she had done such a thing; and that her husband being often absent on long journeys, she was compelled, in self-defence, always to keep a loaded rifle in the house; and that before she had taken this precaution, she was one day obliged to beat off a bear with no other weapon than a frying-pan.

ELLEN. Were you ever under the necessity of sleeping in the open air?

MARIA. Yes, we several times camped out, as it is called, when we were unable to reach a house, and when it was too warm and close to sleep in the waggons. We then ignited some dry leaves, with sparks produced from the gun-flints, and kindled a fire against the trunk of a fallen pine-tree, which served for a back log, and was sometimes set in a blaze from one end to the other. Here we cooked and ate our supper, having with us both coffee and chocolate, which we drank out of our tin cups, after boiling it with water from the nearest brook. We spread blankets on the ground, suspending a sheet or coverlet to the branches of a tree above us, or fixing an umbrella over our heads, to keep off the dew; and putting our feet to the fire, we slept comfortably till day-light, assured that the light of the flame would frighten away the wild beasts.

ELLEN. Did you never meet any other travellers on the road?

MARIA. Very frequently. Sometimes we met a western store-keeper going to one of the Atlantic cities to buy goods, riding thoughtfully along on horseback, with a blanket under the saddle, another upon it, and a great coat and umbrella strapped behind, and sometimes a daughter or sister on another horse beside him, in a calash and riding habit. We were once much amused all day by a Yankee tin-man, who drove his little cart beside our waggon, and from whom we bought a few articles of tin ware. His name was Increase Penny, and he had all the words and phrases peculiar to the lower class of his countrymen; he was, besides, a very acute and entertaining fellow, and had travelled with his tin-cart nearly all over the United States. We often met other waggons loaded with settlers; and once we saw a family that carried nearly their whole property upon a horse, on which the wife and child were perched on the top of a scanty bed, with a bag and a basket behind them; the husband walking beside with his axe and his gun, and a cow following after.

ELLEN. Those must have been the very poorest of settlers.

MARIA. They were what are called squatters—people who, having no means of buying land, go into the new country, and establish themselves upon any unoccupied tract they find convenient. There they clear the ground, build a dwelling, raise crops, and live rent free, till the land is claimed by the right owner, or till they hear of another place that they like better.

ELLEN. But how did you always find your way through the wilderness?

MARIA. What was intended for the road had been blazed; that is, the trees were marked by having a piece of the bark hewn off with an axe.

ELLEN. How did you employ yourselves on this tedious journey?

MARIA. We had some books with us. My mother and Phillis knit stockings, and Fanny and I made patch-work, as we sat in a waggon. When we were tired of riding, we got out and walked. The boys generally rambled on far a-head with the guns, and were very successful in shooting. In the evening, when it was too dark to do any thing else, Fanny and myself generally crept to the back part of the waggon, beside Phillis, who entertained us with long stories, of which she had an inexhaustible variety.

ELLEN. How glad you must have been when you arrived at the end of your journey!

MARIA. We were indeed, though we had not found our journey unpleasant. When we came to our own land, there was no habitation to receive us. My father had hired two men, as we came along, to assist in cutting down trees and building a log-house; and till this was accomplished we lived out of doors and in the waggons. My father took his axe, and struck the first stroke in cutting down the tree. My uncle attacked another, and soon levelled it with the ground: the hired men were very industrious, and sufficient employment was found for my brothers. The logs were stripped of their bark, laid on each other, and the interstices filled with clay. A chimney, with a very large fire-place, was constructed of stone, and shingles and boards were brought from a saw-mill about twenty miles distant. In a short time the house was completed. It had but two rooms, and there was no upstairs, not even a loft. As we sat at table we looked up to the joists of the slanting roof; and as we stood in the corner of the wide chimney we could raise our eyes and see the sky.

ELLEN. What sort of furniture had you?

MARIA. We had brought with us as many articles as could conveniently be packed in the waggons; and my father and uncle (who are both very ingenious) made us some pine tables and shelves; and the boys, following their example, constructed benches and stools. Blankets and quilts were nailed up round the walls to keep off the damp of the clay plastering. During the day we lived almost out of doors, when the weather was fine; and we generally breakfasted and dined at a table set under the shade of the trees. Fortunately there was a spring of excellent water close to the house, which supplied a never-failing brook that ran before the door. The remainder of the season was devoted to clearing the ground for cultivation. Cows, pigs, and poultry, were purchased at the nearest settlement, and also corn, which had to be carried twenty miles to be ground.

ELLEN. And what did you generally eat?

MARIA. The first summer our food was coarse enough, consisting chiefly of bacon, Indian cakes baked on the girdle,[2] and mush and milk; but we had no vegetables, no wheat-flour, and no fruit but such as we found in the woods. Sometimes the boys went out with the guns, and brought home wild turkeys and other birds, and my uncle and father shot several deer. We were once put to great inconvenience for want of Indian meal, having used all we had, and the waters being so swelled by a freshet that there was no crossing them to get to the mill.

ELLEN. What could you possibly do?

MARIA. In the yard, near the door, was the stump of a tree, which the boys hollowed out by burning a deep cavity in it. The corn was put in this, which served for a mortar, and it was pounded with a large heavy stick, made of the branch of a tree. It was very laborious work, and we all took our turn at it. For several days this pounded corn was our only substitute for Indian meal.

ELLEN. I wonder you were able to eat it.

MARIA. In the autumn, when the cold obliged us to live more within doors, we found our house rather small; but we soon got accustomed to that inconvenience. Many things that were not in constant use we were obliged to keep in the yard; and a box containing our china, and my mother's silver tea-set, remained all winter in the adjoining woods; for there was no danger of thieves, and we had no room for it in the house.

ELLEN. Were there no wild beasts in the surrounding wilderness?

MARIA. We were not troubled with them in the summer; but in the long winter nights, when they rove every where in search of prey, they frequently came very near our habitation. The howling of the wolves was sometimes terrible, and we often heard them prowling round the house, and scratching at the doors and windows to get in. Our dogs were afraid of them, and shrunk silently into their kennels.

ELLEN. Oh! how dreadful! I am glad there are none in the neighbourhood now.

MARIA. We often, in the morning, found their tracks in the snow. One night, when we were all at supper, we heard a great noise like wood falling down, and running to the door, we saw by the light of the moon a large bear, who had scrambled to the top of the wood-pile, and was trying to reach the fowls that roosted on a tree which grew over it. Harry immediately ran in for a gun, and taking a very accurate aim, he fired, and the bear fell down dead in a moment, bringing half the wood-pile with him. Next day some of the bear's meat was cooked for dinner; but we found it very coarse, and did not like it much; the lean was like hard beef, and the fat like hard pork. The boys made wolf-traps, something like large rat-traps, and two wolves were caught in them in the course of the winter.

ELLEN. Did any Indians ever come about the settlement?

MARIA. Often, though none lived within fifty miles of us; but we treated them well, and always, as soon as they entered the house, we set before them the best food we had; and my father often purchased furs of them, which he afterwards sold advantageously. Several times two or three Indians passed the night with us, lying on the floor wrapped in their blankets, with their feet to the large fire that blazed all night in the chimney, and their tomahawks by their sides. These tomahawks they used also as pipes, the handle being hollow to afford a passage for the smoke, and communicating at the back of the hatchet with a bowl or socket which contained the tobacco. My father and uncle smoked these pipes with them, in token of friendship; and we all took care to offer them our hands as soon as we saw them. They often brought us maple-sugar, very nicely put up in small baskets of coloured chip. We bought buck-skin moccasins of them, which we found very comfortable and convenient.

Once we had a visit from two Indian men, accompanied by a squaw, who carried on her back a little child or papoose, with its head peeping out from under her blanket. It was tied in a sort of small cradle of basket-work, made concave, that the child might fit in; its arms being stretched down close to its sides, and confined with buck-skin bands, so that it could not move. When the squaw came in, she stood the cradle with the infant in it against the wall, and shortly afterwards she passed a string through the handle at the top, and hung it up to the branch of a tree before the door, that the child might have the benefit of the air and shade, and be amused with what was passing in the yard.

ELLEN. We had once some old-fashioned bed-curtains, pictured all over with William Penn's treaty with the Indians; and there was on them a squaw nursing a papoose, tied in a cradle of that description. I have often, when a little girl, gazed, as I lay awake in the morning, on these bed-curtains; and it was from them I acquired my first ideas of William Penn and of the origin of Philadelphia.

MARIA. Yes, the scene engraved for this calico was taken from a fine picture by Mr. West.[3] It would advance the improvement of children, if the practice still prevailed of selecting the devices for furniture chintz from good historical pictures.

ELLEN. Was not the Indian baby pretty? I think I could kiss a little Indian.

MARIA. I did kiss him. There was a plaything of beads and shells suspended from the top of the cradle; but while his arms were tied down he could only look at it. His mother fed him with maple-sugar.

ELLEN. Perhaps that very child will grow up to be a great warrior.

MARIA. In an opening of the woods, about half a mile from our house, was a mound or burial-place, where in former times a great number of Indians had been interred; I suppose, according to their custom, wrapped in skins and sitting upright. All the Indians that came within twenty miles of the place, repaired to this mound to lament their forefathers, who had been buried there perhaps a century before. And here they bewailed them so loudly, that we frequently heard their lamentations as far as our house; and they seemed to mourn them as deeply and sincerely as if they were their own parents, and had recently died. We took care not to disturb the mound, as that would have drawn on us the resentment of the Indians. In ploughing, my father and uncle frequently turned up arrowheads of flint, broken tomahawks, and other things of a similar description.

ELLEN. How far were you from any other settlers?

MARIA. The nearest house was a store, nine miles off, inhabited by a very good family, whom we thought it pleasant to visit occasionally on horseback. Here a post-office was kept; and every Saturday one of my brothers went there for the newspaper and letters. You may be sure the paper was a great treat to us all; though, by the time it reached our part of the country the news was not of a very recent date.

ELLEN. In what manner did you generally pass your time?

MARIA. Our time was never tedious, for we were always fully occupied. My mother, myself, and Phillis, sewed and attended to the household affairs; and little Fanny was soon old enough to become useful. My father, my uncle, and my brothers, were constantly engaged in clearing and cultivating the ground, and the soil was found to be the finest imaginable. My father, you know, is a man of strong sense, and has made the very best use of an excellent plain education. He took great pleasure in instructing us of evenings, and his method was so judicious that it was impossible for us not to improve. We had brought some books with us, and we sometimes got new ones from the store.

ELLEN. What a happy event the arrival of a new book must have been to you!

MARIA. It was indeed. My father had great success in his farming, and found it very profitable; so also did my uncle. After a while we were able to build a better house. Other settlers came into the neighbourhood; other houses were built; and eventually a town was laid out on my father's land. The place grew and flourished; and now, instead of a forest, we have a long street of good houses, and three cross streets. We have stores, a church, a market-house, a court-house, a female school, a fine hotel, several taverns, and no scarcity of lawyers and doctors.

ELLEN. And in the spot where your log-cabin once stood is now your father's large stone mansion, handsomely furnished, and replete with every thing necessary to the enjoyment of life, even unto a fine library. Your uncle Robert is making the tour of Europe, the boys are at the University, and your father is at Washington, attending his duty in Congress.

MARIA. Such is the career of hundreds who have sought their fortunes in the backwoods of a country, where the road to prosperity and distinction is open to all who are intelligent, industrious, and enterprising.

Eliza Farnham, or The Love Letters

Part I

Eliza Farnham was sister to a physician who resided in the western part of the state of New York, at a large and flourishing town which bore the Grecian name of Peloponnesus. She had been placed, when a little girl, at a fashionable boarding-school, located somewhere on the banks of the Hudson, and having lost both her parents before she attained her fourteenth year, her brother had succeeded to the charge of herself and her fortune of twenty thousand dollars. On quitting school at the age of sixteen, our heroine had spent a winter in the city of New York by an invitation from the family of her fellow-pupil and most intimate friend, Maria Copley. There she became acquainted with Horace Montacute, a Bostonian, of fine appearance, high connections, and independent fortune, who devoting much of his attention to public affairs, was what is called a "rising young man." Fascinated by the beauty of Eliza Farnham, he fell immediately and desperately in love. Perceiving that he had made a favourable impression, he became eager to secure his conquest, and before his return to Boston, he addressed her and was accepted.

When Dr. Farnham came to convey his sister home (his house at Peloponnesus was to be her residence while unmarried) he found her engaged to Horace Montacute. Having learnt, on inquiry, that the young gentleman was, in every sense of the term, an excellent match, Dr. Farnham willingly gave his consent, upon condition that the marriage should not take place till Eliza had reached the age of eighteen; justly considering that, as yet, their acquaintance was too short, and the lady too young. Montacute accompanied them to their home, passed a week at Peloponnesus, and then returned to Boston, with the intention of beguiling the term of probation by frequent visits to the mistress of his heart.

Dr. Farnham was a widower without children. His establishment was superintended by his mother, a plain simple-minded dame of the old school, and an active and excellent house-wife. After bringing home his sister, Dr. Farnham was not long in discovering, to his great disappointment, that though her style of dress was elegant, that of her conversation was very much the reverse: that in the cultivation of a few showy accomplishments the improvement of her mind had been entirely neglected; that she knew nothing of any books except those from which she had been obliged to learn the words of sundry lessons repeated with the comprehension of a parrot and forgotten the next day. Her winter in the city had been passed in a very gay circle, where all her time was devoted to a perpetual round of frivolous company, (including balls and crowded parties) and to the adornment of her person. Her numerous deficiencies as they dawned upon the observation of her brother (who had a quick perception of the ridiculous) sometimes diverted as well as grieved him: but he had a great aversion to lecturing, as he called it; and he comforted himself with the reflection that Eliza was going to be married to a very accomplished and intelligent young man, and that it would then be her husband's business to improve her. In the mean time, Dr. Farnham concluded that now that his sister had left school, and had passed the "ordeal of her coming out," and of a season in New York, she would insensibly and gradually improve without any particular exertion: and that at eighteen she might probably arrive at a tolerable mediocrity.

A few days after the departure of her lover, Eliza Farnham, holding an open letter in her hand, and with a very unhappy countenance, entered the apartment in which her brother was reading, and her grandmother seated at her knitting.

"What is the matter, Eliza"—said the good old lady—"why do you look so uncomfortable. I suppose that letter is from your sweetheart; so it ought to make you glad instead of sorry."

"I hope the course of true love continues to run smoothly"—said Dr. Farnham—"whatever Will Shakspeare may tell us to the contrary, with his universal knowledge of every thing in the world."

"Mr. Shakspeare had better keep his information to himself,"—said Eliza, pettishly—"I know not who he is, or what right he has to be meddling with every body's business and talking to you about Horace and me. I have often heard people repeat things they had got from him. I don't wish his acquaintance, and I hope I shall never see him."

"I rather think you never will"—said Dr. Farnham, laughing. "But is it really possible you have never heard of Shakspeare's plays?"

"If I have, I neither listened nor remembered"—replied Eliza. "We never went to the theatre from Mrs. Copley's, except when operas were to be performed, and none of us had any time for reading. As to Mrs. Holloway, you cannot suppose *she* would permit a play-book of any sort to come within the walls of her school, for she said plays were still worse than novels. All our reading books were what she called good books; but we were not good enough to take any interest in them. Besides, when our studies were over, we were too tired to read any thing at all. To be sure, several of the young ladies used to bribe the servants to get them fashionable novels from the circulating library, which they said let them into all the secrets of English high life, but I thought it too troublesome a business to read by stealth, and to take snatches of books at odd minutes, always in fear of being found out; so I never tried it at all."

"Well, well"—said Dr. Farnham—"we need no ghost to tell us that. There is no need of your taking so much pains to prove that you have read nothing. Let us now return to the main question. Why has that letter discomposed you? Horace Montacute is well, I hope?"

"He says nothing to the contrary."

"And faithful, of course?"

"Oh! very faithful indeed!"

"None of his relatives in Boston offered any objection when they heard of his engagement to Miss Farnham?"

"Oh! no indeed—why should they—and even if they had, he is his own master, and is not obliged to ask any body's leave for any thing. He has plenty of money, and is well able to do as he pleases, and marry as he chooses."

"To be sure he is.—But what then is the cause of your present annoyance?"

"Why the truth is—Horace Montacute expects me to answer this letter."

"Well—of course he does.—and will it not be a very delightful task?"

"Not so very."

"Why!—I always thought separated lovers found their only happiness in pouring out to each other the effusions of their hearts, by means of long and frequent epistles—'Heaven first taught letters for some wretch's aid'—as my friend Pope says."[1]

"I am not a wretch at all"—replied the young lady—"and as to your friend Pope, I don't care what he says, and I hope he don't visit here."

"He does not I assure you"—said the doctor. "But a truce with all this nonsense, and explain why you have any reluctance to answer your lover's epistle."

"If I answer this letter"—replied Eliza—"he will send another as soon as possible, and then I shall have to answer that. I don't want to encourage this continual letter-writing."

"But what is your objection to a correspondence with the man to whom you have engaged your hand, and I hope your heart; and with whom, after a certain period, you are destined in all probability to pass the whole of your life?"

"The truth is, dear Arthur"—resumed Miss Farnham—"I am no great scratch at my pen—in short I am a poor scribe."

"Two very bad expressions—a great scratch and a poor scribe. But as boarding-school girls seldom presume to talk in presence of their governesses, I suppose they have no one to correct their language, and among themselves they probably indulge in a sort of conventional slang. Yet the four letters we received during your visit to New York, were not bad: only there seemed to be a great deal in them that referred rather to Baltimore, and was somewhat puzzling to your grandmother and myself."

"To tell you the truth"—said Eliza, colouring—"Maria Copley's eldest sister Louisa, was spending the winter with some friends in Baltimore, and she is rather clever at writing—so whenever a letter came from her, I borrowed it to read in my own room, and then I took the opportunity of copying it, and sending it in my own name to you or grandma'—and perhaps sometimes I may have overlooked Baltimore, and forgotten to change it into New York."

"Well!—if ever I heard the like!" exclaimed the old lady, dropping her knitting needles—"Then those letters were all a cheat."

"I am very sorry to hear it," said Dr. Farnham, seriously—"very sorry indeed. But still while you were at boarding-school, we received an epistle from you every two weeks."

"Well, all Mrs. Holloway's scholars wrote home once a fortnight—but school letters and real letters are very different things. Mrs. Holloway's eldest daughter, Miss Catherine—(whom we all hated)—attended to the letter-business, and told us what to say; and after we had done, she took them all away to correct at her leisure; and then we never saw them again, for *she* sealed them and sent them to the post-office."

"So then"—said the doctor—"this accounts for your epistles generally giving tolerable satisfaction when they were received at home.—to be sure there was no great variety in them—they always contained the same things—excellent health, perfect happiness, praise of Mrs. Holloway, love for her daughters, and want of pocket-money."

"Well"—continued Eliza—"the girls all knew in their own minds that when Miss Catherine got our letters to correct, she made some one of the teachers re-write them in a proper manner, with good spelling, and the stops all minded, and the capitals placed right; and then as I told you, they were sent off without our seeing any more of them."

"And so you never knew where the faults were, and what corrections were made?"

"We neither knew nor cared."

"But had you really no other practice in the art of committing your ideas to paper?"

"Do you mean composition?"

"Yes—composition, then."

"Oh! yes, indeed—every other Saturday we wrote composition pieces.—But the subjects were always Friendship, and Benevolence, and Gratitude, and Modesty, and other such things that we knew nothing about. We took some of our composition from Miss Hannah More's Essays.[2] But we had an old book among us called the Rambler, that helped us greatly, though we had carefully to avoid all the parts that were the least amusing, or that seemed any thing like stories.[3] And the girls that wrote for premiums generally copied out of Zimmerman on Solitude."[4]

"Is it possible that these tricks were never discovered?"

"If they were, Mrs. Holloway and her people never let on; they pretended not to see, and so saved themselves a great deal of trouble. Besides, on Saturday every thing was hurried through as soon as possible: it being the chief day that Mrs. Holloway and her daughters had for going to the city, and leaving cards at the doors of their *friends*, as they called all the rich people they knew."

"I am seriously grieved to hear all this"—said Dr. Farnham—"after supposing for so many years that Mrs. Holloway's pupils were receiving a first-rate education."

"Well—so we were"—replied Eliza—"and that is the reason we had no time for reading and writing. We had our harps and pianos and guitars to practice, and our dancing and our theorem painting and our poonah painting,[5] and our bead-work and our worsted-work; and worse than all, our French, and Italian, and Spanish, and German."

"If you were so unskilful at your pens, how did you manage to write your exercises in those languages?"

"Oh! we only pretended to write our exercises.—The truth is, we got them done by one of the teachers, Mademoiselle Annette de Jaquesonne, whom the girls called Nancy Jackson. They said she was an Englishwoman that had travelled all over Europe as a countess's lady's maid, and so picked up all sorts of languages. *She* wrote our exercises for us; and we paid her by now and then the gift of a worked collar, or a cambric handkerchief, or a pair of white kid gloves, or a silk scarf, or some such thing."

"But did not the sameness of the hand-writing excite suspicion?"

"Oh no—school girls write pretty nearly alike; and if our language-master *did* suspect the truth, he never wasted his time by making a fuss about it."

"Your language-master—did one man teach all those languages?"

"Yes—Mr. Von Smatter (he was a German baron in his own country)—he knew all languages in the world, one just as well as another; only that his American, as he called it, was not very good."

"Is it really possible that your exercises were written by this Mademoiselle Annette, alias Nancy Jackson?"

"To be sure they were. But she did not help us with our composition, for she could write nothing out of her own head: though she was quite a smart woman at foreign languages. Another way we had of obtaining her services was to plague her about Mr. Von Smatter, and that always put her into such a good humour that she would do any thing we asked her."

"And is it absolutely true, Eliza, that you apprehend any difficulty in composing an answer to Horace Montacute's letter."

"It is true enough. When I am to write about any thing real, (be it ever so trifling,) I am always at a dead stand how to word it, so as to make sense on paper. And if I have to do it all by myself, I am puzzled about the spelling, and the stops, and the capitals, and how to finish one sentence and begin another. It is in vain to tell me to try and write just the same as I talk. When it comes to the pinch I can do no such thing. Talking is very different from writing: at least it is to me. When I was in New York, if any of my dresses did not fit and required alteration, I was obliged, after I had sent back the dress to the mantua-maker, who lived at the world's end (as they all do) to go all the way there myself: because when I tried to give her directions by writing a note, somehow I could not make out upon paper the least idea of what I wanted. And worse than all, when Miss Humdrum used to send me stiff hard invitation notes to her select parties of the same twelve stupid people always, (every one of whom I hated) I had to go, because for my life I could not manage to write a billet of excuse that would not have made her throw back her hands and turn up the whites of her eyes, and thank heaven that *she* had been taught the proper use of her pen."

"Yours is indeed a hard case"—said Dr. Farnham—"I grieve to find that the essentials of your education have been so totally neglected, and I take shame to myself for not having more particularly inquired into your progress as you went along. I can only excuse myself by saying that nearly my whole time and attention has for many years been devoted to my professional duties; and that as I found you always looking well when you came home at the vacations, I concluded that if your health did not suffer, your studies could not be very hard; and that in short, as Mrs. Holloway's boarding-school was considered quite as good as the majority of such establishments, I supposed that you would turn out quite as well as the generality of young ladies."

"But dear Arthur"—resumed Eliza Farnham—"all this talk amounts to nothing. Let us go back to the main point. I am in a scrape about answering this letter (which he begs me to do by return of post) and I want you to help me out of it."

"I hope"—said the doctor—"you do not wish me to send an answer in your name."

"No, no—not precisely that. But I wish you to write a letter *for* me, and I will copy it exactly, spelling and all; and *my* copy shall go, not yours."

"It is beneath the dignity of a man, to assist a woman in any such deception"—said the Doctor, essaying to look sternly.

"Well then—what is to become of me; and what will Horace Montacute think on receiving no answer. If *you* will not do it, I must get somebody else to write and say that I have cut my right thumb, or that I have a dreadful inflammation in both eyes."

The old lady looked up from her knitting in silent horror.

"Shocking!"—exclaimed the Doctor—"has your moral sense been as little cultivated as your mental powers. Have you no idea of the sacred obligations of truth?"

"Let me see—I once wrote a composition upon Truth, copied out of the Rambler."

"Really, Eliza"—said the Doctor—"you mortify me more and more every moment."

"You had better help me out of my difficulty"—exclaimed Eliza, bursting into tears.

"Poor dear"—said the old lady, in a softened voice—"I declare if she is not crying about it."

The doctor was going to reply, when a message was brought, requesting him to repair immediately to a house at the other end of the town, for the purpose of relieving a child that had swallowed a button—of course he departed instantly.

"How I pity that poor child's mother"—said Mrs. Farnham. "It is well that such accidents have happened before; and Arthur is very clever at poking things down people's throats."

Eliza continued to sob and hold her handkerchief to her eyes: and her kind grandmother viewed her with deep commiseration, and said—"Dear—dear—what can I do for you, poor thing?"

"Grandma"—cried Eliza, suddenly brightening up—"you that have lived so long in the world, and have had so much experience of the troubles and difficulties of life, and take such pleasure in making young people happy—cannot *you* write a letter to Horace Montacute, that will be fit for me to copy, and send him as my own. You know it *will* be my own after all, as the very letter that he receives will actually be written by my own hand. Do write one for me, dear, dear grandmamma."

"Who, I!"—said the old lady. "Bless your heart, my writing days are over long ago. To be sure, I *was* considered a pretty good writer when a girl like you: but writing is like making puff-paste: if you don't practise at it almost every day, your hand gets out. I never write any thing now but receipts, and you know I have three long books nearly full of them. If a receipt was what you wanted, I could easily supply you."

"I wish with all my heart there were receipts for writing love-letters"—said Eliza. "How such a book would sell![6] But dear grandma'—did you never write a letter to grandpa'?"

"I had no occasion—after we were married we were always together."

"But before marriage. It is a letter from a young lady to a young gentleman, *before marriage*, that I particularly want just now."

"Why those are love-letters, mostly."

"To be sure they are. In plain terms, Horace Montacute has sent me, of course, a love-letter, and expects an answer: and as I cannot make such things out of my own head, I want a good one to copy."

The old lady simpered. "Well—since you are in such a bad way, I do not care if I do accommodate you with one. My dear deceased Savegood Farnham, your beloved grandfather, was careful to keep all the letters I ever wrote to him, which were three: and after his death they came to me with the rest of the property. I had them for many years put away in my great queen-stitch pocket-book. But I lent one to a chambermaid of ours, who was going to be married, (just like you,) and wanted it, just to see how love-letters ought to be written. She had it about the kitchen, and the cook, not knowing its value, singed a turkey with it. Another of these letters was begged of me by Mr. Seizall, a newspaper man that was on a visit here two or three years ago, and was so kind as to say it was too good to be lost: so he carried it away with him, and I heard afterwards that he had printed it in his newspaper, only he did not put the right names."

"But the third letter, grandma'—the third"—asked Eliza, impatiently.

"That's the only one that is left—I will go and get it for you—I wrote it to the dear deceased soon after we were engaged, when he went down to the city on business, and stayed there a whole week. I remember very well that he offered himself no less than eleven times before I consented to accept him, though I intended it from the very first. But, in those days, young ladies were not so easily won as they are now, when they jump at a man the moment he asks them, and sometimes even before."

Mrs. Farnham then left the room, and soon returned with the great queen-stitch pocket-book in her hand, from which she produced a letter carefully enveloped in a sheet of tissue-paper. "Now, Eliza"—said the old lady—"you are to remember that this letter is not to be copied out and out, as you did those Baltimore letters, for that would be deception, and deception is next a-kin to lying, so you are to change some of the words, and preserve only the meaning."

Neither Mrs. Farnham nor Eliza had perceived that just at this time one of the servants, a black girl, named Belinda, had entered the room. She had brought a message from the cook, but observing how the ladies were engaged, she slipped silently into a corner, and lingered and listened. Mrs. Farnham unfolded the long-cherished letter, and read aloud as follows:

Poughkeepsie, July 18th, ——.

My dear Savegood—I embrace this opportunity of taking up my pen to acquaint you that we are all in good health at this present writing, and I hope this will find you the same. I have nothing particular to inform you of, except that absence is generally an affliction to all constant lovers, and I hope we shall be till death do us part. The time seems very long till it shall fall to our happy lot to meet again in this vale of tears, which I hope will be next Tuesday, July the 23d, according to the promise you made in our parting moments; but we must all look for disappointments in this life.

Permit me, my dear Savegood, to advise you to keep always in the path of rectitude, to set your face against evil counsellors, and to fly from the amusements and stage-plays of New York as you would from a roaming lion seeking to devour you. Allow me to mention that I think it will be best for you to stay chiefly in solitude, for in my humble opinion, there is nothing so good for erring man as the examination of his own sinful thoughts. Alas! poor human nature!—What wretched worms we mortals are!

Having nothing more of importance to communicate, I now hasten to conclude this tedious epistle, hoping you will excuse all faults, and pardon my encroaching so long on your valuable time and patience, and favour me with a lengthy answer by return of post. Father and mother join me in love to you and all enquiring friends, and also sister Mary and sister Margaret, and Jane, and John, and likewise little Peter. Aunt Charity and uncle Daniel, also desire to be remembered to you, and our dear cousins Samuel and Angelina send their best respects, as well as

Believe me, yours sincerely, (in haste)
FRANCES DOROTHEA POWERS.

"There"—said the old lady—"to be sure it is a sin to praise ourselves—but that is a real true love-letter, written just as love-letters ought to be between respectable young people that are engaged. Of course you will leave out father and mother, and the children, and aunt and uncle and cousins, and put in Arthur and me instead. And you will date from Peloponnesus instead of Poughkeepsie. You see there is a great deal of good advice in the letter, for which no doubt Horace will thank you. In the roaring-lion part you can change New York to Boston, which I dare say is not without its amusements and stage-plays as well as other cities. The solitude part means you know, that while he is away from home he had better stay chiefly in his own room. However, manage it as you think proper. When Horace gets the letter, I am sure he will never guess that it was taken from one of your grandmother's."

The girl, Belinda, now presented herself, and delivered her message from Chloe the cook, in consequence of which the old lady repaired immediately to the store-room, leaving Belinda to follow her with the white sugar-box!

Part II

Eliza Farnham saw plainly that her grandmother's letter was not available in the present dilemma, so she folded it up and sat turning it about in her hand, and looking sadly perplexed. The girl Belinda was originally from Philadelphia, but she had lived awhile at Mrs. Holloways's boarding-school, where she was on very familiar terms with the young ladies, in consequence of executing for them numerous confidential matters, library books, &c. She knew our heroine perfectly well, having been in many of her little secrets, all of which she had kept as people of her class usually keep them. Instead of obeying Mrs. Farnham's order with regard to the sugar box, Belinda loitered in the parlour, fully aware of the circumstances that were causing so much annoyance to the young lady. She now came forward and said—"Miss Eliza, if I was you I wouldn't have nothing to do with that old foolish letter of your grandma's—I'm sure it's not at all fit to send to no young gentleman now-a-days; and the better they're advised the worse they are. If you want to take the pattern of a true lover's letter, (such as young ladies writes now) I'll lend you one of mine, that I writ last night, setting up till twelve o'clock to get through. You know I'm engaged to Mr. Sodus, that handsome coloured gentleman that pays attention to the people what stops at the Independence Hotel. He has gone to New York to accept of a place as one of the seven head-waiters in the Amboy boat, where the passengers begins and finishes. And when we are married he is to be put on at the other end of the line, and we are to go to housekeeping in Philadelphia—I needn't send off this letter for a few days, for it makes no difference whether he gets it now or any other time; so you're quite welcome to borrow it, if it will do you any good. I'll just run and get it, before I attend your grandma' with the sugar-box. I guess she is tired of waiting already, up there in the store-room; but she may get through the time a putting the shelves to rights. As for old Chloe's wants, I don't care a cent for them."

Belinda then hastened out of the room, and shortly returned with a huge letter which she put into the hands of our heroine, who was still sitting in moody silence, and who took in despair the black girl's epistle; thinking it just possible that she might collect a few ideas from it. Having carried it to the privacy of her own chamber, she threw herself on the bed, and commenced the perusal of this delectable missive.

Pelicaneasus—may the 1st.

Dear and belovid Mr. Sodass.

The thyme seems particularly long since we parted, as all thyme does when loviers are a way. Since I can no longer Grace my eyes with your Hansom bewty every day seems most a Year, for the hour is Long a coming that will store us to one a nother—I hasten to Tell you that I met with a Fatal Axident yesterday, which will Make your hare Stand on end when you here it. Every Buddy had gone out, and I had just run to the front parlor to sea the long Stage go by that runs to Cunningjoeharry, and I saw my Deer friend Mirandy Woolwitch a setting on the frunt Seat, going Off with a lady as child's Maid. So I was quite Afected, and kept waving my Towel at her long after the Stage was out of site. But I happened to lean out too far, so I lost my Ballence, and the sloping Sellar door was just under that window, and Down went my head and Up went my Heels, and out I fell foremast, and I went Slanting down the Sellar door till my forrad came to the pavement and broke one of the Brix. It is a Mersey I was not hurt—The boys Next door and Opposit came all round me as I was a Picking myself Up, and had the impedence to Sing—"Poor Belinda fell out of the window"—This meloncolly Axident put me in mind of the Day when Me and you was a wawking Together and a krossing the Logg over the branch, and your foot Slipped and you tumbled in to the watter and started the phrogs; and as you Splashed in, they Hopped out. I saw one grate big green and yaller phellow Jump right over your Back—I am Still true and konstant to my favourite Sodass. I waste my thyme mostly in Smelling the flour you put into my hand at Parting and adorning my Head with it, and as it was a bluming Rose it still keeps its good Smell. I mostly Sing love songs now. Yesterday Mrs. Farnum was rather Hard upon me when she found me Stirring buttor and shugar for a Kake, and Singing—"Ah don't mingul"—exactly like Mrs. Wood. The old lady says I do not Mind my dooties no Longer and sweeps dirty. Young persons in Love should not have no dooties to mind, and should not be expected to wurk, for love ellevates the human sole, and wurk is only Fit for low-minded peeple, them as likes to Grovel with brumes and breshes in their Hands. For my part I Hold myself above it, but I Guess I shall have to keep on till after we gets Married, and then I shall Kick away the kitchen in short order. You prommist I should Live like a lady and give Balls, and go to Filladelfy to live. Word has just come from Filladelfy that rents is riz in Squinch street, and that wicturals is very High and so is wedgetables. I was quite Afected when I heard such Bad news, but I suppose it will Make no difference to loviers Enamelled as we are. But let what will Happen—"Our days and Knights and months and years Fly round the cedar Pole."[7] This to conclude, as my paper has come to an End, though I Bought a Grate big Sheet on purpose, and write small. I send you inclosed Heaps of love and a lock of my hare for you to Kiss in Absence as you desired, put up in White paper.

I remane
my deerly Belovid Sodass
your ever Afected sweatheart,
And Sincerest admirer
BELINDA BROADHEAD.

N.B. P.S. I forgot to Tell you that most all the grate Peeple belonging to this town are Now in love—So look Out for weddings—You know Judge Bardley that tawks so Much about a man named Scot, and not general Scot neither—The other Evening at our house I heard him saying in the Middle of a long Rigmeroll—"Love rules the Court"—If that is the Case I do not Wonder so many poor peeple don't get Justis done them when they comes to their Trials.

"Pshaw"—thought Eliza—"what nonsense!—and yet, after all, there are really more ideas in this foolish black girl's letter than in my good grandmamma's.—Well, I will put off the evil moment, and not write till to-morrow.—It is really too much for men, because they are engaged, to expect answers by return of post; and I shall not encourage Horace Montacute in any such absurdity. I wonder why it is the custom for lovers to write to each other at all. I wish it were considered improper."

When she met them at tea, Eliza Farnham informed her brother and grandmother that she had concluded to defer writing till the next day, in consequence of a violent head-ache; and that she had no doubt she could manage the business very well by herself, if she took sufficient time.

Our heroine lay awake half the night, pondering on the task of the morrow, and trying to plan a beginning, a middle, and an end for this dreaded epistle. She was afraid to copy a letter out of a book, for she knew Horace to be a great reader, and there was danger of his detecting the deception. At breakfast, Eliza heard with joy that Dr. Farnham would be out the whole morning, and that her grandmother was going to preserve rhubarb, and would be busily engaged till dinner-time. Eliza, therefore, took possession of the library, and resolved with vigorous determination to set desperately to work, and accomplish this formidable letter. She justly doubted her correctness in orthography from having, when at school, been generally near the tail of her class; and as she had read little or nothing, the appearance of words was but faintly impressed on her mind; so she armed herself with Johnson and Walker on one side of the desk, and Webster's and Entick's Dictionaries on the other.[8] She then set about a rough sketch of her letter.

After writing the date and beginning "Dear Horace," she found herself already at a loss, and was unable to devise a single idea for a commencement; and she sat biting the feather of her pen (she could not write with a steel one) and looking up at the ceiling for near ten minutes. She then contrived to proceed through one line, during which, being doubtful of two words, she stopped to consult all the dictionaries, in case these authorities might differ. Her next difficulty was to finish the sentence, which she finally accomplished after looking out two more words in all the dictionaries. This business appeared so laborious that our poor heroine thought she could get along faster by making the rough sketch without regard to the spelling, &c., and correcting the whole in a fair copy.—"Ah!"—thought she—"if people could only be allowed to spell just as they choose."

The dinner bell rung before she had completed her sketch (rough as it certainly was) and she carried it to her room and locked it up carefully. In the afternoon, she was too tired to resume her pen; therefore she took a long nap: and in the evening there came some visiters. After the company had gone, Mrs. Farnham inquired of Eliza if she had finished her letter; but she replied—"Dear grandma' be so kind as to ask me nothing more about it. I shall hate the very name of a letter."

"Well, well"—said the good old lady—"I will not teaze you"—adding in a low voice—"and you may keep mine to look at as long as you please, and don't be afraid to copy out of it whatever you choose."

"Horace Montacute will wonder that the answer to his epistle is so long in arriving—" observed Dr. Farnham.

"Well, it will not be the first thing he has wondered at, and I dare say it will not be the last"—was the sensible reply of our heroine.

Next morning, Eliza Farnham was glad to find that the doctor had been sent for to attend a consultation of physicians at a place thirty miles distant from Peloponnesus, and would not return home till next day. "Now"—thought she—"I can have the free use of the library—desk—dictionaries—grammars and all. I can write much better there than in my own room."

At length the rough sketch was finished, and on reading it over she found it much rougher than she had supposed; and so full of errors, and containing so many things that must be changed entirely, that she determined on making another sketch that should not be quite so long. But as she drew near its completion, she perceived that the second sketch would be still longer than the first; and on revising it she discovered that the faults were still more numerous. She almost cried with vexation; but at last, consoled herself with the hope of being able in the fair copy to correct all errors.

"Now came the tug of war."—With a tremulous hand she took a sheet of fine letter paper, and as she could not write straightly without the assistance of lines, she ruled them with a pencil and ruled them crooked, which she did not perceive till with much care and pains she had written several sentences. She then called Belinda, and sent her to the stationer's to buy a sheet of printed black lines to slip under her paper. But Belinda brought some lines that were quite too far apart. She was sent back for some that were closer together, but none such were to be had. The girl, however, informed Miss Farnham that she had seen at the store some paper that was ready-ruled. This was delightful news, and a quire of it was immediately procured. It was, however, of the size called foolscap, and Eliza had to *razée* a sheet of it down to the dimensions of letter paper.

She now set to work again, beginning with another new pen, but inadvertently commenced too near, as she thought, to the top of the page. Unpractised writers always think it *comme il faut* to begin very far down, even when they know that they have a great deal to say, and at the risk of being obliged at the last to write on the margin for want of space, and to fill up every inch of the spare paper on the direction side. She now prepared another sheet, and began with—"Dear Horace"—half way down the page.

As this was to be the fair copy, it was now that the orthography was to be corrected; but she forgot this important business till she had written three or four sentences and reached the bottom of the page. Then, on consulting the dictionaries, she found that half her words had been spelt wrong. Of her faults of style she was unconscious; notwithstanding that at school she had been made to study Blair's Lectures,[9] that is to learn the words by rote and repeat them parrot-fashion. She now determined on writing a third sketch, which was to include correct spelling, &c., and was to serve as an *exact* model. This performance, with much trouble and difficulty, she at last achieved. Again she set to work at the formidable fair copy, and made a mistake in the date and left out a word in the first line; and not willing to disfigure her letter by erasures or interlineations, she took another fresh sheet and commenced anew.

It would be painful to follow her through the remainder of that weary day, the whole of which was devoted to accomplishing a copy fair enough to dispatch to her love. She laboured at it both morning and afternoon.

> And when they rang the evening bell
> The *letter* scarce was done.

Finally, she determined not to fold it, direct it, or seal it till next morning, that she might go quite fresh to that arduous part of her task. At first, Eliza thought of reading her letter aloud to her grandmother, but was deterred by the apprehension that it would not at all suit the taste of the old lady. She could not, however, resist her inclination to communicate its contents to Belinda, when the girl came to her room at night with a pitcher of fresh water.

"Well, Belinda"—said the young lady, after finishing this

lecture—"what do you think of my letter? You see I have managed it at last, all entirely by myself."

"I think it's a most beautiful letter"—replied Belinda—"only I don't know what it is about. Somehow, I can't tell what it means."

"That is the fault of your understanding, Belinda"—said Miss Farnham.

"May be so"—replied Belinda. "But I have often heard things read that I could not understand at all, and somehow they sounded prettier than *that*. Somehow the words don't seem to go right, and the same words seem to come in too often. And then you don't tell your lover the least bit of news, and there is not a single happening in it from one end to t'other. However, they say gentlemen are always blind when they're in love, and may be Mr. Montacute will not find out there's no sense in the letter, and people can't help being weak-minded."

"Come, come, Belinda"—said Miss Farnham—"you are going quite too far. Let me hear no more such talk. There is your own letter—of course I made no use of it, and I shall give grandmamma's back to her in the morning. And now, you must not, for your life, dare to breathe a syllable to any living creature about these letters. Say not a word to a human being about my having read yours, or about my reading mine to you. Be secret as the grave upon the whole business."

"Lor, Miss Eliza"—said the maid—"if ever I breathes a breath about the letters, if ever I tells any human quadruped what a dreadful nonplush you've been at because you did not know to write a letter to your sweetheart, and had to borrow patterns of every body both white and coloured, if ever I tells a word of this to either cat or dog I'll give you leave to cut my tongue out."

"I have no desire to perform such a job as that"—said Eliza—"but I assure you it will be the worse for you if I find you have betrayed this secret."

"And the better for me if I don't"—inquired the girl.

"Yes"—replied Eliza, going to her bureau—"here is a pink silk handkerchief for you, that I have worn but once."

Belinda received the handkerchief with many thanks and curtsies; and then hastened to the kitchen to display it to the other servants, saying—"See what I've got—Miss Eliza, with all her schooling, don't know how to write a letter, was at her wit's end about answering one she got from her sweetheart away at Bosting. So she had to borrow mine that I writ to Mr. Sodass, for a pattern. And she took and copied it out and out, word for word, only leaving out the news and the happenings—I told you what a great scribe I am always counted—so she could find no letter to suit her but mine. She got one from her grandmother first, but it was all stuff and she despised it. But now don't for your lives, any of you, go to say one word about all this to any living soul, neither coloured folks nor white trash: for if you do, we shall have our tongues cut out all round; and as her brother's a doctor she can easily get him to do the job."

The servants all put their fingers to their tongues.

Next morning the letter was to go to the post-office, and our heroine set about folding, directing, and sealing it. Her school-letters had always been folded, directed and sealed by Miss Catherine Holloway. Poor Eliza, after many unsuccessful attempts, found it impossible to fold it straight and evenly, but consoled herself with the hope that Horace would not notice so trifling a circumstance. She then wrote the direction in a very straggling and awkward manner, somewhat as follows: the name being so small as to be scarcely legible, except to the practised eyes of post-men.

Horace Montacute, Esquire,
tremont Street,
Bos.

This done, she sealed it roughly and raggedly, letting two drops of wax fall on the paper.

This letter was dispatched without being shown to either the doctor or Mrs. Farnham, and now that the long and irksome task was over, Eliza felt as if relieved from the pressure of a mountain.

"Really"—thought she—"if I had foreseen this correspondence, I do not believe I would have engaged myself to Horace. A lover that lived always in one's own town, would have been every way more convenient."

Her grandmother, as they sat at dinner, alarmed her by saying—"I should not wonder if there is another letter from Horace now on the road, inquiring why you have not answered his first one."

"If there is"—said Eliza—"I will not answer *that*, I am determined."

We will now transfer the scene to Horace Montacute's residence in Boston, and advance the time to the important hour on which he received the first letter of his lady-love, after having been for several days in anxious expectation of it. Our heroine's hope that his impatience to see the contents would cause him to disregard the outside was not exactly realized, for he glanced at it with some surprise. Then hastily tearing it open, he read as follows:

Dear Horace—The time seems very long since we parted, and I have thought of nobody else hardly but you since our parting. Your Eliza always thinks a great deal about you, and hopes that your thoughts are chiefly turned on me as mine are chiefly upon my dear Horace, and ever will be until the happy moment when you and I shall have the happiness to meet again. It is a pleasing task to communicate and exchange all our thoughts, feelings, &c., with one another, writing often to one another frequent sincere letters, for letters, as a friend of my brother's told him very properly the other day, are supposed to be sent from heaven to save us from being wretches, and we should be poor wretches certainly if we could not write letters, and very unhappy also. I am so fond of letter-writing I should like to keep it up all the year round, and it is such a great pleasure for Eliza to write letters to Horace, that I almost wish you to be absent that we may correspond. It is really a pleasure to me to let all my thoughts, feelings, &c. flow out in the epistolary style all smooth easy and without the least trouble, for your Eliza was always considered ready at my pen and composition. Your ever welcome letter was not received until this very morning, and I hastened to reply to it instantly, so you will excuse haste if you please. Brother says the post-office should be called on account for keeping it back, and none of us can by any means imagine their motive for keeping it back unless they have a spite at me, or you Horace perhaps. If your next letter, which I hope sincerely is now on the road, is not answered soon, it will certainly be because I did not get it in time to write soon, and we may all blame the post-office again because of it. I make haste to answer your last letter by return of post, as I have done, for fear you might think me false if your Eliza did not reply quick. I am so used to my pen that I can run off a letter of length in a few minutes and it is really quite play with me to use my pen. I hope it is the same to dear Horace, but if you have any difficulty in writing love-letters, or no time, you need not trouble yourself to write very soon an answer to this. Two or three weeks hence will be quite time enough to answer this letter, as I of course shall suppose you remain in good health, and have nothing particular to say. Indeed, as I know you are a healthy gentleman, I shall not be uneasy if dear Horace does not write again till you come on your next visit to Peloponnesus, and then as your Eliza will certainly see you, you need not write to me at all. She is not one of those impatient young beings who are always expecting letters: it is a bad habit. I now bid you adieu, Horace, and waft you a long farewell. I assure you your absence is felt by me: and of course it is the same by you. When we meet again, all griefs will be forgot by you and me. Believe me

Your bride that is to be,
Sincerely,
ELIZA FARNHAM.

To make this letter more intelligible to our readers, we have found it necessary to improve the punctuation. Also the orthography of the minor words, which Eliza thought she could spell correctly, because they were small; her researches in the dictionaries being confined to such as had not less than two syllables. To make her lover believe that she took pleasure in writing, she had (notwithstanding her commencement half way down the page) filled up every inch of the paper, that was not visible on the outside.

Horace Montacute was startled at the first sentence of this delectable epistle, and his amazement increased as he proceeded. When he had finished, he found himself grinding his teeth and grasping a handful of his hair. For a moment he hoped it might be a forgery; but it was post-marked Peloponnesus, and the impression on the wax was that of a seal-ring he had caused to be made for her in New York, with a device and motto of his own invention. "It is too true"—thought he, crushing the letter between his clasped hands, and stamping about the room. "It is Eliza Farnham's, and she is a fool.—Yes—a silly, illiterate, shallow-headed simpleton, and her clumsy excuse about the post-office is a wilful falsehood.—I cannot—I will not marry her—I will not have a wife that I am ashamed of. And yet she is so beautiful—and she dresses well, and plays well, and dances well. What of that—I cannot be always gazing at her dress, and her beauty, and she cannot always be singing and playing: but always, always should I be annoyed with her ignorance and folly. No—no—I never could introduce her to the Cressinghams, and the Erlingfords, and the Heathfields, and the Lanesboroughs—I should dread to see her open her lips before them, and should sink with mortification ere she had done speaking. This absurd letter is a true picture of her mind. It has opened my eyes, and saved me from the abyss into which I was blindly about to throw myself. How could I possibly be so fascinated with her beauty?—I shall detest the sight of beauty for the rest of my life."

"Let me see"—he continued—throwing himself into a rocking chair, and rocking violently—"Did I ever hear her say any thing that denoted mind or information? Did I ever hear her talk sensibly on any subject?—No—never—I can recollect nothing that was the least worthy of remembrance. It is too true that instead of listening to Eliza Farnham, I was always occupied in looking at her. Still, if she had ever said any thing worthy of remark, I must have observed it at the time, and thought of it afterwards. What did she talk about?—Nothing, unless she could get aside with one of her cronies—then they seemed to gossip. When I addressed her (fool that I was) she only simpered—I took it for smiling innocence or youthful modesty. I recollect now at all our interviews *I* talked, but *she* said nothing and only looked silly—sweetly, as I then thought. No, no—she does not love me—she never did. All that she cares for is my station and my fortune. She has not sense enough, or refinement enough, or heart enough to love any one. No—I cannot marry Eliza Farnham. I should be miserable myself with such a companion, and therefore I could not make her happy. She is too silly to have any feeling, and she only engaged herself to me for the sake of what women call an establishment. I wish I had never seen her. But what excuse can I make for breaking off the marriage. I can think of none."

Such was the perturbed soliloquy of Horace Montacute, in his first moments of grief and disappointment at finding that he had placed his affection on a woman whose intellect and acquirements seemed to him so far below the average standard of her sex, and whom he now felt it impossible ever again to regard as the companion of his life. Gradually he grew calmer, and after long and painful deliberation, he came to the conclusion that the straightest course was the best, and that he would write to Dr. Farnham, candidly stating the truth, but in as delicate a manner as possible. This he did by return of post; requesting Dr. Farnham to acquaint Eliza that finding on perusal of her letter no indications of that congeniality of mind and affinity of taste, without which there cannot be happiness in married life, he had thought it best for both parties that their engagement should be cancelled. He therefore returned her letter, and requested that his should be sent back to him.

We need not describe the regret and vexation of Dr. Farnham on reading Horace Montacute's letter and the epistle which it inclosed. And he blamed himself for not having taken more account of the education of his sister. It was a severe task to break to Eliza the mortifying subject of her lover's rejection.

He consulted the old lady, whose chagrin was still greater than his own, except that it was unmixed with self-reproach.

"Poor thing—poor thing"—exclaimed Mrs. Farnham—"how I do pity her—how she will feel. What can be done!—How shall we tell her!—Why did not she take a copy of *my* letter?—All would have been right then. However, I will go to her room and let her know all about it; for the sooner it is over the better. It will break her heart, that's certain. She is dressing for Mrs. Gaylove's party. But I am very sure after such news as this, she will not be in a state to go there or any where else. I am certain it will cost her a long fit of sickness. I must see first if there is plenty of arrow-root, and tapioca, and sago in the house. Perhaps I had best tell Cato to go to the coop and catch a fowl to-night, for I dare say chicken-broth may be wanted for her to-morrow. Poor dear girl!—I expect she will faint dead away the moment she reads Horace's letter. I will take the camphor bottle with me, and also a few bed feathers to burn under her poor nose."

At this moment, Dr. Farnham was sent for to go immediately to a patient, and the good old lady, provided with a plentiful supply of remedies for fainting fits, repaired to Eliza's apartment, and found her grand-daughter before the glass, while Belinda was fastening the back of her dress.

"Dear, dear Eliza"—said Mrs. Farnham—"I have bad news for you. There, sit down in the easy chair. Belinda, go out."—Belinda obeyed, but remained on the other side of the door, and applied her ear to the key-hole.

Mrs. Farnham then put Horace's letter, inclosing Eliza's own, into the hand of her grand-daughter, who started, changed colour, and having read it over, paused a few minutes. She then returned to the mirror, whirled round a few steps, singing a waltz, and proceeded to put an additional flower into her hair, saying—"Well, grandmother, if Horace Montacute won't have me, somebody else will—I am not the least afraid but I shall get quite as good a match, and perhaps a better still. I should not have had much peace with so particular a husband—I don't believe we are at all suited to each other. So you and Arthur may announce, as soon as you please, that the engagement is broken off, and I am again free. It is just as common now to proclaim a breaking-off as an engagement. His love was very great, to be sure, when it went entirely by letter. Yes—I think we are best apart."

"Eliza"—said the old lady—"don't you feel faint?"

"Not at all, grandma'."

"No choking in your throat?"

"Not the least."

"No sickness about your heart?"

"None whatever, grandma'."

"Perhaps you had better take a few drops of camphor and water."

"What for, dear grandma'."

"Why—for fear."

"No—I hate camphor."

"Don't say that, dear—it's wicked to hate medicine."

"Well, grandma'—don't be uneasy about me—I am going to the party; and I shall have beaux enough there to put that impertinent fellow Horace Montacute quite out of my head. If he is to choose a wife by her letter-writing, he had better take Katy Holloway with her pug nose and horse-shoe mouth. I am sure I can wish him nothing worse."

Belinda would have listened longer at the key-hole, only that she was so impatient to communicate what she had already heard: and hastening to the kitchen she made her report to the other servants. Her version of the story was, that Miss Eliza's sweet-heart had given up on her because she wrote him a bad letter, and that the young lady did not mind it at all, but pranced about the room, and said, "there's as good fish in the sea as ever was caught"—and that she had seven other beaux waiting for her at the ball-door, and that her old sweet-heart was going right off to marry somebody named Katy, with a horseshoe nose and a pug mouth."

"I guess"—added Belinda—"Miss Eliza is sorry enough now that she did not copy more out of *my* letter. But I'll just step over to Mrs. Gaylove's kitchen, and let Venus and Diana know how things has turned out."

Eliza Farnham came home from the ball in far worse spirits than when she went. She had seen many beaux, but she had made no conquest. She went to bed, but found it impossible to sleep. Her first emotions of resentment and bravado were now succeeded by a deep sense of mortification; she felt that the loss of her lover was not such a trifle as she had been willing to suppose, and the dawn of morning found her still awake, and in tears.

At breakfast, she looked very pale and was unusually silent; and though her good grandmother, finding that she did not eat, went to a closet and brought her a saucer of gooseberry jelly, still nothing could tempt her appetite, or restore her smiles.

When the old lady had left the room to give orders for dinner, Dr. Farnham entered into a serious conversation with his sister on the deficiency which had led to the recent rejection of her hand by her fastidious lover. She seemed much touched; and her brother obtained from her a promise that she would set about the improvement of her mind with earnest assiduity. He advised that she should unfailingly devote her forenoons to reading and writing, and relinquish the idle practice of receiving and paying morning visits: and he proposed that she should every day address to him a letter about something that she had seen, heard, or read. This, he assured his sister, would greatly improve her in composition, and in every thing appertaining to epistolary correspondence. Eliza at first shrunk from the task, but her brother urged her to persevere. It soon grew comparatively easy, and eventually it became one of her greatest pleasures. In a short time she began to delight in books; and the more she read, the more she improved in conversation as well as in writing.

Horace Montacute received from Dr. Farnham, by mail, his own letter to Eliza: that first and only letter, the reply to which had produced such important consequences. It was inclosed in a blank envelope, to signify that no further communication could take place between them; the doctor feeling, (though he did not tell *her* so) that his young and inexperienced sister had been treated with too much severity by her double-refined lover. In a few days after the return of his first and last love-letter, Horace Montacute embarked in one of the Havre packets, with the resolution of spending several years in Europe. During the voyage, he found it more difficult to banish Eliza Farnham from his mind than he had at first supposed; but he consoled himself for the turn his love-affair had taken by reflecting on her absurd and ridiculous epistle, every word of which seemed indelibly engraven on his memory. "No"—thought he—"all is for the best—I never could have been happy with such an illiterate simpleton, beautiful as she certainly is: and a man that is ashamed of his wife had better be without one."

After passing two years on the European continent, Horace Montacute made a second visit to London, and there he found in the person of Mrs. Amwell (an American lady, who, with her husband, had been living there a twelvemonth) the ci-devant Miss Copley at whose house in New York he had first met Eliza Farnham. Mrs. Amwell, though formerly a very giddy girl, devoted to dress and parties, had married a sensible man, and now bid fair to become a sensible woman. She had seen much of Eliza shortly before leaving America; and our heroine had, with many tears, confided to her friend the mortifying cause of her estrangement from Horace Montacute. It had been settled that the two ladies should correspond regularly while separated by the Atlantic.

Montacute took an early opportunity, though with flushed cheek and downcast eyes of inquiring after Miss Farnham. "She was well when I last heard from her"—answered Mrs. Amwell. "She sends me a letter once a month, and I expect one from her by the next arrival."

"What curious letters they must be!"—thought Horace.

Just then Mr. Amwell came in with a smiling face, and threw on the table half a dozen American letters. Mrs. Amwell, having first gone through one from her own mother, took up an epistle folded, sealed, and directed with remarkable neatness. "Ah!"—said she—"this is from Eliza Farnham." Montacute felt as if he would have given worlds to look at the inside; and was unable to understand any thing that Mr. Amwell was telling him about the Bank of the United States. He was not, however, kept very long in suspense as to Eliza Farnham's letter, for Mrs. Amwell having hastily perused it, put it into his hand, saying—"Mr. Montacute, there is nothing in this that may not be seen by you."

Our hero read the missive with much emotion and equal surprise. The hard, awkward, straggling chirography had now become free, graceful, and regular: the spelling and punctuation were perfect, the style was easy, euphonous, and critically correct; and the matter sensible and entertaining. She told of her occupations at home, and of the books she had last read, spoke of her brother with affectionate respect, and of her grandmother with overflowing kindness, and descanted amusingly upon the *on-dits* of the day.[10]

Horace Montacute was charmed, enchanted, and read the letter so often over, that Mrs. Amwell kindly offered to make a present of it, and also showed him from the same young lady, several others equally interesting. He felt all his love for Eliza Farnham return with redoubled warmth; or rather it was a new and superior sort of love, based on a more secure foundation than mere personal beauty.

In another week our hero found himself on board one of the steam-packets; and in a fortnight he had landed on the wharf at New York. He proceeded immediately to Peloponnesus, made his peace with Eliza Farnham (a task by no means difficult), and in less than a month, the old lady was preserving a water-melon *whole* to grace the centre of the supper-table at her grand-daughter's wedding. And a few days after that joyful event, Horace Montacute had the happiness of introducing to his relatives a bride whose intellectual acquirements would pass muster even in Boston.

Mr. and Mrs. Woodbridge

A STORY OF DOMESTIC LIFE

Part First

The morning subsequent to their arrival in Philadelphia, Harvey Woodbridge proposed to his bride (a New York beauty, to whom he had recently been united, after a very short acquaintance) that she should accompany him to look at the new house he had taken previous to their marriage, and which he had delayed furnishing till the taste of his beloved Charlotte could be consulted as well as his own. Meanwhile they were staying at one of the principal boarding-houses of his native city.[1]

Ten o'clock was the time finally appointed by the lady for this visit to their future residence: and her husband, after taking a melancholy leave (they had been married but seven days) departed to pass an hour at his place of business.

When he returned, Mr. Woodbridge sprang up stairs three steps at a time (we have just said he had been married only a week) and on entering their apartment he was saluted by his wife as she held out her watch to him, with—"So, after all, you are ten minutes beyond the hour!"

"I acknowledge it, my dear love"—replied the husband—"but I was detained by a western customer to whom I have just made a very profitable sale."

"Still"—persisted the bride, half pouting—"people should always be punctual, and keep their appointments to the very minute."

"And yet, my dearest Charlotte"—observed Woodbridge, somewhat hesitatingly—"I do not find you *quite* ready to go out with me."

"Oh! that is another thing"—replied the lady—"one may be kept waiting without being ready."

"That is strange logic, my love"—said Woodbridge, smiling.

"I don't know what you call logic"—answered the beautiful Charlotte. "I learnt all my logic at Mrs. Fooltrap's boarding-school, where we said a logic lesson twice a week. But I am sure 'tis much easier for a man to hurry with his bargaining than for a lady to hurry with her dressing; that is if she pays any regard to her appearance. I have been pondering for an hour about what I shall put on to go out this morning. I am sadly puzzled among all my new walking-dresses. There are my chaly, and my gros des Indes, and my peau-de-soie, and my foulard—"

"If you will tell me which is which"—interrupted Woodbridge—"I will endeavour to assist you in your choice. But from its name (foulard, as you call it,) I do not imagine that last thing can be a very nice article."

"What fools men are!"—exclaimed the lovely Charlotte.—"Now that is the very prettiest of all my walking-dresses, let the name be what it will. I always did like foulard from the moment I first saw it at Stewart's. I absolutely doat upon foulard. So that is the very thing I will wear, upon my first appearance in Chesnut street as Mrs. Harvey Woodbridge."

"Don't"—said her husband, surveying the dress as she held it up—"it looks like calico—"

"Say don't to me"—exclaimed the bride, threateningly—"calico, indeed!—when it is a French silk at twelve shillings a yard—a dollar and a half as you foolishly say in Philadelphia."

"Well, well"—replied Woodbridge, pacifyingly—"wear whatever you please—it is of no consequence."

"So then, you think it of no consequence how I am drest!

I dare say you would not grieve in the least if I were really to go out in a calico gown—I *did* suppose that perhaps you took some little interest in me."

"I do indeed"—answered Woodbridge.

"You confess then that it is but *little.*"

"No—a very great interest, certainly—and you know that I do. But as to your dress, you, of course, must be the best judge. And to me you always look beautifully."

"To you, but not to others—I suppose that is what you mean."

"To every one"—replied the husband—"I observed this morning the glance of admiration that ran round the breakfast table as soon as you had taken your seat. That little cap with the yellow ribbon is remarkably becoming to you."

"So then, it was the cap and not myself that was admired!"—said the wife.—"I am sure I am much obliged to the cap. *Yellow* ribbon, too!—to call it yellow when it is the most delicate primrose. As if *I* would wear a yellow ribbon!"

"Indeed, my love"—answered Woodbridge—"you must forgive me if I am not *au-fait* to all the technicalities of a lady's toilet.[2] I acknowledge my ignorance with due humility."

"You well may—I was absolutely ashamed of you one evening at our house in New York, when Mrs. Rouleau and the two Miss Quillings and Miss Biasfold were present, and we were all enjoying ourselves and discussing the last fashions. And thinking you ought to say something by way of joining in the conversation, you called my deep flounce a long tuck."

"I'll never do so again"—said Woodbridge, imitating the tone of a delinquent school-boy.

The foulard silk was energetically put on; the fair Charlotte pertinaciously insisting on hooking it up the back entirely herself: a herculean task which, in his heart of hearts, her husband was rather glad to be spared. And not knowing that spite gives strength, he stood amazed at the vigour and dexterity with which his lovely bride put her hands behind her and accomplished the feat. When it was done, she took a long survey of herself in the glass, and then turned round to her husband and made a low curtsey, saying—"There now—you see me in my calico gown."

Woodbridge uttered no reply: but he thought in his own mind—"What a pity it is that beauties are so apt to be spoiled!"—He might have added—"What a pity it is that men are so apt to spoil them."

At length, after much fixing and unfixing, and putting on and taking off the finishing articles of her attire (particularly half-a-dozen pair of tight-fitting new kid gloves, none of which were quite tight enough) her ignoramus of a husband again offending by calling her pelerine a cape and her scarf a neck-cloth,[3] and mistaking the flowers in her bonnet for little roses when he ought to have known they were almond blossoms, Mrs. Harvey Woodbridge sullenly acknowledged herself ready to go out.

During their walk to the new house, our hero endeavoured to restore the good-humour of his bride by talking to her of the delightful life he anticipated when settled in a pleasant mansion of their own. But his glowing picture of domestic happiness elicited no reply; her attention being all the time engaged by the superior attractions of numerous ribbons, laces, scarfs, shawls, trinkets, &c., displayed in the shop-windows, and of which, though she could now take only a passing glance, she mentally promised herself the enjoyment of making large purchases at her leisure.

They arrived at their future residence, a genteel and well-finished house of moderate size, where all was so bright new and clean, that it was impossible for the bride not to be pleased with its aspect, as her husband unlocked the doors and threw open the shutters of room after room. Mrs. Woodbridge rejoiced particularly on observing that the ceilings of the parlours had centre circles for chandeliers, and she began to consider whether the chandeliers should be bronzed or gilt. She also began to talk of various splendid articles of furniture that would be necessary for the principal rooms. "Mamma charged me"—said she—"to have silk damask lounges and chair-cushions, and above all things not to be sparing in mirrors. She said she should hate to enter my parlours if the pier-glasses were not tall enough to reach from the floor to the ceiling; and that she would never forgive me if my mantel-glasses did not cover the whole space of the wall above the chimney-pieces. She declared that she would never speak to me again if my centre-tables were not well supplied with all sorts of elegant things, in silver, and china and coloured glass. And her last words were to remind me of getting a silver card basket, very wide at the top that the cards of the best visiters might be spread out to advantage. The pretty things on Mrs. Overbuy's enamelled centre-table are said to have cost not less than five hundred dollars."—"Was it not *her* husband that failed last week for the fourth time?"—asked Woodbridge.—"I believe he did"—replied Charlotte—"but that is nothing. Almost every body's husband fails now. Mrs. Overbuy says it is quite fashionable."—"In that respect, as in many others, I hope to continue unfashionable all my life"—remarked Woodbridge.—"That is so like pa"'—observed Charlotte.—"He has the strangest dread of failing; though ma' often tells him that most people seem to live much the better for it, and make a greater show than ever—at least after the first few weeks. And then pa' begins to explain to her about failing, and breaking, and stopping payment, and debtors and creditors, and all that sort of thing. But she cuts him short, and says she hates business talk. And so do I, for I am exactly like her."

At this information Woodbridge felt as if he was going to sigh; but he looked at his bride, and, consoled himself with the reflection that he had certainly married one of the most beautiful girls in America; and therefore his sigh turned to a smile.

They had now descended to the lower story of the house. "Ah!"—exclaimed Charlotte—"the basement, back and front, is entirely filled up with cellars. How very ridiculous!"—"It does not seem so to me"—replied Woodbridge—"this mode of building is very customary in Philadelphia."—"So much the worse"—answered the lady.—"Now in New York nothing is more usual than to have a nice sitting-room down in the basement-story, just in front of the kitchen."—"A sort of servants' parlour, I suppose"—said her husband. "It is certainly very considerate to allot to the domestics, when not at work, a comfortable place of retirement, removed from the heat, and slop and all the *désagrémens* of a kitchen."

"How foolishly you always talk"—exclaimed Mrs. Woodbridge.—"As if we would give the basement-room to the servants! No we use it ourselves. In ma's family, as in hundreds of others all over New York, it is the place where we sit when we have no company, and where we always eat."

"What!—half under ground"—exclaimed Woodbridge—"Really I should feel all the time as if I was living in a kitchen."

"It is very wrong in you to say so," replied the lady—"and very unkind to say it to *me*, when we had a basement-room in our house in New York, and used it constantly. To be sure I've heard ma' say she had some trouble in breaking pa' into it—but he had to give up. Men have such foolish notions about almost every thing, that it is well when they have somebody to put their nonsense out of their heads."

"I never saw you in that basement-room"—observed Woodbridge.

"To be sure you did not. I do not say that it is the fashion for young ladies to receive their beaux in the basement room. But beaux and husbands are different things."

"You are right"—murmured Woodbridge.—"If always admitted behind the scenes, perhaps fewer beaux would be willing to take the character of husbands."

They now descended the lower staircase, and went to inspect the kitchen, which formed a part of what in Philadelphia is called the back-building. Woodbridge pointed out to his wife its numerous conveniences; upon which she told him that she was sorry to find he knew so much about kitchens. They then took a survey of the chambers; and on afterwards descending the stairs they came to a few steps branching off from the lower landing-place, and entered a door which admitted them into a narrow room in the back-building, directly over the kitchen. This room had short windows, a low ceiling, a small coal-grate, and was in every respect very plainly finished.

"This"—said Woodbridge—"is the room I intend for my library."

"I did not know I had married a literary man"—said Charlotte, looking highly discomposed.

"I am not what is termed a literary man"—replied her husband—"I do not write, but I take much pleasure in reading. And it is my intention to have this room fitted up with bookshelves, and furnished with a library-table, a stuffed leather *fauteuil*, a reading-lamp, and whatever else is necessary to make it comfortable."

"Where then is to be our sitting room?"

"We can seat ourselves very well in either the back parlour or the front one. We will have a rocking-chair a-piece, besides ottomans or sofas."

"But where are we to eat our meals?"

"In the back parlour, I think—unless you prefer the front."

"I prefer neither. We never ate in a parlour at ma's in spite of all pa' could say. Down in the basement story we were so snug, and so out of the way."

"I have always been accustomed to eating quite above ground"—said Woodbridge—"I am quite as much opposed to the burrowing system as you say your good father was."

"Oh! but he had to give up"—replied Charlotte.

"Which is more than I shall do"—answered her husband—looking very resolute. "On this point my firmness is not to be shaken."

"Nobody asks you to eat in the basement story"—said Charlotte—"because there is none. But this little room in the back-building is the very thing for our common sitting-place—and also to use as a dining-room."

"We can dine far more agreeably in one of the parlours."

"The parlours, indeed!—suppose somebody should chance to come in and catch us at table, would not you be very much mortified?"

"By no means—I hope I shall never have cause to be ashamed of my dinner."

"You don't know what may happen. After a trial of the expenses of housekeeping, we may find it necessary to economize. And whether or not, I can assure you I am not going to keep an extravagant table. Ma' never did, in spite of pa's murmurings."

"Then we will economize in finery rather than in comfort"—said Woodbridge. "I do not wish for an extravagant table, and I am not a *gourmand*; but there is no man that does not feel somewhat meanly when obliged, in his own house, to partake of a paltry or scanty dinner; particularly when he knows that he can afford to have a good one."

"That was just the way pa' used to talk to ma'. He said that as the head of the house earned all the market-money—(only think of his calling himself the head of the house,) and gave out a liberal allowance of it, he had a right to expect, for himself and family, a well-supplied and inviting table. He had some old saying that he who was the bread-winner ought to have his bread as he liked it."

"And in this opinion I think most husbands will coincide with Mr. Stapleford"—said the old gentleman's son-in-law.

"There will be no use in that, unless their wives coincide also"—remarked the old gentleman's daughter. "However, to cut the matter short, whatever sort of table we may keep, this apartment must certainly be arranged for an eating-room."

"But we really do not require it for that purpose—replied her husband, with strange pertinacity—"and I must positively have it for a library."

"The truth is, dear Harvey"—said Charlotte, coaxingly—"I am afraid if I allow you a regular library, I shall lose too much of your society—think how lonely I shall be when you are away from me at your books. Even were I always to sit with you in the library, (as Mrs. Deadweight does with her husband,) it would be very hard for me to keep silent the whole time, according to *her* custom. And if, like Mrs. Le Bore, I were to talk to you all the while you were reading, perhaps you might think it an interruption. Mrs. Duncely, who has had four husbands (two lawyers, one doctor, and a clergyman) all of whom spent as little time with her as they could, frequently told us that libraries were of no use but to part man and wife. Dear Harvey, it would break my heart to suppose that you could prefer any thing in the world to the company of your own Charlotte Augusta. So let us have this nice little place for our dining-room, and let us sit in it almost always. It will save the parlours so much."

"Indeed my dear Charlotte, I do not intend to get any furniture for the parlours of so costly a description that we shall be afraid to use it."

"What!—are we not to have Saxony carpets, and silk curtains, and silk-covered lounges, and large glasses, and chandeliers, and beautiful mantel-lamps; and above all, a'n't we to have elegant things for the centre-table?"

"My design"—answered Woodbridge—"is to furnish the house throughout, as genteelly, and in as good taste as my circumstances will allow: but always with regard to convenience rather than to show."

"Then I know not how I can look ma' in the face!"

"You may throw all the blame on me, my love."

"Pray, Mr. Harvey Woodbridge (if I may venture to ask) how will these plain, convenient, comfortable parlours look when we have a party?"

"I do not furnish my house for the occasional reception of a crowd of people, but for the every day use of you and myself, with a few chosen friends in whose frequent visits we can take pleasure."

"If you mean frequent tea-visits, I can assure you, sir, I shall take no pleasure in any such trouble and extravagance—with your few chosen friends, indeed! when it is so much cheaper to have a large party once a year (as we always had at ma's): asking every presentable person we knew, and every body to whom we owed an invitation; and making one expense serve for all. Though our yearly party was always an absolute squeeze, you cannot think how much we saved by it.—Pa' called it saying grace over the whole barrel—some foolish idea that he got from Dr. Franklin."

"For my part"—remarked Woodbridge—"I hope I shall never be brought to regard social intercourse as a mere calculation of dollars and cents. I would rather, if necessary, save in something else than make economy the chief consideration in regulating the mode of entertaining my friends and acquaintances."

"Then why do you object to saving our parlours by using them as little as possible?"

"When our furniture wears out, or ceases to look *comme il faut*, I hope I shall be able to replace it with new articles, quite as good and perhaps better—particularly if we do not begin too extravagantly at first."

"I suppose then *your* plan is to fit up these parlours with in-grain carpets, maple-chairs, and black hair-cloth sofas: and instead of curtains, nothing but venitian blinds."

"Not exactly—though young people, on commencing married life in moderate circumstances, have been very happy with such furniture."

"More fools they!—For my part, I should be ashamed to show my face to a morning visiter in such paltry parlours. That sort of furniture is scarcely better than what I intend for this little upstairs sitting-room."

"If this little room is devoted to the purpose you talk of, we must there show our faces to each other."

"Nonsense, Mr. Woodbridge!—How can it possibly signify what faces married people show to each other?"

"It signifies much—very much indeed."

"To put an end to this foolery"—resumed the bride—"I tell you once for all, Harvey Woodbridge, that I must and will have this very apartment for an eating-room, or a dining-room, or a sitting-room, or whatever you please to call it—to take our meals in without danger of being caught at them, and to stay in when I am not drest and do not wish to be seen."

"The hiding-room I think would be the best name for it"—murmured Woodbridge.

"Only let us try it awhile"—persisted the fair Charlotte, softening her tone, and looking fondly at her liege-lord—"think how happy we shall be in this sweet little retreat, where I will always keep a few flower-pots—you know I doat on flowers—imagine your dear Charlotte Augusta in a comfortable wrapper, seated on a nice calico sofa, and doing beautiful worsted work:

and yourself in a round jacket, lolling in a good wooden rocking chair either cane-coloured or green, with slippers on your feet, and a newspaper in your hand. We can have a shelf or two for a few select books. And of an evening, when I do not happen to be sleepy, you can read to me in the Summer at Brighton, or the Winter in London, or Almacks, or Santo Sebastiano.[4] I have them all. Brother Jem bought them cheap at auction. But I never had time to get to the second volume of any of them. So we have all that pleasure to come. And I shall be delighted to have those sweet books read aloud to me by you. You will like them far better than those Scotch novels that people are always talking about."

Woodbridge looked dubious. Finally, being tired of the controversy, he thought best to end it by saying—"Well, well—we'll let this subject rest for the present."—But he resolved in his own mind to hold out for ever against it.

At their boarding-house dinner-table, Mrs. Woodbridge informed a lady who sat opposite, that she was delighted with her new house; and that it was a love of a place; particularly a snug little apartment in the back-building which Mr. Woodbridge had promised her for a sitting-room, to save the parlours, as they were to be furnished in very handsome style. Woodbridge reddened at her pertinacity, and to divert the attention of those around him from a very voluble exposé of what she called her plans, he began to talk to a gentleman on the other side of the table about the latest news from Europe.

From this day our heroine spoke of the little sitting-room as a thing of course, without noticing any of the deprecatory lookings and sayings of her husband. And she succeeded in teazing him into allowing her to choose all the furniture of the house without his assistance: guided only by the taste of one of the female boarders, Mrs. Squanderfield, a lady who had been married about a twelvemonth, and after commencing house-keeping in magnificent style, her husband (whose affairs had been involved at the time of their marriage,) was obliged at the close of the winter, to make an assignment for the benefit of his creditors; and the tradesmen who had supplied it took back the unpaid furniture.

After her parlours had been fitted up in a very showy and expensive manner (not forgetting the centre-table and its multitude of costly baubles) Mrs. Woodbridge found that these two rooms had already absorbed so large a portion of the sum allotted by her husband for furnishing the whole house that it was necessary to economize greatly in all the other apartments: and to leave two chambers in the third story with nothing but bare walls. This discrepancy was much regretted by Mr. Woodbridge, even after his wife had reminded him that these chambers could only have been used as spare bed-rooms, which in all probability would never be wanted as they did not intend keeping a hotel; and that as to encouraging people to come and stay at her house (even her own relations) she should do no such expensive thing.—"You may depend on it, my dear,"—said she—on the day that they installed themselves in their new abode, "I shall make you a very economical wife."

And so she did, as far as comforts were concerned, aided and abetted by the advice of her friend Mrs. Squanderfield who counselled her in what to spend money; and in what to save it she was guided by the precepts of Mrs. Pinchington, another inmate of the same boarding-house, a widow of moderate income, whose *forte* was the closest parsimony, and who had broken up her own establishment and gone to boarding ostensibly because she was lonely, but in reality because she could get no servant to live with her. The advice of these two counsellors never clashed, for Mrs. Squanderfield took cognizance of the dress and the parlour arrangements of her pupil, while Mrs. Pinchington directed the housewifery: and both of them found in our heroine an apt scholar.

We need not tell our readers that the fair bride carried her point with regard to the little apartment at the head of the stairs, which she concluded to designate as the dining-room, though they ate *all* their meals in it; and it became in fact their regular abiding-place, her husband finding all opposition fruitless, and finally yielding for the sake of peace.

It took Mrs. Woodbridge a fortnight to recover from the fatigue of moving into their new house: and during this time she was denied to all visiters, and spent the day in a wrapper on the dining-room sofa, sometimes sleeping, and sometimes sitting up at a frame and working in worsted a square-faced lap-dog, with paws and tail also as square as cross-stitch could make them; this remarkable animal most miraculously keeping his seat upon the perpendicular side of an upright green bank, with three red flowers growing on his right and three blue ones on the left. During the progress of this useful and ornamental piece of needle-work, the lady kept a resolute silence, rarely opening her lips except to check her husband for speaking to her, as it put her out in counting the threads. And if he attempted to read aloud, (even in Santo Sebastiano) she shortly desired him to desist, as it puzzled her head and caused her to confuse the proper number of stitches allotted to each of the various worsted shades. If he tried to interest her by a really amusing book of his own choice, she always went fast asleep, and on raising his eyes from the page he found himself reading to nothing. If, on the other hand, he wished to entertain himself by reading in silence, he was generally interrupted by something like this, preluded by a deep sigh—"Harvey you are not thinking now of your poor Charlotte Augusta—you never took up a book and read during the week you were courting me. Times are sadly altered now: but I suppose all wives must make up their minds to be forgotten and neglected after the first fortnight. Don't look so disagreeable: but if you really care any thing about me, come and wind this gold-coloured worsted—I want it for my dog's collar."

The fortnight of rest being over, Mrs. Woodbridge concluded to receive morning visiters and display to them her handsome parlours: which for two weeks were opened every day for that purpose during the usual hours of making calls. Also she availed herself of the opportunity of wearing in turn twelve new and beautiful dresses, and twelve pelerines and collars equally new and beautiful.

Various parties were made for his bride by the families that knew Harvey Woodbridge, who was much liked throughout the circle in which he had visited: and for every party the bride found that she wanted some new and expensive articles of decoration, notwithstanding her very recent outfit; she and her ma' having taken care that the *trousseau* should in the number and costliness of its items be the admiration of all New York, that is of the set of people among which the Staplefords were accustomed to revolve.

When the bridal parties were over, Woodbridge was very earnest that his wife should give one herself in return for the civilities she had received from his friends; for though he had no fondness for parties he thought they should be reciprocated by those who went to them themselves, and who had the appliances and means of entertaining company in a house of their own and in the customary manner. To this proposal our heroine pertinaciously objected, upon the ground that she was tired and worn out with parties, and saw no reason for incurring the expense and trouble of giving one herself.

"But"—said her husband—"have you not often told me of your mother's annual parties. Did she not give at least one every season?"

"She never did any such thing"—replied Charlotte—"till after *I* was old enough to come out. And she had as many invitations herself, *before* she began to give parties as she had afterwards. It makes no sort of difference. Ladies that dress well and look well, and therefore help to adorn the rooms are under no necessity of making a return (as you call it) even if they go to parties every night in the season. Then, if, besides being elegantly drest, they are belles and beauties (here she fixed her eyes on the glass) their presence gives an *eclat* which is a sufficient compensation to their hostess."

"But if they are *not* belles and beauties"—observed Woodbridge, a little mischievously.

"I don't know what you are talking about!"—replied the lady with a look of surprise.

"Well, well"—resumed the husband—"argue as you will on this subject, you never can convince me that it is right first to lay ourselves under obligations, and then to hold back from returning them, when we have it amply in our power to do so."

"I am glad to hear you are so rich a man. It was but last week you told me you could not afford to get me that case of emeralds I set my mind upon at Thibaut's."

"Neither I can. And excuse me for saying that I think you have already as many articles of jewelry as the wife of a Market street merchant ought to possess."

"Are the things you gave me on our wedding-day to last my life-time. Fashion changes in jewellery as well as in every thing else."

"It cannot have changed much already, as but a few weeks have elapsed since that *giorno felice*.[5] However, let us say no more about jewels."

"Oh! yes—I know it is an irksome topic to husbands and fathers and all that sort of thing. Pa' was always disagreeable whenever Marquand's bill was sent in."

"To return to our former subject"—resumed Woodbridge—"I positively cannot be satisfied, if after accepting in every instance the civilities of our friends, we should meanly pass over our obligation of offering the usual return. I acknowledge that I do not like parties; but having in compliance with your wishes accompanied you to so many, we really *must* make the exertion of giving one ourselves."

"If you disapprove of parties you ought not to have a party. I thought you were a man that always professed to act up to your principles."

"I endeavour to do so. And one of my principles is to accept no favours without making a return as far as lies in my power. I disapprove of prodigality, but I hate meanness."

"It is wicked to hate any thing. But married men get into such a violent way of talking. When pa' *did* break out, he was awful. And then, instead of arguing the point, ma' and I always quitted the room, and left him to himself. He soon cooled down when he found there was nobody to listen to him: and the next day he was glad enough to make his peace and give up."

Woodbridge could endure no more, but hastily left the room himself: and Charlotte walked to the glass and arranged her curls, and altered the tie of her neck-ribbon; and then sat down and worked at the everlasting dog.

Part Second

Finding it utterly impossible to prevail on his wife to consent to a large party, Woodbridge next endeavoured to persuade her to invite a few families at a time (sociably, as the ladies call it,) till they had thus gone round all their acquaintances.

"Why this is worse than the other way"—exclaimed Charlotte—"really, Mr. Woodbridge, I am surprised at you. Did I not tell you, when we were first married, that ma' never had any evening company whatever, except when she gave a squeeze once in the season. The expense of having a few people at a time is endless, and there is no *eclat* in it either, as there is with a large general party; so it is an absolute throwing away of money."

"Then let us have a large general party."

"Harvey you really make me sick. Will you never cease harping on the same subject. Is it an affair of life and death, our paying back again what we owe to the people who saw proper to invite us. Shall we lose our characters if we do not?"

"Yes."

"Was there ever such nonsense."

"Our characters will so far suffer that we shall be justly considered mean, sordid, and inhospitable."

"Will any one ask us why we do not invite company. How can they know what reasons we may have? And then again how business-like to regard the thing as an affair of debtor and creditor! But men will be men."

"Charlotte"—said Harvey Woodbridge—"I am tired of this foolish contention—and I insist—(yes—I positively insist) on a few of our friends being invited to take tea with us to-morrow evening. Next week we will have a few more, and so on, till we shall have entertained at our own house, the whole circle of our acquaintances."

"But when these people paid me their bridal visits"—said Charlotte—"I carried my politeness so far as to hint to every one of them a general invitation to come and see us of an evening without ceremony, as soon as they chose."

"No matter"—returned her husband—"why should they hasten to avail themselves of a mere general invitation, when there is no reason for their not receiving a special one. Among women, I know very well that volunteer visits are only made where there is a very familiar intimacy; and never when the parties are but newly or slightly acquainted.—Again—supposing that any of these ladies or gentlemen were to take you at your word—are we ever prepared for unexpected guests?—Could we receive them in this vile room that you insist on living in; or in the cold dark parlours, with the fire out, and no lamp lighted."

Mrs. Woodbridge began to conclude that, for this time, she had best give up to her husband; and therefore, with a very ill grace, she finally consented to his desire; and he felt so happy at having carried his point, that he apologized for the epithet he had bestowed on the sitting-room; and conceded that, used in moderation, there was some convenience in having such places.

Accordingly, invitations were given to three married couples, one widow, two young ladies and three young gentlemen; all of them being among those of our hero's friends, who stood highest in his esteem, from whom his wife had received the utmost civility, and in whose eyes he was most anxious that she and her domestic arrangements should appear to the greatest advantage. In the interim, he took particular care to be as amiable to her as possible: only once giving her occasion to say that "all men were fools."

Harvey Woodbridge came home from his store in excellent spirits, anticipating the most pleasant evening he had yet enjoyed in his own house. Anxious to keep his wife in good humour, he had foreborne during the day to offer any suggestion as to the preparations for the evening; merely hinting his hope that every thing would be arranged in a liberal and convenient manner.

"Why should you doubt it?"—replied Charlotte—"But I am not going to tell you a word beforehand. Perhaps I shall surprize you."

"So much the better"—said Woodbridge gaily—and he resolved to trust entirely to his wife, and to ask no questions: calculating greatly on this surprise that was in store for him, and feeling persuaded that, on this their first reception of evening company, she would take care that all should be *séIon les régles.*[6]

But, "a change came o'er the spirit of his dream" when he found that at seven o'clock the parlours were not lighted; Mrs. Woodbridge, who had not yet began to dress, averring that people never arrived till at least an hour after the time specified, and that she would encourage no useless waste of oil. About ten minutes past seven the door-bell rang, our heroine flew to her toilet, and Mr. Woodbridge had the mortification of seeing the first detachment of visiters make their entrance by the light of a dim and newly-kindled fire; the ladies leaving their cloaks and hoods in the entry, Charlotte having given orders that nobody should be shown up stairs. The servant man now hurried to light the lamps which stood on the centre-tables, in each parlour, omitting those on the mantel-piece, because he knew that they were unfurnished with oil, as they had never yet been prepared for use.

In a very short time, all the guests had arrived, and Woodbridge was obliged for nearly an hour to entertain them entirely himself; his consort not being ready to make her appearance. Finally, the beautiful Charlotte came down elegantly and elaborately drest: and smiled, and looked sweet, and expressed to the company her regret at not being aware of their intention of coming so early, and her delight at their having done so, as by that means she should have the pleasure of enjoying a larger portion of their society.

Then she took her seat, changing it occasionally so as to afford each of the guests a share of her talk. They were all intelligent people, with cultivated minds and polished manners, and Woodbridge, who was well able himself to sustain a part in rational and amusing conversation, thought his wife had never talked with less tact and more folly. She discoursed with untiring volubility on new style bonnets, new style shawls, and remembered with surprising accuracy the exact figures of certain new style mousselines de laine, embroidered chalys, and brocaded satins.[7] And she varied her declamations by describing divers patterns for worsted work, particularly the new style dog that she was doing for the cover of a tabouret, and to which she was going to give a companion in the shape of a basket of fruit, to be taken in hand for another tabouret as soon as the present occupant was out of the frame.

After a while, the attention of the visiters began to flag; all seemed to grow dull and tired, and our hero felt that he was becoming dull and tired himself, and in fact quite out of spirits. The truth was, he wanted his tea, and thought that all the company did the same; and his only hope was now in the exhilarating influence of "the cups that cheer but not inebriate."[8] The time-piece showed the hour of nine, and still there was no sign of tea. He wondered that it did not appear, and was at a loss to conjecture what had retarded it.

At last, the conversation subsided into silence, and after a dead pause, Mrs. Woodbridge proposed music. For herself she had never been able to acquire any proficiency in the art, and therefore did not profess to play. But she had insisted on the purchase of a highly ornamented instrument as an elegant piece of furniture for the back parlour, and because, as she said—"No decent house is without a piano."

She sat two young ladies down to the overture to La Cenerentola played as a duet, and which she said was "ma's favourite."[9] During the move which generally takes place when music is about to commence, Woodbridge found an opportunity of saying in a low voice to his wife—"I wish the music had been deferred till after tea. We have already waited too long, and want something to brighten us."

"People must be badly off when their brightness depends upon tea"—replied Charlotte, also *sotto voce*[10]—"is that the only excuse you can make for being so stupid this evening—you and your select friends. But sensible people are always stupid—at least *I* find them so."—Then turning away from her husband, she walked into the other parlour, and taking her seat beside a lady who was looking over the splendid annuals that lay on the table, our heroine remarked that a figure in one of the plates reminded her of a celebrated actress then performing at the Chestnut street theatre; and from thence she ran into a minute description of the costume of that actress in every character in which she had seen her. The truth was that our fair Charlotte never observed or remembered any thing concerning a play, except the habiliments of the performers: her eyes being chiefly engaged in wandering round the boxes, and taking cognizance of the caps, turbans, feathers, flowers, and other head ornaments there displayed.

The overture to La Cenerentola was played mechanically well, the musicians (like the hearers) being tired before it began. When it was over, the young ladies rose from the instrument, and returned with the rest of the company to the other room: and it was well they did so, for in a few minutes the back-parlour lamp died out, self-extinguished for want of sufficient oil.

At length, Mrs. Woodbridge desired her husband to touch the bell, and he obeyed with alacrity, thinking to himself—"Now we shall have tea, to a certainty."

The servant man made his entrance: and (to the utter dismay of our hero) he handed round a waiter set out with diminutive glasses of weak sour lemonade, and a silver basket half-filled up with a large thickly folded damask napkin, upholding some very small thin slices of stale tasteless sponge-cake.

"Is this the surprise she promised me"—thought Woodbridge—almost betrayed into an audible exclamation. But he checked himself, and with heightened colour proceeded to do the honours of the banquet, imagining (and it was not altogether "fancy's sketch") that he perceived a look of disappointment in the countenances of the whole company, none of whom had taken their tea at home, having all understood that Mrs. Woodbridge's invitation included that refreshment. His wife, however, smiled on; and assured the ladies that they would not find the lemonade too strong, and that if any cake could be considered wholesome, it was sponge-cake eaten in moderation.

The remainder of the evening dragged on still more heavily than the former; Woodbridge being too much annoyed either to talk himself or be the cause of talking in others; and also watching anxiously, but vainly, for the appearance of something else in the way of refreshments. It was scarcely ten o'clock when one of the married ladies signified to Mrs. Woodbridge that she must go home on account of her baby. All the other guests seemed eager to avail themselves of the first symptom of breaking up, and hastened to take their leaves; their hostess assuring them that it was quite early: that she had not enjoyed half enough of their company: that she hoped they had spent as pleasant an evening as she had done: and that she trusted it would not be long before they repeated their visit, and that they might rely on being always treated in the same unceremonious manner. "You had better not put that in"—thought her husband, as he glanced at her with ill-concealed disapprobation.

When all the company had departed, and the husband and wife were left to themselves, our hero (making an effort to throw as much mildness into his tone as possible) inquired why there had been no tea for the visiters.

"Because I did not choose to go to any unnecessary trouble and expense"—was the reply.

"You went round yourself,"—said Woodbridge—"and gave the invitations verbally. Of course you asked them to come to tea."

"There is no 'of course' in the case. I do not remember saying anything about tea. Perhaps I did, and perhaps I did not. None of ma's friends ever gave tea, whether the company was large or small. And Mrs. Pinchington told me herself that when *she* kept house she always expressly asked her friends to come *after* tea. I wish *I* had done so, and then these people would not have expected any."

"But why should they not expect any? At their own houses they on all occasions have tea. Is tea and its appendages so enormously expensive that we cannot afford to give them to our friends?"

"I am always at a loss to know what you can afford, and what you cannot. When after a great deal of trouble I had made you understand what blond was, did you not object to my giving eight dollars a yard for seven yards of blond trimming to go round the skirt of that gros d'Afrique I had made for Mrs. Hillingdon's ball. To be sure I *did* get the blond notwithstanding: and it was not my fault if it caught in the flowers of Miss Wireblossom's skirt and was half torn to pieces that very evening. Then when I fell in love with that superb gold card-case at Thibault's, did you not meanly refuse to let me have it, merely because you had given me a silver one already. And now when I try as much as I can to economize in things that are of no consequence, you are displeased at my not giving to these people, as if they could not just as well have all drank their tea at home."

"Undoubtedly they would have done so, had it been possible for them to foresee that they would get none at our house. Did you not invite them to come at an early hour?"

"Yes—but I did not suppose they would be so simple as to take me at my word. And I asked them to come *socially*, just to meet half a dozen friends. Therefore they need not have expected any thing."

"Socially!—Yes, we were all very social indeed. The truth is that persons accustomed to the refreshment of tea, feel the want of it in the evening after the fatigues of the day are over. And if they chance to go without it, they always miss its exhilarating effects. I wonder you did not want it yourself."

"Oh! I am not such a fool as to let my vivacity depend on a cup of tea. Besides—I had some made for myself, and I drank it in the sitting-room before I came down. When I had done, the pot was filled up with water, and left by the fire—I dare say it is there yet, and if you are in distress for tea, you can go and get some of that. For my part I am very sleepy, and very tired of all this nonsense, and I will not hear another word on the subject. But I can assure you this is the last time you shall ever prevail on me to invite evening visiters. If *my* society is not good enough for you, I shall not assist in bringing other people here to entertain you."

So saying, she flounced up stairs, and her husband sighed, and went out to a restaurant in quest of something by way of refreshment: experience having taught him that nothing was to be had in the house. The lovely Charlotte did not speak to him all next day, and gave no token of her knowledge that he was in existence, except that she contrived for dinner something that she knew he particularly disliked. Finally, he was fain to bribe her into good humour by the gift of a turquoise ring.

Time passed on, and Harvey Woodbridge became sadly apprehensive that for him the bonds of married life would never be "golden chains inlaid with down."[11] As his mental vision cleared, the beautiful Charlotte Augusta seemed every day to grow less and less beautiful. And too often his recollection dwelt on some favourite adages of his grandmother, such as—"Handsome is that handsome does"—and "Marry in haste and repent at leisure."

No home could be more cheerless than that of our hero; notwithstanding that his wife piqued herself greatly on her domestic qualifications, after the pattern of her ma'. But her housewifery consisted only in the perpetual practice of a mean sordid and annoying parsimony, carried into the most minute details of every thing connected with comfort. While at the same time there were no limits to her extravagance in all that related to the adornment of her own person. And her passion for dress, increasing by indulgence, soon surprised even her love for fine parlour furniture; taking care only to preserve what they had already by using it as little as possible. Till they learn by experience men have but a faint idea of the sums that can be expended on the external decoration of a woman who is resolved on being the first to adopt every new fashion, and the first to throw it aside for another, and who takes a silly pride not only in the costliness but in the number of her dresses. As Mrs. Woodbridge never gave any thing away, a spare room (or rather a room which could not be spared, and ought to have been appropriated to a better purpose) was filled with receptacles for her discarded finery: discarded in many instances after having been worn but two or three times.

With the usual selfishness and folly of women whose ruling passion is a love of dress, our heroine seemed to think that almost every cent expended for any other purpose was taken wrongfully from the fund which ought to be devoted exclusively to the adornment of her own person. Now that her parlours were furnished, she appeared to consider all expenditure for the comfort or convenience of the establishment as an encroachment on her self-assumed right to be indulged in every new and costly vanity that fashion and ostentation was continually introducing into female attire. Yet though her milliner and mantua-maker were the most modish, and therefore the most extravagant in their charges that Philadelphia could support, if she wanted any other sort of work to be executed, she would walk to the most distant suburbs of the city in all the torture of tight shoes, to make a hard bargain with a cheap seamstress; or she would absurdly hire a carriage for the purpose of conveying her to cheap (or rather low-priced) stores in remote places: where, by Mrs. Pinchington's account, she could buy articles of household necessity at a cent or two less than in the best part of the town.

In charity Mrs. Woodbridge gave nothing. When her feelings sometimes prompted her to afford relief in a case of severe distress that chanced to fall in her way, her hand was stayed by some such reflection as that a quarter of a dollar would buy her a yard of ribbon, or a half dollar the same quantity of narrow edging: that seventy-five cents would pay for a pair of white kid gloves, and that a dollar would purchase a flower sprig. Therefore the money remained in her purse to be expended in some article of similar utility to the above.

A book was one of the last things she would have thought of purchasing for herself; and she even looked displeased whenever her husband bought a new one for his own reading; and wondered what people that had the Athenaeum to go to, and also a share in the City Library, could possibly want with any more books.

As is usually the case in families where the practice is ultra economy our heroine was always in difficulties about servants, some of whom left her or were dismissed by her in two or three days: and few that were worth having remained more than a week, for good servants can easily obtain good places. She usually began her daily routine by keeping her husband waiting an hour or more beyond the appointed breakfast time, for it was always a difficult task to her to get up in the morning, and it was deferred and delayed as if it could be dispensed with altogether. On this subject no remonstrance on the part of her husband ever made the slightest impression; her pretence being that early rising was injurious to her health. And if he resorted to the desperate measure of eating his breakfast without her, he was punished by her not speaking to him for the remainder of the day. When breakfast was over, Mrs. Woodbridge devoted an hour to scolding the servants, and five minutes to arranging her scheme of parsimony for that day. This she called superintending her household affairs. Then, having taken off her wrapper, and spent two hours in making a very *recherché* toilette, she issued forth in a superb dress-bonnet, with every thing to match, and passed the remainder of the morning in costly visits to the fashionable shops, and to the fashionable milliners and mantua-makers; and in leaving cards at the doors of such of her acquaintances as lived in handsome houses, and dressed expensively. The only persons with whom, on making her calls, she desired an interview, were her cronies Mesdames Squanderfield and Pinchington. Friends she had none.

About three o'clock Mrs. Woodbridge went home and undressed for dinner, which in her house was always a paltry and uninviting repast: such as her husband would have been really ashamed of if seen, and which it was certainly politic to serve up in the privacy of the little dining-room. As it was, he thought that at his own table he never felt exactly like a gentleman; and his genteel feelings were brought still lower at times when for a day or two he found his house without a single domestic: a condition to which a *ménage* of this description is not unfrequently reduced.[12] Indeed, their servants very often left them on account of the scanty supply of kitchen utensils, averring that they were not allowed things to do their work with.

On afternoons, the fair Charlotte, continuing in her dishabille, and establishing herself permanently up stairs for the remainder of the day, pursued her worsted work for a while, and then took a nap till tea-time, and another after tea, while her husband went to the Exchange to read the news by the eastern mail. During the remainder of the evening, by the glare of a small, low, shadeless lamp, she made herself an occupation with a bit of trilling and useless sewing, interrupting him every few minutes with some querulous remark if he was reading to himself, and falling into a doze if he was reading aloud.

About nine o'clock, (and sometimes before) she always began to be very fidgetty on the subject of having the lights and fires extinguished, the house shut up, and preparations made by all within it to go to bed with the utmost dispatch: implying that she saw no use in wasting fuel and oil any longer: and always worrying without ceasing till she had carried her point of a general retirement at an unseasonably early hour.

If a gentleman called in the evening to see Mr. Woodbridge, the parlour fire had gone out, no lamp had been lighted there, and all below was gloomy and cheerless. It was a formidable undertaking to clear out the grate and rekindle the fire, and to make an astral lamp burn which was not in order for want of being in nightly use; and our aggrieved hero soon found that of the two evils, the least was to entertain his friends in the ever obnoxious dining-room: Mrs. Woodbridge, to avoid being caught in dishabille, always taking flight to her own chamber before the guest could find his way up stairs. Under these circumstances, it was not surprising that their house was soon relieved from the inconvenience of visiters, and that the husband and wife were left to the full enjoyment of each other's society; except when he occasionally indulged himself by going to the Athenæum for an evening of quiet reading in a well-warmed and well-lighted room: even though sure to incur the penalty of finding his lady speechless all the next day.

Mrs. Stapleford had several times volunteered to quit for a while the delights of her beloved New York, and make a visit to her daughter even in Philadelphia; but was always put off with some trifling excuse from our heroine. Mrs. Woodbridge was well aware that notwithstanding the close parsimony that prevailed in the paternal (or rather maternal) mansion, her mother, when a guest at the house of another person, was greatly displeased if all things were not conducted on the most liberal scale.

Finally, however, Mrs. Stapleford was allowed to come. She disappointed her daughter by not admiring sufficiently the handsome parlour furniture, which (on inquiring the prices of all the articles) she took much pains to prove could have been purchased for better and infinitely lower in New York. In return, Mrs. Woodbridge resolved to make no alteration in her domestic arrangements during the visit of her mother; saying when any thing was unusually mean or comfortless—"You see, ma', I keep house exactly on *your* plan."—and indeed she rather outdid her pattern.

Mrs. Staplefood sometimes hinted a desire that this strict adherence to *her* plan might be dispensed with, but her dutiful daughter would make no improvement, and endeavored to persuade her mother that, in Philadelphia, servants and all other things were far worse, and more difficult to procure than in New York. Woodbridge was annoyed, ashamed, and angry nearly the whole time. The visit was by no means a satisfactory one to any of the parties: and Mrs. Stapleford, instead of remaining a month (as she had at first intended) stayed but a week; alleging that she was obliged to hurry back to New York that she might not lose Mrs. Legion's grand annual ball, for which there were never less than six hundred invitations sent out.

Each of the two brothers of our heroine came at different times on business to Philadelphia, but wisely stayed at a hotel. Both were invited to take a family dinner at their sister's house: she assuring them that they need not expect any thing more than she would have had for her husband and herself—"As you know"—said she—"that one never stands on ceremony with one's brothers."—This entire absence of ceremony was indeed so very apparent that the young Staplefords concluded, for the future, not to forego an excellent dinner at an excellent hotel for the scanty and unpalatable repast provided by their sister.

On the first of these occasions, our hero bore his vexation in silence; on the second he expostulated with his wife when they were alone in the evening. But she replied that the dinner was quite as good as any they ever had in ma's house, and just as her brothers were used to at home; adding—"Harvey Woodbridge, I wonder you are not tired of continually trying to make me change my plans. What reason have you to suppose me one of those trifling, weak-minded persons that can be persuaded to any thing? No—from my earliest childhood I was always distinguished for firmness of character. I remember when only five years old, because pa' bought me a doll for a Christmas gift, when he knew I wanted a pearl ring, I held out for a whole week; and all that time I would neither play with the doll or even look at it, nor kiss pa' at bidding good night. So that on New Year's day he was glad to get the pearl ring for me, as ma' had been advising him all the while. No—no—have you yet to learn that firmness is my forte?"

"That obstinacy is, I have learnt most thoroughly"—replied her husband—"and *that* united with your other fortes is fast wearing away the peace of my life. You really seem to be trying your utmost to make my home irksome to me."

"Then you will have the more excuse for spending your evenings at your beloved Athenaeum. You had better go there now."

"I will take you at your word"—replied Woodbridge, rising to depart.

"Harvey"—said his wife, as he was about to leave the room—"as you have to pass Mustin's in your way, you may as well take this bit of brown worsted and try to match it for me—I can't go on with my work to-morrow, till I get some more of it."

"Confound the worsted!"—exclaimed her husband, turning angrily away from her.

And as he hastily shut the door and precipitately ran down

stairs, she struck up melodiously the *refrain* of "Sweet—sweet home."

Part Third

During a slight access of graciousness (purchased by the gift of a diamond pin) Harvey Woodbridge prevailed on his consort to engage a cook that had lived a long time in his father's family; and also to take a waiter that had been for many years a servant to the brother of our hero, a gentleman residing in Baltimore. Both these domestics were excellent in their way, and (as far as permitted by what Mrs. Woodbridge called her plans) they performed their duties well. Her husband now thought that he would avail himself of the convenience of having a very good cook and a very good waiter, and invite some gentlemen to dine with him: trusting that the displeasure he had evinced on the occasion of the evening visiters, &c., would operate as a warning to his wife and induce her to make a proper provision for the dinner party.

But the dinner party, as soon as he ventured to propose it, met a decided disapproval from the lady, who said she did not see the use of a parcel of men dining together, and that if money *must* be spent, there were better ways of spending it: and that she fully expected she should have to live all her life without an India shawl. Her husband, being very anxious to carry his point, reminded her that they had not yet had an opportunity of displaying their fine French china dinner set and other elegancies appertaining. And then he called her Charlotte Augusta, and assured her that a pretty woman always looked peculiarly well presiding at her own table, and doing the honours to a company of gentlemen.

At length, after much assenting and dissenting, and agreeing with a bad grace and disagreeing with no grace at all, the dinner was finally undertaken, and fixed for the following Thursday.

Interviews between Mrs. Woodbridge and Mrs. Pinchington commenced forthwith.

In the mean time, as the appointed day drew near our hero had frequent and increasing misgivings, and at last ventured to question his wife concerning her preparations.

"You need not be afraid to leave every thing to me"—replied Charlotte—"pa' often has gentlemen to dine with him (much as it annoys ma') so I know very well what arrangements to make. And I have very good advisers, beside my natural judgment. Even if I were incapable of preparing for dinner-company, men have no business to be cot-betties."

"What is a cot-betty?" asked her husband.

"I wish you were as ignorant of the character as you are of the name"—replied the lady sharply.—"A cot-betty is what ma' used to call pa.' A man that meddles with house affairs, and undertakes to advise his wife about her domestic concerns; instead of sticking to his store or his office (or whatever place he goes to) and giving his whole attention to providing the money for his family expenses, as all men ought."

Harvey Woodbridge did not like to be classed among the cot-betties; though, as young ladies are *now* brought up, a capable cot-betty may prove a very valuable husband. Therefore, he, after this, held his peace with respect to the dinner-party: which forbearance he was only enabled to exercise by closing his eyes, ears, and understanding against much that he saw, heard, and suspected.

At length the eventful afternoon arrived, and Mr. Woodbridge left his store at an early hour, and repaired to his dwelling-house to be ready for the reception of his guests. To his surprise he found that no table had been set in the back-parlour. This was a thing that he could not on this occasion have anticipated: and hastily running up stairs, he found it laid in the more-than-ever obnoxious little dining-room, which looked even smaller and meaner than usual. His vexation was intense, and hastening to the apartment of his wife, whom he found at her toilette. "How is this"—said he—"I had not the most distant idea of the dinner table being set to-day in any other place than the back parlour. That vile little room will not do at all. It is too small, too narrow, and the ceiling is too low."

"I did not expect we were to dine on the ceiling"—replied Mrs. Woodbridge. But this attempt at a witticism did not succeed; and her husband plainly expressed his displeasure at finding that his friends were to be entertained in what he called in his anger "that abominable hole."

"It is neither a hole nor abominable"—answered the lady—"but a nice comfortable apartment. And you pay me a great compliment of talking of it in that outrageous manner, when you know it is my pet place, where you have spent so many happy hours in my society."

"Fudge!"—exclaimed Woodbridge, turning away from her, completely out of patience.

"If domestic happiness is fudge"—resumed his wife—"I shall be sorry enough for having quitted ma', and left my own city to go away to a new place and live with a strange man."

"It is true"—said her husband, with a sort of sigh—"we *were* almost strangers to each other when we married."

"And all this fuss"—pursued Charlotte—"is about dining in a dining-room, as if it was not always the most proper place. Do not we continually read of dining-rooms in English fashionable novels. The very lords and ladies do not dine in their parlours or drawing-rooms, even when they have company."

"The dining-rooms of English gentry"—replied Woodbridge—"are very different apartments from that paltry little place of ours. I have no objection to a dining-room, provided that it is commodious and pleasant, and that it has an air of gentility as well as convenience. But I cannot endure the idea of making my guests eat their dinner in the worst apartment of my house, though I have yielded to the infliction myself."

"And I"—said Mrs. Woodbridge—"cannot endure the idea of having our parlour furniture greased or stained or injured in any way, even by one single dinner. Never supposing such a thing would be wanted, I did not get a parlour crumb-cloth, and the one we have up stairs is too small to save any carpet than that of the dining-room."

"And this is the reason you have set so small a table. Worse than all, my friends will not have elbow-room."

"I never saw a man yet"—replied Charlotte—"who could not somehow or other manage to convey his dinner to his mouth. When a large table is set, there must be a great deal to cover it: and it is not my way to provide more than is necessary. I know very well how ma' managed when pa' *would* have dinner company. And besides, I have consulted Mrs. Pinchington. She was so kind as to accompany me to market yesterday."

"Surely on *this* occasion"—said Woodbridge, with a look of alarm—"you are not going to mortify me before my friends with the sight of a mean and scanty dinner."

"There will be dinner enough"—replied his wife coolly—"and even if there should not, (as I heard a man say in a play,) nobody called for more at another person's table. The fact is, I so hate extravagance that, as I have often told you, it is really a pleasure to me to save in every little thing as much as I can."

And she finished adjusting before the glass a new laced pelerine that she bought the day before, and which Mrs. Squanderfield assured her was cheap at forty dollars.

"You Philadelphians"—she added—"think there can never be too much on the table, and I am told that the further south the worse."

"Two of my guests are southern gentlemen"—said Woodbridge—"and I am convinced that all who dine with me to-day have been accustomed to 'sit at good men's feasts.'"

"Harvey"—said his wife—"do not make me uncomfortable, or I won't come to table. I feel very much like hysterics already. I have been annoyed enough with Phillis this morning."

"Phillis, who was brought up by my mother"—exclaimed Woodbridge—"there cannot be a more excellent cook."

"Rather too excellent for me"—replied Charlotte, "I have been thinking for some time of parting with her. Mrs. Pinchington tells me (and I have found it so myself,) that it is cheapest to keep cooks that are not considered very good. And as to particularity about food, it is a thing I am not going to encourage. Ma' never did. Phillis is the last professed cook I shall ever be troubled with. This morning she was so vexed at my not having things as extravagant as she thought proper, that she said something that made me angry, and I packed her out of the house. So then I had to coax Mary to get the dinner."

"What, Mary—the raw Irish girl—the chambermaid. Surely she knows nothing about cooking. It would have been better at once to have sent out and hired a professed cook for the day."

"So Caesar had the assurance to tell me, and he did prevail on me to let him go for an aunt of his, who goes out cooking at what she calls a low price, a dollar a day. But, as Phillis had already made a beginning, I was determined not to give more than sixty-two cents, so we could not agree; though at the last I *did* offer her seventy-five. As for my giving a dollar for cooking one dinner, it was quite out of the question: so there was nothing to be done but to set Mary about it."

"I would rather have given ten dollars! Mary is little better than an idiot."

"How *can* you say so, when she came from New York, where she had lived a whole month with ma'. And even if she *is* rather stupid, there is the less danger of her objecting to any thing I tell her to do. Ma' could never get along with smart servants. But I wish you would go down stairs. Your friends will be arriving presently."

"Caesar, of course, has obeyed the orders I gave him about the wine"—said Woodbridge.

"He wanted to do so"—replied the wife—"but between you and him I found there was wine enough got out for twenty people instead of eight. So I made him put back the half of it. He began to look gruff, and then—"

"Charlotte! Charlotte!"—exclaimed the alarmed husband—"if you have turned Caesar out of doors—Caesar who lived ten years with my brother, and is so useful and so faithful—"

"Do not be frightened"—replied Charlotte—"Caesar would not go. He had the insolence to say he should wait till Mr. Woodbridge came home."

"He is a good fellow"—said Woodbridge—"and I am obliged to him for not deserting me this day."

"Don't talk of his goodness. When I threatened to tell Mrs. Pinchington of him, he held down his head to keep from laughing in my face."

A ring at the door-bell now announced that the guests were beginning to come, and Woodbridge smoothed the discomposure of his countenance, and hastened down stairs to receive them. His lady did not appear till the gentlemen had all assembled, and she then made her entrance through the folding-doors of the back-parlour, and proceeded gracefully to the front; elegantly drest, and looking as sweet and innocent as if incapable of uttering one unamiable word, or conceiving one unamiable thought. Just so she had looked when Woodbridge was first introduced to her at a party in New York.

All the gentlemen having arrived, Woodbridge took an opportunity of asking his wife, in a low voice, if it was not time that dinner should be announced. Upon which, she whispered to him that she was waiting for Mrs. Pinchington, who had kindly volunteered to come and support her on this her first appearance as hostess at a gentleman's party. In about half an hour

Mrs. Pinchington came, excusing herself for being detained by an unexpected visiter; but in reality having prudently stayed to secure a good dinner at her boarding-house. Mr. Woodbridge, though she had become his besetting antipathy, was obliged to offer Mrs. Pinchington his arm; and his face flushed with shame as Charlotte, all smiles and sweetness, accompanied by his principal guest (a gentleman from Virginia) led the way up stairs into the paltry dining-room: and he bit his lips at the first glance at the table, though it was profusely ornamented with flowers.

The festive board was so short, that the guests could scarcely squeeze into their places, and the dining-room was so narrow that the said table had to be set over to one side, that Caesar might have space to pass along on the other. When all were with some difficulty seated, Mrs. Woodbridge with great *sang froid* began to send round some thin greasy ash-coloured broth, being a decoction of cold veal with a few shreds of vermicelli floating in it, and highly-flavoured with smoke; Mary having forgotten to cover it while it was simmering over an ill-made fire. This potation, Mrs. Pinchington, after swallowing a spoonful or two, announced to be a delicious white soup. The unfortunate man whose duty it was to perform the part of host, proceeded to help a piece of boiled halibut served up without draining, but it looked so sanguinary that no one chose to try it: for even the lovers of what is called *rare* beef seldom have a fancy for rare fish. For the second course, the soup was replaced by a small tough round of *par-baked* beef, black on the outside, and raw within, and denominated *bœuf-a-la-mode*: the a-la-moding being a few cloves stuck over the top which had been previously rubbed with powdered allspice: this beef Mrs. Pinchington declined tasting lest it should prove too rich for her. The bottom dish was a meagre roast pig, (called "delicate" by Mrs. Pinchington) accompanied by a little tureen of watery panada, termed, on this occasion, bread-sauce. After the company had pretended to eat of these things, Caesar was desired to bring on the third course. The third course was a dish of hard bony mutton chops, which were to have been *cotelettes à la Maintenon*, but which Irish Mary had produced *au naturel*: and also a dish of something begun as *croquettes*, but ended as mere minced veal, washy and tasteless. Afterwards was introduced as a *bonne-bouche*, two pair of split birds sprawling on greasy slices of ill-made toast, and called game by the ladies but known to be pigeons by Caesar and the gentlemen. All the vegetables prepared for this dinner were few in number, small in quantity, half-boiled, half-drained, and mixed with that disgrace to a lady's house, *cooking* butter, its disagreeable taste predominating through all disguise, and rendering every thing unpalatable. The fourth course was at the top a superb glass bowl *half* full of a pale lilac liquid, consisting of faintly sweetened milk that had been skimmed till blue, and was then tinged with something pinkish. This was dignified by the name of floating island; the island being a spoonful of cream taking from the said milk and beaten up with sufficient white of egg to give it "a local habitation and a name," by forming a small heap in the centre of the bowl. At the bottom sat a dish containing a few cones of boiled rice that had been moulded in wine-glasses, the summit of each cone decorated with a red spot made by sticking on a mashed cranberry. This part of the dessert was highly recommended to the company by Mrs. Pinchington, who assured them that rice was a delicious thing and "so pure." The centre confection was a flat leathery pancake denominated *omelette soufflée*, the very sight of which would have made Fossard tear his hair. This strange affair had been manufactured under the immediate superintendence of Mrs. Woodbridge herself, who did it exactly "ma's way." The side-dishes held a few very small state single tartlets about the size of a half dollar procured at a low-priced cake-shop, each containing a half tea-spoonful of mysterious marmelade, made of some indescribable fruit mounted in marvellous heavy paste. These tartlets Mrs. Pinchington called "little loves."

We need not attempt to depict the sufferings of our excitable hero during the progress of this dinner, or to tell how continually his resolutions to bear it manfully were on the point of giving way. In vain did he try to repress the outward and visible signs of vexation, mortification, indignation and all the other *ations* that in spite of his efforts to conceal them were flushing his cheek, knitting his brow, compressing his lips, and trembling in his voice. Once he found his hand rambling through his hair, and once he found his teeth gritting against each other; but on both these occasions he recollected himself in time to smile an unnatural smile, and to talk some random talk.

But Mr. Woodbridge's disgust and anger did not quite rise to its climax till he tasted the madeira which, when he purchased it, he knew to be of the first quality, and which he now found had been greatly diluted with water after being decanted; evidently to make it go further. On glancing at his wife he met her eye watching his, and he saw by her guilty look to whom he must attribute the adulteration. Had she been able to draw the corks, it is most probable that the hock and champagne would not have escaped a similar *allongement*.[13]

Poor Caesar well understood and deeply sympathized in the numerous annoyances that assailed Mr. Woodbridge at this unhappy dinner: to say nothing of the griefs that were more particularly his own. He prided himself greatly on his skill and alertness in the art of waiting on company, on his *savior faire* in arranging, on his dexterity in executing, and in the harmonious but unquestionable authority with which he could give a tone to the movements of the apt and well-tutored "coloured gentlemen," that on similar occasions had always been employed to assist him. Mrs. Woodbridge having persisted in not hiring a single additional waiter, Caesar had so much to do that he had no chance of doing any thing well, or of displaying his usual tact in seeing without seeming to see, and anticipating the wishes of the guests. To-day he felt "his laurels withering on his brow," but his crowning horror was the sight of Irish Mary, when he had to receive from her the dishes at the door of a little back staircase that led down to the kitchen. Having put on her worst costume to cook in, she presented herself in full view, slip-shod, and bare-heeled, in an old dirty gown its sleeves dipped in grease, a ragged and filthy apron, her handkerchief pinned awry over one shoulder and leaving the other exposed, and her elf-locks hanging about her ears. On handing in each dish she took an opportunity of standing awhile with her stupid whitish eyes and her large heavy mouth wide open, to stare at the company, till Caesar shut the door in her face; upon which affront her murmurs and threats were audible all the way down stairs.

This dinner appeared endless to all concerned in it, except to Mary, who taking no note of time, and being unprovided with the organ of clock-knowledge, had nothing ready when wanted, or indeed for a long while after. The dusk of evening had darkened the table, and the guests were feeling about among the spotted oranges and worm-eaten apples, the *cooking* raisins and the stony-shelled almonds that had been set on subsequent to the removal of the cloth. Mr. Woodbridge after waiting in vain for his wife to order lights till it became so dark that he could scarcely discern her, gave several hints to that effect: but she continued hint-proof. He then audibly desired Caesar to bring them. Caesar on passing near Mrs. Woodbridge was detained a few moments by a low talk from her, and the result was two candles only. Immediately after their introduction, she made a signal to Mrs. Pinchington, and both ladies left the table; Mrs.

Woodbridge taking an opportunity of telling Caesar it was not worth while to light the entry-lamp as the gentlemen would soon go. Having reached her own apartment Mrs. Woodbridge changed her dress and threw herself on the bed, exclaiming that she was dead with fatigue: and Mrs. Pinchington prepared to go home, escorted by Caesar, who was run up for the purpose. She took an affectionate leave of her hostess, assuring her that she should report every where how delightfully the dinner had gone off, and expressing her hope to be at many more exactly like it. "Oh! Jupiter!" exclaimed Caesar, for a moment forgetting where he was. Mrs. Woodbridge frowned, and Mrs. Pinchington stooped down to tie her walking-shoes.

In consequence of having to walk behind this lady to her lodgings, Caesar to his great vexation was unable to superintend the making of the coffee, and when he got home he found that Mrs. Woodbridge, in her impatience to hurry the departure of the gentlemen, had ordered Irish Mary to prepare and carry it in herself; and the weak, cold and muddy beverage was left in every cup, almost untasted by the company.

The guests departed: and Caesar cleared away the table sighing heavily over the disgraces of the day; and confirmed in his resolution of seeking another place when he found his Hibernian colleague lying intoxicated on the kitchen floor.

Harvey Woodbridge passed the remainder of the evening extended on one of the parlour sofas, and endeavouring to devise some plan for expanding the mind and heart of his wife, improving her disposition, and rendering her ideas and practices less mean and less selfish. Knowing, however, that she could not have been blind to all the inconveniences and vexations which, on this occasion particularly, had arisen from her ill-judged parsimony and her willful perseverance in it, he imagined her touched for once with compunction, and perhaps sincerely disposed to try and do better for the future. "This after all"—thought he—"may prove a salutary lesson to her. She cannot always be incorrigible. I will spare her feelings to-night, and refrain from all expostulation till to-morrow; and then I will reason with her as calmly and mildly as I can."

He rose early next morning and took a walk to Schuylkill, willing to defer a little longer his intended remonstrance. On his return, breakfast was not ready, and Charlotte had not come down. He tried in vain to read the newspaper: but threw it aside, and traversed the room till she made her appearance; and Caesar at the same time brought in the tray.

As soon as the repast was over and the breakfast apparatus removed, our hero commenced his expostulation, making a strong effort to control his feelings and to speak with calmness. Without referring to former subjects of similar annoyance, he tried to confine himself entirely to the dinner-party: setting forth with all the eloquence of truth the shame and mortification she had caused him by her unhappy notions of ultra-economy, so absurdly and annoyingly put in practice on that much-to-be-regretted occasion; lessening both her and himself in the eyes of his guests, all whom, as he said, had a just right to consider themselves treated with disrespect at being set down in a gentleman's house to so paltry an entertainment, and in so paltry a room.

"If you talk this way, Harvey"—said Charlotte Woodbridge—"I shall go off into strong hysterics."

This threat, however, had lost its effect; for though Harvey had often heard of hysterics he had never seen them.

"Charlotte"—said he—"this is no time for folly. Believe me when I assure you that I am now seriously determined to insist on a general reform in the whole tenor of household arrangements. I am completely disgusted with living in this manner, and I will submit to it no longer. My patience is exhausted with the vain effort of suppressing my vexation, and in trying to endure in silence the innumerable petty annoyances with which you contrive to embitter every hour of my life; and I am still more tired of ineffectual remonstrances, and useless bickerings about trifles."

"Why then do you bicker?"

"Nonsense!—Is not domestic misery composed chiefly of trifles: each a unit in itself, but the whole when added together making a large sum total."

"I despise business talk."

"Charlotte—Charlotte!—I doubt if in reality you are as silly as you would seem to be."

"Yes, I am—and so you will always find me. As I never had the least wish to be sensible, I did not trouble myself to try. Ma' always said that sensible girls got but few beaux, and did not go off well. Her only care was that I should grow up pretty, and be handsomely and fashionably drest. So I always had plenty of beaux, and I did go off—to be sure it was no great go. And, now, though I am a married woman, I see no reason why I should not wish to look well and be admired just the same as before. As to the management of the house and all the sort of thing, I again assure you that I shall not make the least change in my plans now or ever—do *you* attend to *your* business, and I will manage mine."

"Oh! Charlotte"—exclaimed her husband, having listened to this *tirade* as much in sorrow as in anger, "Can nothing make any impression on you. Or rather, why are all your sayings and doings so perverse and wilful, when there must at the bottom of your heart be some latent touch of tenderness for the man who loving you sincerely, was willing to take you upon trust, without any previous knowledge of your temper and habits; and who so frankly and fondly entrusted his happiness to your keeping."

"'Nobody asked you, sir,' she said"—

was the reply of our wayward heroine, singing a line from a well-known ballad,[14] and making a low curtsey; "did you not fall in love the moment you were introduced to me at Mrs. Vanvernigen's party, where I wore my rose-coloured ærophine with the satin corsage and the coquille trimming, and carried in my hand a silver bouquetaire with six dollars worth of hot-house flowers in it? And did not you steal a sprig of heliotrope from my bouquet, and put it to your lips instead of your nose—I saw you do it!—and did you not follow me all about the room, and talk to nobody else, and give me your arm to the supper-table, and go without your own supper that you might accompany me back to the front drawing-room and get a seat on an ottoman beside me? And did not you wait at the door to put me into the carriage, though my pa' and brothers were along? And then you know very well how you came next morning the moment the clock struck eleven, (a full hour before any reasonable creature thinks of making a visit:) and how you bespoke yourself to escort me to Miss Semibreve's musical soirée; and whenever a song finished and a piece began did not you look delighted, because then you could talk to me all the while, as nobody is bound to listen to pieces? Did you not from that time visit me twice a day, and go every where with me even to church, and actually come to a proposal on our way home, at the corner of Broadway and Warren street. And did not you detain me on the door-step till I consented, scrambling hold of my hand and tearing my white kid glove? And the very moment we were engaged did not you bounce after me into the front parlour and ask pa'?"

"I plead guilty to all this—"replied Woodbridge—"Next time I will be less precipitate."

"So will I"—said Charlotte.

"We are talking very absurdly"—resumed Woodbridge—after a short pause—"I began this conversation with an earnest desire to make a serious impression on you, and to awaken your good feelings; for I hope and trust you are not entirely without them."

"Feelings"—replied our heroine—"I do not know why I should be suspected of want of feeling. I am sure I always cry at the theatre when I see other ladies with their handkerchiefs to their eyes, for then I am certain there is something to be cried at. When I was a little girl I actually sobbed one night at the play, when Cinderella's sisters made her stay at home from the ball. It is not a month ago that I looked very serious when every one else was laughing at that wicked Petruchio not allowing his wife to have her new gown and cap. However, I suppose I had best say nothing about Petruchio—as it may not be quite safe for me to put him into your head."

"Charlotte—Charlotte"—exclaimed her husband—"no more of this folly: but listen attentively to what I am going to say. In the first place I insist on your giving up Mrs. Pinchington and Mrs. Squanderfield."

"What, my best friends!—my most intimate friends!—the only true friends I have!"

"Your husband is your best and truest friend."

"You really make me laugh—as if husbands and friends were not totally different things!—Do you think I could ever talk to you, and consult you on all occasions, as I do these two ladies."

"Supposing then that that were impossible—have you not become acquainted with other ladies far superior to these for all purposes of conversation and consultation."

"How should you know—men are no judges of women. I can assure you that of all the ladies I have met with in Philadelphia, Mrs. Pinchington and Mrs. Squanderfield are the most to my taste."

"I am sorry to hear it."

"I tell you again that I shall always regard them as my best and dearest and only friends. Both of them are so fond of me that they actually grieve if they do not see me every day. They have nothing so much at heart as me and my good."

"I wish they would let you and your good alone!"

"That is not your own wit, Mr. Woodbridge—I heard a man say something like it in a play. No—the interest they feel in me is quite astonishing, and they always give me proper advice, just as I like to take; and as they have nothing to do but to go about and see people, they always have a great deal to tell me of such things as I like to hear. As to this dinner that has so much affronted you, *I* have the most cause to be offended at your finding fault with it after all the trouble it gave me. So I assure you it is the last dinner party I will ever preside over."

"Would you wish me to invite my friends to dine with me at a hotel, as if I had no means of entertaining them at home."

"No, indeed—when ma' was on here, she told me that pa' had tried that experiment, and that the expense was enormous; and besides, the leavings were all lost, as they could not be had to furnish family dinners afterwards. People can *live*, I suppose, without having dinner company, or indeed any company at all. And much as you despise yesterday's entertainment, the expense of it actually frightened me. However, I can tell you, for your comfort, that we dine to-day upon the cold things that were left."

"What cold things?"

"No matter what. When pa' *would* have dinner company, ma' never sent to market for a week afterwards."

"And was he contented to dine on scraps for a week?"

"Contented or not, he had to do it for years and years. To be sure at last he got into a very provoking way of dining at a hotel whenever he expected a scrap dinner (as you call it,) at his own table."

"I will follow your worthy father's example, and dine to-day at a hotel."

"Are you in earnest."

"Yes, I am. If you will not listen to talking, I will try what virtue there is in acting."

"Why it will cost you a dollar or more."

"I know it. But I shall at least obtain a dollar's worth of comfort, and have a chance of composing my temper, and dining in peace."

"I have no more time to waste with you"—said his wife, seeing that he was determined on accomplishing this new feat. "I must go to Madame Tourtelot's at eleven o'clock, to be fitted for my pearl-coloured figured satin and my fawn-coloured luster-silk. But to think of your throwing away a dollar upon a dinner for yourself.—The extravagance of men is awful."

She then repaired to her own apartment; and her husband too much ruffled to pursue his expostulation with the temper he desired, prepared to go out.

In the entry he was way-laid by Caesar, who informed him that he wished Mr. Woodbridge would suit himself with another waiter by the end of the month, adding—"Indeed, sir, I am sorry to leave you, but I seem as if I could not stand things no longer, 'specially Irish Mary. Her head is so muddled from yesterday, that I found her, when she was getting breakfast, haggling at the loaf with the side of a fork instead of a knife, and saying—"Oh! but it's hard this bread is to cut, then." And I catched her greasing the griddle with the end of a candle, and when I stopped her short in her wickedness, she said—"Ah! and what would ye have then—grase is grase all the world over." Indeed, sir, you don't know how hard it is to live day in and day out with a woman that's a born fool."

"Yes, I do"—thought Woodbridge—"and he almost sighed to think that he had not, like Caesar, the resource of changing his home. However, he merely replied—"Very well, Caesar—you may refer to me for a character"—and with a heavy heart he walked to his store.

That day, resolving to put his threat into practice, our hero *did* dine at a hotel. His wife, after finishing her dress-fitting, shopping, and card-leaving, went to take her dinner, as the guest of Mesdames Squanderfield and Pinchington, at their boarding-house. She found that both those ladies had gone together up the river; one on a visit to an acquaintance at Burlington, the other to see a relative living at Bristol. Nevertheless she accepted the slight invitation of her former hostess, the mistress of the establishment, to stay and dine with *her*, as the dinner-bell was about to ring.

Towards evening, Mr. Woodbridge came home in much better temper; and was disposed to enter into a cheerful conversation with his wayward Charlotte. But she kept a sullen silence; and at the tea-table she steadily put aside every thing he offered her, helping herself to it immediately after. When their uncomfortable tea was over, her husband again tried to reason with her on the subject of that perverseness which was undermining his affection, and destroying their peace. She made not a word of answer, but lay motionless and speechless, reclining on the sofa. After a while, she turned to the wall and threw her handkerchief over her head.—"She is touched at last"—thought Woodbridge.—"To hide her face and weep in silence is a good symptom. I have hopes of her yet."—He then softened his tone, and made a tender and powerful appeal to what he called her best feelings. In conclusion, he rose from his chair, went to her in much emotion, and taking her passive hand, addressed her as his beloved Charlotte. Still, she replied not. He gently withdrew the handkerchief from her face.—She was fast asleep.

Her husband sighed—replaced the handkerchief; resumed his seat before the full and ashy fire; folded his arms: and gazed awhile on the ceiling. Then he took up a book, but held it unconsciously for half an hour, forgetting to open it. At last he started up, and went out to revive himself by a walk in the open air. Finally, on passing one of the theatres he strolled in and placed himself in the back of a box; but though his eyes were fixed on the stage, he had no perception of any thing that he saw, and no comprehension of any thing he heard. He only knew when the performance was over by finding that the lights were extinguishing and the benches vacated. He then went to his cheerless home, and found that his wife had retired for the night and was sleeping with her usual tranquility.

Next morning their breakfast passed exactly like the tea of the preceding evening, and Woodbridge went to his store in silent despair. When he again came home he found that though yesterday he had dined at a hotel to escape the threatened leavings of a vile dinner, his wife, with *malice prepense*, had kept these "shadows of a shade" to set before him to-day, and as long as they could be made to last.

Part Fourth

It chanced that just at that time Mr. Stapleford, the father of our heroine, had some commercial business which made it necessary for him to visit Philadelphia and Baltimore. He left New York in the earliest morning line, and having reached the Delaware and dined in the boat, his attention, as he sat reading on deck, was withdrawn from the newspaper by the conversation of two ladies who occupied seats just in front of him. One of the dames proved to be Mrs. Squanderfield. She had come on board at Bristol, and expressed great delight at meeting her friend, Mrs. Pinchington, who had been taken in at Burlington. Both ladies talked in a very audible under-tone, and Mr. Stapleford thought of changing his place 'till he was startled by hearing the name of his daughter. Curiosity then triumphed over every other consideration, and, keeping his eyes on the paper, he sat still and listened.

"*A-propos*, my dear Mrs. Pinchington"—proceeded Mrs. Squanderfield—"you have not yet told me the particulars of the great Woodbridge dinner. I was out when you came home from it—and yesterday morning, as we went up the river, you know how I was beset by that persevering man, Mr. Bulkworthy, who monopolized me the whole time; as, to say the truth, he always does whenever we meet."

"You seemed very well pleased to be thus monopolized"—replied Mrs. Pinchington, with a Sardonic smile.—"If you had chosen to change your seat, he could not have made much progress in following you, with his immense size and gouty foot. However, my dear Squanderfield, let me advise you, as a friend, to take care what you are about. Old fat men are not always rich: though silly girls and dashing widows seem to think so. Neither is the gout always caused by high living, and therefore a proof that they have a great deal to live on. Besides, by not paying their debts, they may get the gout at other people's expenses."

"How you run on"—answered Mrs. Squanderfield—evidently desirous of changing the subject.—"But do tell me how the Woodbridge dinner-party went off. I suppose, as usual, Mrs. W. was superbly drest. I know she got every thing new for the occasion, for I was with her when she bought all her paraphernalia. That pearl-coloured figured satin could not have cost less than fifty dollars by the time it was made up—and that laced pelerine was forty. What a passion she has for laced pelerines. I know that she has six others, all equally elegant and costly. Then the blond cap and French flowers, that she bought to wear on the back of her head, was fifteen. When I am out shopping with Mrs. Woodbridge, it almost makes my hair stand on end to see how readily she agrees to buying the most extravagant things, and things which she cannot possibly want. I cannot imagine where she finds room to stow away all her dead stock.

Her husband will find that dressing alone of his pretty doll will add to his annual expenses, not merely hundreds of dollars, but actually thousands. I was telling my friends at Bristol all about the Woodbridges; and they agree with me that the poor man little knows what is before him. I have asked several New Yorkers about her family, and they say that old Stapleford's wife is a bye-word, even there, for her extravagance in dress."

Mr. Stapleford changed colour, and looked off from his paper, and could not suppress a deep sigh—and then made an effort to appear more intent on his reading than ever.

"I have heard, also"—continued Mrs. Squanderfield—"(and from persons who have been at her house,) that in her domestic concerns there never was a meaner skin-flint than that same Mrs. Stapleford. One of my New York friends told me she had a cook that had once lived at Stapleford's. On some grand occasion, when they were to have an apple-pie, Mrs. S. gave out six apples to pare and a quarter; and then she came into the kitchen and counted the bits of apple, and because there was only twenty-two pieces instead of twenty-four, she scolded the cook violently, and ended by calling her a thief. So the woman went right out of the house, leaving the dinner at a stand. Of course she told the apple-story every where, and in a day or two it was all over New York."

Mr. Stapleford's sigh was now audible—for he remembered the cook, (the best they ever had,) and he was well aware of the circumstances attending her departure. The ladies, however, were sitting with their backs that way, and did not observe him. After pausing a minute to take breath, Mrs. Squanderfield proceeded—

"But about this dinner—it must have gone to Mrs. Woodbridge's heart to get it up. I long to know all the particulars."

"It would take me till to-morrow morning to tell the whole"—replied Mrs. Pinchington—"so at present, I can only give you a slight sketch. Well—in the first place we were ushered into that wretched hole that she calls the dining-room: though it's their sole abiding-place, morning, noon, and night. There was a little bit of table set cater-cornered to give more space; notwithstanding which we were all squeezed flat by the time we had got wedged into our seats. The only waiter was their man Caesar, for she could not open her heart so far as to hire even on that extraordinary occasion, the first dinner company they have ever had. The dishes were handed in by a horrid Irish girl, all filth and rags, who stood staring, open mouthed, the whole time—never having seen such great things before."

"But do tell what they had by way of eatables"—cried Mrs. Squanderfield.

"Why there was a soup which tasted exactly like smoked dish-water. And a hard, tough, black-looking piece of beef—and a morsel of half-raw fish. The chief dish seemed to be a pig, that looked as if he had been killed just in time to save him from dying, and which I know she got at half-price, for I went to market with her myself. Then, by way of game, were some pigeons, with scarcely a mouthful of flesh on their bones, split in half, and looking as flat as boards. The butter was detestable, and would have spoiled every thing, only that every thing was spoiled before. The dessert was utter trash—milk—and rice—and froth—and a few miserable cheap tarts, made of nothing: and a little decayed fruit, turned with the best side uppermost. And as dusk come on, we had to poke about among the things all in the dark, for she would not allow us candles to eat by. But the wine—the wine above all—I forgot to tell you of the wine. It had actually been watered to make it go further. Think of gentlemen at a dinner party filling their glasses with wine and water!"

"Wretched, indeed!—But how did the sensitive Mr. Harvey Woodbridge live through all this?"

"Oh! poor miserable creature"—replied Mrs. Pinchington—"he really moved my compassion—I absolutely felt for him. I wish you could have beheld his face when his eye first glanced over the dinner-table—I could scarcely keep from laughing all the time, to see how ashamed he was of every thing, and how he labored to conceal his mortification; the natural man peeping out in spite of himself. It was really too good to see how he tried to smile, not knowing that his smile was only a ghastly grin. And how he twinkled his eyes and essayed to look pleasant, when he felt the fire flashing from them; and how he twitched his brows to smooth them, when he found they were contracting into a frown; and how he endeavoured to soften his voice and talk agreeably, lest he should break out into an open fury."

"And how did his wife take all this?"

"His wife—it was best of all to see how she sat in her finery, with a coolness that really amounted to impudence, and looking as sweet and amiable as if she was presiding at the best spread table in the world, and enjoying the satisfaction of the company. That woman has not an atom of either sense or feeling. For my part, I was glad to get away as soon as I possibly could, that I might indemnify myself at our own tea-table for the miserable dinner I had *pretended* to eat. Young as she is, Mrs. Woodbridge is certainly the meanest woman I ever yet met with—and I have a good chance of knowing, for she consults me about all her plans, as she calls them."

"And she is also the most extravagant"—rejoined Mrs. Squanderfield.—"I ought certainly to know, when I so often go shopping with her."

"The fact is"—rejoined Mrs. Pinchington—"she will drive that husband of hers to desperation before long."

Mr. Stapleford could listen no more. He threw down his newspaper, started up, and walked the deck in unconcealed perturbation: forgetting where he was, and regardless of all observers. In the mean time, Mesdames Squanderfield and Pinchington continued to regale each other with alternate and exaggerated anecdotes of the meanness and extravagance of their friend Mrs. Woodbridge, till the boat arrived at Chestnut street wharf—from whence the two cronies proceeded to their lodgings, arm in arm.

The unhappy father of our heroine had been too much absorbed in his own irritated feelings to be conscious of the progress of the boat. He looked not at either shore—he recognized none of the landmarks; and he only started from his painful reverie when the boat touched the pier and the roaring of the steam announced that its work was over for that day. On landing, he almost unconsciously replied to the importunities of a hack-driver, threw himself and his baggage into a coach, and repaired to the dwelling of his son-in-law.

On arriving at the house, the front door was opened by Caesar, (who yet lingered in the establishment) and the old gentleman exclaimed—"Where is that dining-room—I know she is there." He then, before Caesar could show him into the parlour, ran straight up stairs, and found the place intuitively.

The young couple had just concluded their slender dinner, at which Woodbridge (to whom nothing was more intolerable than silent anger, and who already longed to conciliate his wife, almost on any terms) had been trying in vain to force a conversation. But Charlotte held out, and answered only in sullen monosyllables—it being her way when she knew she had done wrong to behave always as if she was the person that had most cause to be offended. They were both struck with surprise at the unexpected appearance of Mr. Stapleford. When they recovered, Harvey shook hands with him, and Charlotte kissed her pa', and asked him if he had dined.

"Yes"—he replied, struggling to keep down his wrath—"I

dined in the boat—I have had my dinner—Are you not glad? But I am hot and thirsty, and I want some drink."

"What will you have, pa'?"—inquired Charlotte.—"Here is some nice water."

"I want some brandy also"—said Mr. Stapleford.—"Water is weak—it does not drive away care.—Give me some brandy, too—I *must* have it."

Woodbridge rang the bell, and Caesar was desired to bring some cool water; after which our hero silently brought some brandy himself, and placed it on the table, while Charlotte looked pale and amazed.

Mr. Stapleford mixed a tumbler full of strong brandy and water, and then said to his son-in-law—"Shall I mix one for you?—I have become quite clever at the business."

"I never drink brandy"—replied Woodbridge.

"Then I hope to Heaven you never may"—said the old man, fervently, and raising his eyes, in which the tears seemed to glisten. But he passed the back of his hand across them, paused a moment, then snatched up the glass, and hastily swallowed the half of its contents.

"There"—said he, throwing himself into a chair—"you see what I have come to—I—your father-in-law—and *her* father. Have you not heard it?—Don't you know it?—I am a drunkard now—I am—I am. It is a shameful, dreadful vice. It came upon me by slow degrees; but it *has* come—and every body knows it—you see it about my face, don't you?—Look at me—look—I bear about me the unfailing signs—you know I do."

They looked at him—it was too true. There was that redness in his face which never can be mistaken for the honest glow of health.

"Do you know what has made me a drunkard?"—resumed Mr. Stapleford—"A bad wife. A wife may be bad, and yet she may neither play cards, nor tipple, nor betray the honour of her husband.—But she may destroy his peace, she may undermine his happiness, she may wear out his love by the everlasting rubbing of petty annoyances. I have read—(for I once *did* read)—that one of the severest tortures inflicted by the Romish Inquisition, was a contrivance which caused water to fall unceasingly, day after day, week after week, month after month, in single drops, one at a time, upon the head of the miserable captive. I, too, have had my drops—and I know what I have suffered from them. And she that selfishly and heartlessly inflicted that suffering was my wife—your mother Charlotte—and I fear that you are indeed her true daughter."

"Dear pa'"—said Charlotte—"pray don't talk so dreadfully—and, above all, before Harvey."

"I will—I will"—exclaimed her father—"and before Harvey, above all, will I do it. Let him take warning, for I know that he needs the lesson. Do not exchange glances at each other—I am not intoxicated *yet*—I am quite sober still, and I know exactly what I am saying. But while I can yet do so, (for now I have begun with the poison I must keep on) I will tell you what I heard in the Delaware boat to-day. There were two women taken on board, (ladies, I suppose I must call them.) I chanced to sit where I overheard their conversation, and I could not help listening, when my ear was struck with your name, and I found they were talking about my daughter. Perhaps it was dishonourable to sit and listen; but I am not an honourable man now—I do things every day that once I would have shuddered at. I found that these women knew you well."

"Mrs. Squanderfield and Mrs. Pinchington, I suppose"—said Woodbridge, turning to his wife.

"Yes"—continued Mr. Stapleford—"those were their names. One of them had been at a dinner-party, here, in this little room; and she detailed it all to her companion, broadly and coarsely enough, but still I knew that, in her main, her statement was true. She described and ridiculed the paltry, contemptible dinner, and its wretched arrangements; and Woodbridge's ill-concealed efforts to repress his shame and mortification. Then as one of these women talked about your meanness, the other discussed your extravagance: and told of the money you were continually throwing away in useless finery for the decoration of your own person, while you denied your husband the comforts which every gentleman has a right in his own house to expect, if he can furnish the means of procuring them. I listened to their talk, and I understood it all—I felt it all—for I knew by sad experience what it was."

"Is it possible"—said Charlotte, with quivering lips—"that Mrs. Squanderfield and Mrs. Pinchington could have talked of me in that manner—and in a public steam-boat, too!"

"They were your friends, Charlotte"—said her husband—"your dearest, best—your only friends—your aiders and abettors in the practice of your two besetting sins."

"The vile, false, wicked creatures"—exclaimed Mrs. Woodbridge—"I will never speak to them again."

"I am delighted to hear it"—said Woodbridge—"and earnestly do I hope you will keep that resolution."

"Listen to me, Charlotte"—said Mr. Stapleford, trying to speak with more composure—"Listen to me, also, Harvey Woodbridge, and may both of you profit by the lesson. I married Mary Holman when we were both very young. I was then a clerk in a merchant's counting-house—she was the daughter of a poor clergyman. Her beauty first attracted me, and I thought she had been well brought up. Necessity had obliged the family to be notable and industrious, and to economize in superfluities. Her mother often told me of Mary's talent for housewifery, and of her ingenuity with her needle, and how clever she was in the art of making a genteel appearance at a small expense. I thought I had drawn a prize in the lottery of marriage, and I loved her with my whole heart. We took possession of a small plainly-furnished two-story house in a remote street, and I thought we might live respectably and comfortably upon my salary. I soon discovered my wife's innate passion for dress, which in her father's house, she had been unable to indulge. But now that she was a married woman, and emancipated from the control of her parents, she seemed resolved to run her course as she chose. In a very short time, I found a great falling off in every thing connected with household comforts, and a corresponding increase in the finery of my wife's attire. I saw her in silks, and laces, and feathers, and flowers; all being such as were worn by ladies whose husbands had five times my income.—But our servant-woman (we could keep but one) was dismissed for a half-grown girl, at half wages. These girls (we had a succession of them) were changed at least every month, as most of them were found to be worthless, idle, dirty, or dishonest; and all were incapable of doing work. If by chance we obtained a good one, she would not stay above a week in a house where she had to work hard and fare badly, for low wages. Often, when at our late dining hour I came home tired and hungry, I found no dinner—and when, after waiting an hour or two, the repast was at last produced, it was scanty, poor, and unpalatable. My wife had been out nearly all day, visiting, shopping, and going after mantua-makers.—When our dinners were unusually late, she said it would save the trouble and expense of tea, so she went early to bed, and obliged her girl to do the same by way of saving fire and light in the kitchen; and I passed the evening alone in our cheerless parlour, laboriously engaged in extra book-keeping, or some other such job, which I was glad to undertake for the purpose of obtaining a little addition to our income, and which frequently occupied me till midnight. I had hoped by this means to gain some improvement in our way of living. But I found it only encouraged my wife to run up bills for finery, which she knew I would be obliged eventually to pay for. Vain, selfish woman, at what sacrifices was her trumpery obtained? For the price of one or two of her expensive dresses we could have kept a grown servant a whole year. One French bonnet less, and we could have had *good* fires all winter, and the cost of one her embroidered muslin collars would have furnished me every evening with a better light to toil by.

"After awhile I obtained another situation, at a higher salary. I then proposed allowing a certain sum weekly for the household expenses alone—and I made this allowance as ample as I could. It was in vain—she pinched off so much of this money for additional finery, that we lived as badly as ever. At length, the death of my uncle James put me in possession of sufficient property to enable me to emancipate myself from the drudgery of clerkship, and to commence business on my own account. I did so, and was soon considered a prosperous man.

"From the time I went into business there were no bounds to my wife's extravagance—that is, in articles of show. But in all that regarded comfort and convenience, her penurious habits remained unchanged—and so they always will. In a few more years we had a handsome house, and she furnished the parlours elegantly—but she made us take all our meals in a little, low, cheerless room in the basement story; and, in fact, it became our chief abiding place. How I despised it, and how long I held out against it!"

"I wonder you submitted at all"—said Woodbridge.

"I submitted to that, and to all other proceedings of my wife, because I found resistance was in vain—as it always must be with a heartless, selfish, obstinate woman. Often, after the fatigues of the day, I was too tired to undertake the trouble of altercation. Nothing then seemed so desirable as peace and quiet, and, for the sake of present peace, I let the evil grow till it darkened my whole life with its baleful shadow. Naturally my disposition is cheerful, and as I could not be quarrelling for ever, I sometimes tried to laugh at the inconvenience and mortifications to which my wife continually subjected me. But it would not do—the iron, notwithstanding, had entered my soul and was fast corroding it. My affection for my wife was at last worn out. How could I love her, when I had daily proof that she had no regard for me? It was still worse when I was left alone with her—after Charlotte was married and gone, and my son Frank went to live in New Orleans. To James and myself our home was more than ever uncomfortable, for she allowed us no society; indeed, things were so managed that we became ashamed to invite any one to the house. Jem could endure it no longer—so he took lodgings at a hotel, where he is drinking wine every day, and going to destruction. For myself, I became reckless—desperate. I had long ceased to remonstrate with my wife on the sums she expended in dress—but I had grown very tired of the petty squabbling about fires, and lights, and food, and servants, and all other necessary expenses, which for five-and-twenty years had embittered my married life. I hated my home—and I was driven to seek elsewhere for peace and comfort; such, at least, as I could get in houses of public resort. I took my meals at restaurants and hotels—I frequented oyster-cellars—I joined a club. Gradually the vice of intemperance came upon me—wine was not enough, I took brandy also. I drank to raise my spirits, and to drown the sense of degradation that always oppressed me when I was sober. My wife did not care—she dressed more than ever, and went almost every night to a party—making me come for her when I was not fit to be seen—and thus exposing me to her 'dear five hundred friends,' when it was she, herself, that made me what I am.—I shall grow worse—I shall be seen reeling through the streets, with the boys hooting after me—I shall be taken up out of the gutter, and laid dead drunk on my own door-step. I know I shall—I see it all before me—yet, when it comes to that, and my children hear of it, let them remember that it is the fault of their mother. Look at what she has made of me—and what my wife's daughter is going to make of her husband—*She* knows how wretchedly we lived—she knows how all domestic happiness was worried away from her father's house—and still she has been walking fast in her mother's footsteps. Charlotte—Charlotte—do you not tremble?"

Charlotte did tremble—and pale and terrified she threw herself into the arms of her husband, hid her face on his shoulder, and burst into a flood of tears. Woodbridge also was deeply affected. But he saw at that moment a dawn of hope—and he hailed this first inclination of feeling on the part of his wayward wife as an omen of reform and happiness.

"I am glad to see you cry"—said the old man, after a pause.—"I have never seen *my* wife shed a tear, except when a splendid dress has been spoiled by the mantua-maker. I begin to hope that the daughter may be better than the mother."

"Dear sir"—said Woodbridge—"do not persist in speaking so harshly of your wife."

"I will—I will"—exclaimed the old man—swallowing the remainder of the brandy and water. "Has she not embittered my life, and turned to gall the love I once felt for her? What has Mary Stapleford ever done to make me happy? Has she ever cared for *me*—why then should I care for her? Has she ever regarded my tastes, my wishes? Why then should I have any respect for hers? And now I am a drunkard—disreputable, despised—looked at askance by respectable men, (I was once a respectable man myself,) obliged to associate now with those that have degraded themselves as I have done. And my wife has caused it all. She has made me wretched, and she has brought up her daughter to make *you* so too."

Mrs. Woodbridge now threw herself on the sofa, buried her face in one of the cushions, and sobbed aloud: and, on her husband approaching, she motioned him to leave her to herself. Woodbridge, after removing the brandy, prevailed on his father-in-law, (who had sunk back in his chair, and thrown his handkerchief over his face) to go to the spare chamber, and lie down and repose himself: and Charlotte in a faint voice said, *she* would also retire to her room. As she passed her husband she caught his hand and pressed it fervently: but her eyes again overflowed, and she was unable to speak.

Woodbridge having ascertained that the spare-chamber was in order, and conducted Mr. Stapleford to its door, now thought it best to leave his wife for awhile to the retirement of her own apartment. He then repaired to his store, where he recollected his presence at this time was particularly essential; and he endeavoured, but in vain, to occupy his mind with business during the short remainder of the day.

When he came home in the evening, he found that Mr. Stapleford, having requested that some tea might be brought to him, had gone to bed for the night, and was now asleep. Charlotte remained also in her room, and at her desire the tea-table had been set for her husband alone. After he had somewhat refreshed himself with a cup of tea, he went up to see her. He found her lying on the bed, and looking very pale and dejected. "Harvey"—said she—"don't talk to me to-night—I shall feel better in the morning—I know all you would say. I have indeed made you a very bad wife—I acknowledge and regret it: my eyes are opened at last, and I will try to do better in future. But I am so shocked at my father, to see him as he is now, and to hear all that he thinks and feels, and all that he fears. Oh! no—no—you shall never be brought to his condition by *me*. Indeed, indeed you never shall. It is too dreadful. But leave me now, dear Harvey and when I deserve it, I will beg you to forgive me all."

In compassion to the distress of her feelings Woodbridge quitted the room in silence. He passed the evening alone, in perturbed meditation; hope for the future and regret for the past, alternately casting their lights and shadows on his mind. But, the sunbeam of hope rested there at last.

Our heroine passed a restless night of bitter retrospection, and silent tears. Towards morning, she had wept herself into an uneasy slumber. Woodbridge rose with the dawn, resolved to try and compose himself by an early walk, his usual remedy after any extraordinary excitement. On descending the stairs, he overtook his father-in-law who had risen for the same purpose. They walked together as far as the Schuylkill, and had much conversation on the subject that was uppermost in both their minds.

When the two gentlemen returned, they were met in the entry by Caesar, who, while his face shone with smiles, stopped them as they were proceeding to the staircase, and with a flourish of his hand as he threw open the door, said to Mr. Woodbridge—"We breakfast in the back parlour, sir."

They found the table nicely set out with a better breakfast than either of the gentlemen had ever seen in his own house: and Caesar said, with increasing smiles—"Mrs. Woodbridge was up early, sir. She came down soon after you went out. And we have been to market already. And after we came home, I got the breakfast myself, and would not let Irish Mary put her paws to any thing. Mrs. Woodbridge has given Mary a short warning, and I am to get Phillis to come back, for our everlasting cook.—Please to excuse my saying *paws*: but that Paddy woman is enough to make the genteelest coloured gentleman forget himself. People of the best polishment can't be decorumous when they have to deal with Irish."

At these excellent signs of the times, our hero's smile became almost as bright at Caesar's. And Mr. Stapleford said, in a low voice to Woodbridge—"I was just going to ask for my early dram—but I believe I will not take any this morning."

"I have made the coffee very good and strong"—said Caesar. "Mrs. Woodbridge told me to do. And we bought the best butter that was to be had in market; and we took cream this morning instead of milk."

At this moment the lady of the house appeared. Her father and her husband kissed her as they bade her good morning. Her heart and eyes filled and she held her handkerchief to her face, while each of the gentlemen turned to a window and seemed to look out. There were a few minutes of silence: after which our heroine took her seat at the table, and Woodbridge and Mr. Stapleford did the same. Caesar entered with a damask napkin and a silver salver, and waited on table *con amore*. Woodbridge introduced a cheerful conversation, and though he had to sustain it chiefly himself, he was repaid by an occasional smile from Charlotte, and a laugh from her father.

When breakfast was over, and Mrs. Woodbridge had left the room, Mr. Stapleford said to his son-in-law—"She is touched at last. She is going to set about a reform—I only hope she will stay reformed. Ah! there is no touching her mother. I have tried often to work on *her* feelings: but she has none. Vanity, sordidness, and selfishness have hardened her heart till it is like 'the nether millstone.' But Charlotte is not so bad; and I trust she will do well yet. I must have a bottle more than usual to-day at dinner, in celebration of this joyful change."

"Rather celebrate it"—said Woodbridge—"by a day of entire temperance."

"Ah!"—replied Stapleford—"that is easier said than done. I am ashamed to confess that a day of temperance will be a day of suffering to me. The habit of drinking once formed, the craving once acquired, it is hard indeed to abstain. A drunkard is not easily cured."

"Let me beg of you, dear sir," said Woodbridge—"not to give yourself that detestable appellation."

"Do I not deserve it?"—replied Stapleford. "Am I not really what I call myself? But *she* made me so. I know that many men who are blest with excellent and affectionate wives have become sots notwithstanding—to their eternal shame be it spoken.—But that was not *my* disposition. No man was more capable of enjoying domestic happiness if it had been allowed me. However, I cannot trust myself on this theme. So let it drop for the present."

Mr. Stapleford and his son-in-law went out together, but parted at the corner: each going his own way to his respective business. That morning Mrs. Woodbridge did no shopping or visiting, but busied herself at home in improving her *ménage*. Irish Mary, being dismissed, was loud in her vociferations at parting, asserting that she had never seen a real lady or gentlemen since she came to Philadelphia, and that she would never more darken the doors of a Philadelphia house: for she knew scores of places in New York where they would jump out of their skins for joy to get her back again, and where the silver would come pouring into her lap. A week's wages extra, however, somewhat quieted her wrath: but on leaving the presence of Mrs. Woodbridge, she slammed the door, and exclaimed as soon as she got into the entry—"Bad luck to ye any how, and I wish to holy Patrick ye may never have nobody but black nagurs to cook your bit of victuals for you."

"That's a good wish instead of a bad one"—said Caesar, who had just come in at the front-door, triumphantly conducting Phillis.

That day an excellent dinner was served up in the back parlour: and as all were now in good spirits it would have gone off pleasantly, only that Mr. Stapleford filled his wine-glass too often. But he said, as he poured out the last—"I cannot help it—indeed I cannot. It is a dreadful vice—easily contracted and hard to cure. Shame on the woman that brought me to it. Well—well—enough of that—I wish I could forget her always. Come—I'll not drink any thing more to-day. Only I *must* have my glass of hot whiskey punch at bed-time."

As soon as the two gentlemen were alone, Woodbridge told his father-in-law that having now the most sanguine hopes of Charlotte's improvement, he thought it best to make no further reference to what had already passed; and that, unless he saw unequivocal symptoms of relapse, he would gladly consign to oblivion every thing that had hitherto embittered their married life.

"I fear"—said Mr. Stapleford—"her goodness will not last. However, even a little of it is better than none at all. Her mother never had a single fit of goodness—not even for one day. Well—well—I will not trust myself to talk of her."

Next day the old gentleman set out at an early hour for Baltimore; and Woodbridge, (judging from appearances) found that in the future the table was to be set always in the back parlour, and supplied in a liberal manner.

That morning Mesdames Squanderfield and Pinchington made together a visit to Mrs. Woodbridge. Her intention had been to send them each a concise note indicative of her desire that their acquaintance should cease; and she had purposed consulting her husband that very afternoon on the best manner of wording these notes. But they had seen her as they came past the window, and the moment Caesar opened the front door they pushed by him, and with their usual familiarity made their entrance into the room. At the first sight of her two perfidious friends, our heroine determined to meet them with calm and dignified resentment; but this wise determination soon gave way to the passion which she felt burning in her cheeks and sparkling in her eyes.

Mrs. Squanderfield began—"Dear Mrs. Woodbridge, it seems an age since I have seen you. But I was busy the whole day yesterday, shopping all through Chestnut street, with two ladies from the far west (who with their husbands are staying at our house) and taking them to milliners and mantua-makers. They have travelled more than a thousand miles, each bringing a young baby along; and their sole business is to get fitted out with the Philadelphia fashions. They take this journey twice every year, and carry wagon loads home with them."

"For my part"—said Mrs. Pinchington—"I was all day yesterday going about in search of a cheap washerwoman. Mine has raised her price to six dollars a quarter, and rather than give more than five I will wash and iron my own things in my own room. But as Mrs. Squanderfield says, it seems an age since I have seen you. I really believe we have not met since the day of your delightful dinner-party."

"Delightful was it"—said Charlotte, unable longer to restrain herself—"you did not think so in the boat coming down the river, when you were telling Mrs. Squanderfield about it: and I am very sure that you made it out worse even than it really was."

Mrs. Pinchington changed colour, and looked much embarrassed; but rallied in a few moments and said—"My dear Mrs. Woodbridge you must be misinformed. Some vile mischief-maker—some wicked slanderer has been trying to disturb our friendship."

"My informant"—replied Charlotte—"is neither a mischief-maker nor a slanderer. It was my own father, Mr. Stapleford. He happened to be seated near you: and he heard every word. First, you led me on by your own advice to do all sorts of mean paltry things"—

"I found you willing enough to be led"—interrupted Mrs. Pinchington.

"And now"—continued Charlotte—"you have abused me for following your instructions. I should not have been half so bad, had you left me to myself. But my eyes are now opened, and as I intend to act very differently for the future, I shall have the better chance of keeping that resolution by declining all further intercourse with Mrs. Pinchington."

"With all my heart"—said Mrs. Pinchington, rising angrily—"I have no occasion to force my acquaintance on any one. And from what I have heard of her, I am very sure your notions of economy came from your own mother far more than from me. I wish you all possible success in your new scheme of reform; which you will find a very tough job, take my word for it."

So saying, Mrs. Pinchington flounced out of the room, and scuttled out of the house.

"What a strange woman that is"—remarked Mrs. Squanderfield. "I have thought several times of telling you how little she is, in reality, your friend, and how shamefully she talks about you wherever she goes. It is a great pity you asked her to that unlucky dinner-party; the account she gives of it is awful. I own I was a little hurt at your not inviting *me*. I should then have had it in my power to contradict her ill-natured reports."

"Perhaps not"—said our heroine—"for with shame I acknowledge that there was too much foundation for her statements, however unfavourable they might be. But the next time I prepare for company, things will be found very different. I have had a mortifying lesson."

"I must say"—pursued Mrs. Squanderfield—"that I greatly approve of liberality. People in genteel life should not mind expense. By the bye, have you heard of the splendid new style shawls that Levy has just opened. I saw them yesterday, and they are the most divine things I ever beheld. Get ready, and come with me, and secure one before all the best are gone."

"To be plain with you Mrs. Squanderfield"—said Charlotte—"my intention is, in future, to expend less money on dress, and more on things of greater importance. And I know that both my husband and myself will be the happier for the change."

"Really"—observed Mrs. Squanderfield—"I thought all men were happy to see their wives handsomely drest."

"I begin to think"—said Charlotte—"that a woman may be drest handsomely without spending enormous sums, and getting five times as many new things as she can possibly want. My husband has not yet made his fortune: and in the mean time, that our housekeeping may be on a more liberal scale, I shall lessen my own personal expenses. But as I am going to reform both ways, I think it best to relinquish my intimacy with Mrs. Squanderfield as well as with Mrs. Pinchington, for I wish not to be led farther into temptation."

"I declare you are very polite"—exclaimed Mrs. Squanderfield, starting up—"I cannot think what has got into you to-day. You don't seem at all like yourself."

"So much the better, perhaps"—replied Charlotte; "but as my father could not have overheard Mrs. Pinchington, without also overhearing Mrs. Squanderfield, his report has convinced me that *neither* of these ladies has any right to call herself my friend."

"Upon my word"—said Mrs. Squanderfield, forcing a laugh—"it is really amusing to see how new you are. I thought you were old enough to know that in all circles, even in the highest, every body talks of every body without the least scruple. It is the way of the world: and I do not pretend to be better than my neighbours. However, as Mrs. Pinchington says, I have no occasion to force my society on any one. I have more friends already than I can possibly visit, even if I were to do nothing else from noon till midnight. I see we don't suit: but you will lose more than I shall. However, let us part decently, and be civil whenever we chance to meet. So I wish you good morning, and success to your plan of reforming both ways."

"Good morning"—said Charlotte, softening her voice: for in truth, she felt rather better disposed towards Mrs. Squanderfield than to Mrs. Pinchington, whose report of the dinner-party seemed unforgiveable. She accompanied her visiter to the door, and ere they parted, our heroine found herself asking—"Who did you say has just opened these elegant shawls—Levy or Vanharlingen?"

"Aha"—replied Mrs. Squanderfield, with a sneer; "still hankering after new shawls—I saw them at Levy's: and I fear the naughty child is not going to get quite good all at once."

"I wish it were more easy to do so"—said Charlotte, colouring highly, and hastily returning to the parlour, where she sat down awhile and pondered. She then went up to her chamber, and took out some sewing. But her thread knotted and her needle broke, and she found she was not in the humour to sew. So she dressed herself, and went out, and habit directed her steps to Chestnut street. "At least"—thought she—"I may as well stop in at Levy's and *see* the shawls. 'Tis certainly pleasant to look at things that are new and elegant. But I am determined nothing shall tempt me to buy one."

She went into Levy's—saw the shawls—and *was* tempted to buy one. But she thought she would not mention it to her husband for some days at least; and, as a salve, she resolved on paying extra attention to his comforts and wishes.

"My dear Harvey"—said she, after helping him at dinner to a second piece of pie—"would you not like to have a carpenter or a cabinet-maker or some such person, to fit up the dining-room with bookshelves or book-cases. You can have it for a library if you wish, as in future we shall use the parlours entirely."

The delighted husband started from his seat, and replied by a kiss: and the same afternoon he bespoke both shelves and cases; and went to a bookseller's to begin his selection of books.

Next morning, shortly after breakfast, Harvey Woodbridge came home from his store with a look of consternation which much alarmed his wife; and as gently as he could, he broke to her the appalling intelligence of her mother's sudden death. A letter had just arrived from New York, written by her brother James, who stated that on the preceding day while a mantua-maker was fitting her for a new dress, Mrs. Stapleford had fallen down and instantly expired. Great was the horror of our heroine at this unexpected termination of her mother's mortal existence. And she and her husband set out by the first conveyance for New York, leaving a letter for Mr. Stapleford, who arrived that afternoon from Baltimore, and followed them in the mail.

The old gentleman was excessively shocked at his wife being so suddenly hurried to her last account, unprepared as she was for the awful change into eternity. He grieved exceedingly, and never made any further allusion to her faults. The day after the funeral he took the temperance pledge.

The fate of her vain, selfish, and heartless mother made a deep impression on our heroine, and soon completed the work of reformation which her father's representations had begun. The old gentleman was prevailed on to return with his daughter and his son-in-law, and to pass a few weeks with them in Philadelphia. Though her father was completely sobered, Charlotte soon perceived that, after the first shock had subsided, the husband of such a woman as Mrs. Stapleford, could not be inconsolable for her loss: and that (though he said nothing) he soon began to feel it a relief. "Ah!"—thought she—"I must make Harvey happy while I live—or he too will regard my death as a deliverance from misery."

On Mr. Stapleford's return to New York, it was arranged that his sister, an excellent woman who had been left a widow with a small income, should take charge of his house: and that his son James should again reside beneath the roof of his father. This change had a most salutary effect on the habits of the young man, and he found it easy to abandon the incipient vice which as yet had not fixed itself upon him.

Mr. Stapleford found an affectionate and intelligent companion in his amiable and considerate sister, (though she had always been in his wife's aversion) and now that he had a well-ordered and happy home, he had no inclination to seek for pleasure elsewhere. The entire abandonment of liquor soon restored his good looks and his self-respect: and his visits to Philadelphia were always anticipated with delight by his son-in-law and daughter.

We will not say that our heroine had not for a while occasional lapses from her good resolutions: but these aberrations gradually became slighter and less frequent. Love for her husband once awakened, she no longer took pleasure in wilfully annoying him, either by word or deed: and when she showed any indication of her former waywardness, a gentle remonstrance from Harvey always brought her to reason. Also, having so unceremoniously dismissed her two evil counsellors, she felt the advantage of being released from their blighting influence.

She now formed an intimacy with some of the most valuable of her husband's female friends. These ladies set her in every respect an excellent example, particularly in improving her mind, and cultivating a taste for books. Her heart and hand also expanded to the relief of the unfortunate and the indigent. Her reform at length became complete, both with regard to extravagance in dress and parsimony in housekeeping; and there is not, at this day, in Philadelphia, a more happy or a more popular couple than Mr. and Mrs. Woodbridge.

Nothing Morally Wrong

Part First

One warm afternoon in early summer, Mrs. Chesterwood was reclining on a sofa in her own apartment, and enjoying the delights of a loose gown and an entertaining book; believing herself secure from the interruption of visitors; as the heat of the weather seemed to make visiting impracticable while the sun remained above the horizon.

Suddenly, she heard a wheelbarrow stop on her own pavement; and afterwards, a loud and continuous ringing at her own door—the bell being jerked with all the might of somebody, and the peal keeping on and on.

Looking down through the slats of the Venetian shutters, Mrs. Chesterwood beheld a porter, out on the pavement, in charge of a large wooden box painted brownish red, and a square black leather sack resembling a half-sized mail-bag, especially as it was fastened by a very conspicuous padlock. But the porter (who looked rather ashamed) was not the bell-ringer; for a city colored man always understands bells. The performer on the bell-handle (she still had her gloveless hand upon it) was an unknown female of singular appearance, that stood on the door-step, parleying with Vance, Mrs. Chesterwood's waiter, who was strenuously "doubting if it was not some mistake," while she as strenuously insisted that "she knew she was right." The stranger finished by ordering Vance to assist in bringing in her baggage; and after paying the porter, she walked in herself.

Zuby, a much-indulged mulatto girl brought up in the family of Mrs. Chesterwood (who was a native of South Carolina, though now living in Philadelphia), ran up into the chamber of her mistress (for such she still called the daughter of her old master), eager to "tell her the news."

"Ma'am"—said the girl—"there's a very strange stranger below. Did you ever hear such a bell-ringing? She can't be used to bells, no how. Vance has put her in the back-parlor. Please to come down and look at her. She's uncommon queer."

"I cannot go down to a stranger till I have changed my dress"—answered Mrs. Chesterwood. "Give me my blue and white muslin."

"Oh! indeed, ma'am"—resumed Zuby—"you needn't make a bit of a stranger to *her*, at least as far as dress goes. Even her baggage is awful. There she came walking in after it as straight as a pyramid of Egypt, with a dreadful coarse straw basket in her hand, a flat-sided thing stuffed quite full and bulging."

"Did she send up no name?"—inquired Mrs. Chesterwood, arranging her dress before the toilet-glass.

"No indeed. When I asked her if she'd please to give me her name, she said it warn't of no consequence; and that's always a bad sign. People that is what they should be, need never be ashamed to tell their names to nobody. I expect she an't of no consequence herself. I reckon she's bent upon a long stay. Dear mistress, how I pity you. I afeard she'll be worse than them nephew boys of Mr. Chesterwood's which we had here all the Christmas holidays, and a'most broke our hearts with their scamperings and rompings. To be sure she an't likely to scamper and romp; but there's other ways of troubling us, and I reckon she'll show off somehow. There now, you needn't mind fixing your collar; she has none. It an't worth while to brush your hair—hers is all standing on end. She's in a drab-colored grass-cloth thing that's neither gown, nor frock, nor nothing else, (the stuff looks like buckram,) and a great big bonnet of the same. I wonder where she got her fashions?"

Mrs. Chesterwood went down to the back parlor, and there found the stranger walking about, and curiously examining various articles of furniture. The back of her dress was immensely full, much fuller than the forebody, and puffed out between her shoulders like a hump. On the contrary, the skirt was so plain behind, that the gathers actually left off before they reached the middle; and so full before, as to be heaped one gather on another. Also the body was shorter before than behind, and the skirt *vice versâ*. Her bonnet poked down over her face so as nearly to blind her; and behind it was so short as to display nearly all the back of her head and its rough switchy black hair which had once been cropped short, but looked now as if it again wanted the scissors. On seeing in a pier-glass the entrance of Mrs. Chesterwood, the stranger turned round, took off her bonnet and threw it on the piano, and introduced herself as Jonathina Judd from Connecticut; displaying a face that, though very strong-featured, was by no means ugly.

"And now"—said Jonathina, seating herself on an ottoman—"to keep you no longer in suspense (for suspense is painful)—(I presume you are the wife of Chesterwood)—I will just inform you that, having a great desire to see the world, I have come to pass a week or two in Philadelphia with you and your husband, who, you know, is, like myself, a native of Connecticut."

"Are you a relation of his?"—inquired Mrs. Chesterwood.

"No, not quite—though I was once very near being so. I am cousin to a first love of his, Fabiana Faber, to whom he was much attached while at Yale; and they would certainly have been married only she found that a New York merchant was more to her taste; and she went with her husband to Europe, and died there. I never saw Mr. Chesterwood but twice, for I did not live in New Haven. He was desperately in love with my cousin Fabiana; and I dare say for her sake he will recollect me, and show me every sort of civility. First love is always lasting. Men never love so well as the first time. I have forsworn the whole sex since Lawyer Snively deserted me for the Widow Sturgis, a woman noted for nothing but her wealth and finery."

Mrs. Chesterwood looked at her guest, and was not much surprised at hearing of this desertion.

"Now"—continued Miss Judd—"I will explain that an aunt who brought me up, left me, at her death, a small house in a village not far from New Haven, and money enough to support it and myself; and there I have been living for the last seven years, (with very good help, daughter to one of the neighbors,) and doing exactly as I please. I have relations in New Haven, of whom I am quite independent; therefore I do not care for any of their advice, and am determined to go where I please, and act as I please; always taking care to do nothing morally wrong. So every summer I take a journey somewhere to see the world; and having heard that Harry Chesterwood had married a southerner, and settled in Philadelphia, and being cousin to his first love, I have come to make a visit. Now here is a certificate of my respectability, signed by some of the best names in New Haven county, for I never travel without a character. Nobody ever should."

Mrs. Chesterwood, much amused at the *sang froid* and eccentricity of her guest, looked at the certificate, and found it every way satisfactory as to the respectability of Miss Jonathina Judd. She then desired the lady to excuse her for a few minutes, and left the room to give orders concerning the apartment to be prepared for her.

When Mrs. Chesterwood returned, she found Miss Judd had located herself in the front parlor, where, having raised the sashes and drawn up the blinds to their full height, she was seated at one of the windows, with the sun and dust pouring in upon her, and upon everything in the room.

"You see"—said she, on perceiving the entrance of her hostess—"I have begun already to enjoy the sights of Philadelphia. As yet I have seen nothing go by but people, and not many of them."

"The heat of the weather is now go great"—replied Mrs. Chesterwood—"that few persons venture out till after the sun has declined."

"Yes, I know"—resumed Jonathina—"many people have a prejudice against the sun. My idea is that we ought to enjoy everything, and be annoyed by nothing. That is my philosophy."

"Mine is"—replied Mrs. Chesterwood—"that there is nothing meritorious in quietly submitting to any inconvenience that we can easily prevent or remedy. For instance, are you not incommoded, at this very time, by the glare of the sun, and the dust raised by every carriage that passes along? You see how it has come in at the open window."

"I have long since made up my mind"—said Jonathina—"never to look upon the sun as a trouble. And as to the dust, only two carriages have passed by, and three omnibuses. I counted every one; for accuracy is desirable in all things. In the first omnibus were only three men, two women, and a child. In the second were—"

"And now, Miss Judd"—interrupted Mrs. Chesterwood—"your apartment is ready, and a servant is waiting to conduct you to it. You will probably wish to change your dress."

"Why?"—inquired Jonathina.

"After traveling in warm weather"—replied Mrs. Chesterwood—"most ladies wish to refresh themselves by a change of dress."

"I am not a lady"—resumed Miss Judd. "Don't be startled—at least I do not call myself by that absurd title. But I am a perfectly respectable woman, and I am above all the nonsense of empty forms and ceremonies. Now, in our republican country, the terms lady and gentleman are entirely out of place. They belong only to the aristocracies of Europe. We Americans should glory in being men and women. As to dress, I regard it merely as a covering; and I consider the time devoted to it as a mere waste of existence. To dress once a day is enough; and I was dressed clean this morning, before I left New York."

"Would you not like to arrange your hair?"—said Mrs. Chesterwood.

"I had it cut off, purposely to avoid all unnecessary trouble in arranging it."

"But really, Miss Judd, it is greatly disordered."

"So much the better"—(*looking in the glass*). "When it stands on end, the air passes through it, and it is far cooler when thus disordered, as you call it, than if pressed down close upon my head with a comb or brush. Now, that is the philosophy of hair."

"I think"—observed Mrs. Chesterwood—"as there is so little to be seen in the street during the heat of the afternoon, you would find it pleasanter to retire to your room, and repose till tea-time. You will find some new books there."

Then calling Zuby, who was standing just without the parlor door, Mrs. Chesterwood desired the girl to show Miss Judd up stairs, and attend to her. The baggage had already been carried up, and Jonathina sat down on her large box.

"There's chairs plenty"—said Zuby, handing her one. "Maybe you'd like to get something out of your trunk?'

"Good girl"—replied Jonathina, looking at her with great complaisance. "I feel a friendship for you already."

"La! ma'am!"—exclaimed Zuby.

"Yes I do, most sincerely; and early impressions are lasting. I foresee that you and I will be like two sisters."

"Oh! laws a mercy!"—exclaimed the colored girl.

"What name do you rejoice in?"—pursued Miss Judd.

"As to my name"—replied Zuby—"I can't say that I rejoice

in it much. If I'd had the naming of myself I should have chose a prettier. I should like to have been Rosalily or Blanchiflower. And I hate my name worse since the boys that worried us to death here last winter, had a way of saying—'Zuby, Zuby, rhymes to looby.'"

"I see we shall be friends"—resumed Miss Judd. "And now, Zuby, for a beginning, I will treat you with unbounded confidence."

"I don't know what bounded confidence is"—observed the girl—"but if you'll only use me well and be polite to me, that will do."

"No fear of my not being kind to you, Zuby. I take the utmost interest in your whole race."

"I can run pretty fast, to be sure"—said Zuby—"and I *could* race if there was any occasion. But Vance is the one that does most of the arrants.

"Your ideas no doubt are excellent"—remarked Jonathina—"but I see I must assist you in developing them to advantage. Ask me anything you wish to know, and say to me whatever you please."

"That I will"—answered Zuby, with much animation. "So what's the reason you wear such an ugly gown? And where did you get that horrid bonnet? And why don't you travel with a right sort of trunk and a right sort of bag? And what have you stuffed in that big basket? And why did you ring the bell so queer?"

"Stop! stop!"—exclaimed Miss Judd—"you are running on quite too fast. I must answer your questions one at a time."

"Do. So first of all—why did you let your mantuamaker spoil your gown so? Did you pay her? She did not deserve five cents. She must be the worst mantua-maker that ever lived. And your milliner is just as bad, for your bonnet's dreadful."

"The mantuamaker and the milliner were the same person"—said Miss Judd, looking down.

"So I should think. 'Twould be a pity if there were two such."

"It was myself"—said Jonathina. "As there is no reason why all women should not make their own clothes, *I* always do so, by way of setting an example to my neighbors."

"But la! ma'am"—rejoined Zuby—"I should think they would not be willing to follow these examples in their own gowns and bonnets. I guess not many have asked you for patterns."

"I have my own peculiar way of doing everything"—said Jonathina—"just according to my own taste and convenience. Zuby, I can teach all my ways to you."

"Oh! dear no, ma'am"—said the girl, curtseying—"I'd rather you'd not trouble yourself."

"Well, what next, Zuby?"

"And now about your baggage—it looks so uncommon."

"I see no reason for wasting money on handsome leather trunks with brass ornaments, or on showy carpet-bags, when they are exposed to all the accidents and wear and tear of traveling. So I have mine cheap and plain and strong, and such as can bear knocking about."

"There seems some sense in what you've said last. And now, what is it that stuffs out your straw basket so?"

"That is my new silk gown. I forgot it till my box and bag were both as full as they could hold; and there was no other way than to squeeze it into this basket."

"Oh, laws a mercy! did I ever hear the like? Who'd ever think of squeezing up a silk gown so as to cram it into a hand-basket? What a sight it will be! But now about that bell-ringing—why you pulled so long and hard. I don't care much about it myself, but Vance wants to know."

"I always ring a bell powerfully, and long enough to ensure its being heard. What is worth doing at all, is worth doing well."

"That sounds sensible, too. True enough, many people pull

the bell too weak, so that it don't sound; and then they're so vexed at Vance not coming to the door soon enough."

"The world is peopled with fools."

"Pretty much so. That's what Vance is always saying. And now"—continued the girl, emboldened by the familiarity of the stranger—"Vance and me are a good deal 'plexed and puzzled about knowing who you are, and what brought you to our house. To be sure, you're quite welcome—we're so very rich here, and not a bit mean, like the people next door. We could entertain the Queen of Mexico."

Jonathina Judd then very condescendingly (or rather without feeling it a condescension) gave the girl Zuby an account of herself, similar to that she had just related to Mrs. Chesterwood, and showed her also the certificate.

"Oh, la!"—exclaimed Zuby—"how wonderful—for white folks to be traveling with a passport, like colored folks in the southern states."

"'Tis a great pity they don't"—remarked Miss Judd. "It would then be known what they really are."

"That's sensible, too"—observed Zuby. "And now about that hair of yours—do let me fix it in some sort of Christian fashion. I seem like taking pity on you, and I want to see you look as handsome as you can."

Thus flattered, Miss Judd produced a comb and brush from the leather bag, and submitted her head to the dextrous hands of the mulatto girl, who, with no little trouble and perseverance, reduced her hair to a rational form, saying, as she finished—"Now mind and keep your hands still, and don't go rambling them through your head, and spoil all my work. There, now, look in the glass, and see what I've made of you."

"I am much obliged to you, Zuby."

"Not a bit you needn't be. I take pleasure in doing good. And now let me see that silk gown. It must be in a sad bungle, all crushed up and crammed into that narrow flat-sided basket; but maybe it an't quite past cure. Oh, mercy, mercy! what a heart-breaking sight! Just a hard-squeezed lump of striped silk. Why did you get stripes of two browns—red brown and brown brown? I don't know how to begin to open it out. Oh, this must be the body, all bundled up in the skirt. Where's the other sleeve? There *must* be two sleeves—at least there ought to be!"

"It does look somewhat disordered"—remarked Miss Judd, placidly, as Zuby shook out the gown.

"Disordered! It's the rumpledest thing I ever saw in all my born days! And how can it be otherwise?"

"Cannot it be ironed out?"

"I am afraid it's past irons. However, I'll take it down stairs, and try, out of pure pity, what can be done with it. I want Vance to see it. I'll try and make it look decent if you'll promise to put it on this evening, and wear it before mistress. Who knows but company may come in? And I should be so 'shamed here in a genteel house like ours, if strangers were to see you in that horrid thing you have on. Now take care, and keep your head right, and don't dare to lay down, or lean it against the wall, or get it all scrambled as bad as ever. Have you no collars in your box? You *must* have something of the sort. Give me one, and I'll take it down and smooth it over for you. I dare say it will want it."

"I have this plaid silk handkerchief"—said Miss Judd, producing one from her box. "When I am dressed, I wear this instead of a collar."

"Pah! wah!"—exclaimed Zuby. "Silk to silk, and nothing white about your neck? Nobody can look like a lady that way!"

And the mulatto girl was more than half right. No lady (or gentleman either) can possibly look well unless there is something white near the neck or face. It is surprising what an ungenteel effect the non-observance of this fact imparts, even to the most genteel personages.

The silk dress striped with two dull browns was skillfully ironed by Zuby, who, during the process, discovered in it numerous faults of making, which were "past cure, past help."

On her way to Miss Judd's room, she stopped in that of Mrs. Chesterwood, with the gown hanging over her arm, and said she had come to ask "a bit of charity of her mistress." The ever-ready purse of Mrs. Chesterwood was immediately taken out, when Zuby stopped her by saying—"Oh, no, ma'am; it an't for a real right-down beggar—it an't money I want. It's something for poor Miss Judd, who hasn't a white collar on the face of the earth. As for seeing her go about with a dingy plaid silk handkerchief on her neck, after I've had the trouble of damping and ironing this gown and trying to make it look fit to wear, 'tis what I can't give up to, no how. So as I really pity the poor thing, and am willing to take her in charge, and do all I can for her, now she's here in mistress's house, I've just come to ask if you won't lend her one of your collars to look decent in, till she can be made to get something white for herself. You needn't be particular which. Your very worst one will do."

Mrs. Chesterwood took out a neat French-worked collar, and desired Zuby to carry it to Miss Judd, with her compliments and a request that she would accept it.

"Do you give it to her to keep?"—asked Zuby.

"Yes—though perhaps it may offend her."

"Not a bit. She's very hard to affront. I can say anything I please to her already. She says she and me is to be like sisters—but, to be sure, that's all fudge. Besides, I don't want to. Any how, ma'am, you'd better give her up pretty much to me and Vance. He's willing to help me in taking the trouble off your hands. Phillis and Venus declare off, and say they don't want nothing to do with her, for they think she an't genteel. But I tell them they ought to excuse her, for it takes a great many people to make up a whole world full, and we can't expect everybody to be like ourselves, as Vance often tells us. Well, I'll go now and try how decent I can make the stranger person look."

When Mr. Chesterwood came home, his wife told him of the arrival of their extraordinary guest, the cousin of his first love. He smiled, and confessed that, while at college, he had really been smitten with Miss Fabiana Faber, a young lady who had nothing attractive but a pretty face, and who, after jilting himself, had made a very silly, heartless wife to a husband who knew nothing but how to make money, while she knew nothing but how to waste it. Miss Judd, though he had seen her but twice, he well recollected from her singular appearance, strange manners, and disregard of the usages of society. And he remembered the fair Fabiana saying that she was always ashamed of her cousin Jonathina.

"And now"—said Mrs. Chesterwood—"what shall we do with her?"

"We will do the best we can"—replied her husband—"and with a good grace, too. Let us not be annoyed by her peculiarities, but rather regard them as a source of amusement. It is pleasant sometimes to meet with a new and extraordinary variety of the human species."

"But her uninvited visit, with little, or rather no claim on our acquaintance"—remarked Mrs. Chesterwood—"denotes such entire ignorance of the world and its customs."

"Still, my dear Julia"—said Mr. Chesterwood—"think how little will be the annoyance of this visit to us, compared with the enjoyment it will afford to a lonely woman, who does us the honor to confide in our kindness and hospitality."

"What will our friends think of her?"—said the lady.

"Our friends"—he replied—"will soon understand that she is what is called 'a character,' and therefore not to be judged by common rules. I am very sure they will look on her with due indulgence."

"And now, dear Harry"—answered his wife—"I will try to regard this visitation in the most favorable light—at least it will afford me an opportunity of exercising a virtue for which I have hitherto had but little occasion—that of forbearance."

"Very well, my beloved Julia. And the more your virtues develop themselves, the more of course I shall love you."

Miss Jonathina Judd came down to tea, fresh from the improving hands of Zuby, who had managed to make the ill-fitting striped silk look somewhat passable, by means of taking in here and opening out there, and pinning down in some places and pinning up in others. Also, her hair had undergone an additional smoothing, and her neck was graced with the new collar. Mr. Chesterwood came forward, recognized Miss Judd, and talked to her of Connecticut.

As soon as tea was over, Jonathina went to her own room, and not coming down again, Mrs. Chesterwood sent Zuby to see after her.

Zuby carried up a light, and found Miss Judd sitting rocking in the rocking-chair, absorbed in thought, with her head thrown back and the moonbeams shining full in her face.

"Come in, Zuby"—said she—"and take a chair. Being tired of my journey, and wishing to feel quite easy, I have exchanged my silk dress for a loose gown."

"Well, to be sure"—exclaimed Zuby—"that loose gown, as you call it, is the tightest thing I ever saw in my life. It is so narrow that it meets nowhere. It must be hard work to drag it on, and harder still to wear it. But what's that thing on your head?"

"'Tis a new muslin cap of my own invention. It will do either for night or morning. I made it myself."

"More's the pity, for it's like nothing human. It is falling a'most over your eyes in front; and behind, it stands away out loose, and it don't half cover the back of your head. And even if it *was* deep enough in the neck (which it an't), there an't the least bit of a string to draw it in behind and make it sit close. What a cap!"

"The drawing-strings are exactly in front"—explained Jonathina, taking it off. "There are two of them; one just above the other—two strings run into short cases, rather low down on the forehead. See—when I pull this string, one case goes slanting up; and when I pull the other, that case goes slanting down."

"To be sure they will, when there's only one string in each case, and both the cases are run crooked—an infirm sort of bias."

Miss Judd stretched the cap over her knee, and began pulling at the two strings, neither of which were capable of being tied.

"This cap is quite an idea of my own"—said she. "The pattern has never been taken."

"So I suppose"—returned the girl. "'Tis certainly a new notion. I should call it the see-saw pattern—for that's the way the strings go when you pull them, one up and one down, and no way of bringing them together so as to tie decently. If they *are* to go flying, two short bits of tape an't much of ornaments."

"Tastes are different, Zuby"—remarked Miss Judd.

"Yes, yes, I know that very well. As Vance says—'Some men like good meat, and some prefer rank pison.' But I don't think it's the same with caps, for here's one that can suit no Christian taste. However, let me have it, and try if I can make it so that it will stick on your head. If this is your style of caps, no wonder your hair is so scrabbly."

Zuby then took the cap, and endeavored to render it wearable by plaiting in and pinning the back; and forming the front into something like a shape, though obliged to leave the see-saw strings inactive.

"Now, Miss Judd"—said Zuby—"it's my solemon request that you get a new set of things now you've the pleasure of being in Philadelphy, so as not to disgrace us. And let them all be made by Christian people, and not by yourself."

"All my garments are quite good enough for me"—said Jonathina.

"I suppose they are—but then they're not good enough for us. We're very genteel here. And as Vance says—'when you're staying in Roman families, you should try to do like Romans.' Of course, Philadelphy's just the same as Rome. Now, to-night, Miss Judd, when you're laying in your silent bed, think of what I've been a saying to you. Remember, it's all for your own good."

"I'm not going to bed yet awhile"—said Miss Judd. "I'm getting over my fatigue, and I'll go down stairs, and sit with Mr. and Mrs. Chesterwood."

"What, in this rig?"

"Why not? You cannot suppose I'll dress up in my silk again at nine o'clock in the evening?"

"No, no; I don't suppose it—and I don't wish it. And all your hair to be fixed, too? But as for your setting in the parlor in this trim with ladies and gentlemen, it's quite out of all reason, and it won't do. Suppose visitors should come in! What would they think?"

"I'm perfectly indifferent as to what is thought of me, as long as I do nothing morally wrong. That is my philosophy."

"If that's what you call phosophy, I'm glad I han't none of it. My experience is that it's better to act wrong than foolish. Come now, be good, and stay up stairs and look at the moon, or read a book, or go to bed, or do any reasonable thing, and I'll bring you some fruit and cake, for we always have such things in the evening."

Finally, Miss Judd was prevailed on to remain in her room, and be seen no more that night.

Next morning when it was scarcely light enough to discern objects distinctly, a going about was heard in the house, and an opening of doors and windows.

"The servants are up unusually early"—said Mr. Chesterwood.

"I fear"—replied his wife—"it is not the servants, but your first love's cousin. I have no doubt that rising with the lark is 'her custom always in the morning.'"

And Miss Judd it really was. She came down in her grass-cloth gown, threw up the sashes, and leaned far out of one of the front parlor windows, gazing upon the silent street. It was too early even to see the working-people going to commence the labors of the day. Not a horse, not a vehicle was in view; but there was, at times, a distant sound as from another street, of market carts coming into town. The milk-men and the bakers, and the newspaper carriers, had not yet commenced their rounds. It was even too early for the noted pavement-washing of Philadelphia.

When tired of looking at nothing, Jonathina threw open the windows of the *back* parlor, and exercised herself by a promenade through both rooms, and then sat down at a table, and took up a book which lay there.

At length the city began to waken. Mr. Chesterwood's servants were not sluggards, and Vance came in to put the parlors in order.

"I am afraid, ma'am, I shall discommode you"—said the colored man.

"Oh, don't mind *me*"—replied Miss Judd. "Sweep away—brush away—dust away. I wish to see how parlors are cleaned in Philadelphia. I am traveling for improvement; I don't mind trifles. And in the pursuit of knowledge, I am not easily troubled or annoyed with anything. Then I have not the least bit of pride."

"I fear, ma'am, you'll be covered with dust"—said Vance, sweeping round her.

"Then sweep lightly, and raise as little dust as possible"—persisted Miss Judd. "The color of my dress is excellent for hiding it."

She changed from seat to seat, always going to the very place that was most inconvenient, and always most particularly in Vance's way. He brought in a small tub and a house-cloth, and began to wash the summer matting that covered the parlor floors.

"Well, Vance, what are you doing now?"

"I'm washing the floor-mat with salt and water, to keep it from turning brown."

"Well, now, that's a thing I never knew before. 'Live and learn,' says the proverb."

"Yes, ma'am. If we choose to continue living, we must expect to pick up learning."

"Now, Vance, let me wash a little of that matting. I should like to try how it is done."

"Oh, no, ma'am; I'd rather you wouldn't. You know it injures the soup if too many cooks are seasoning at it."

"Now you talk of cooks"—said Jonathina—"I think I'll go into the kitchen and see how *your* cook gets breakfast."

"Excuse me, ma'am, but please don't. I beg your pardon, ma'am—but Venus will be so put out."

"I travel for improvement. I'm seeing the world"—said Miss Judd, pertinaciously walking out of the room.

She found her way to the kitchen; first falling down stairs. Hearing the noise, the women ran out to see what was coming. But she had cleverly picked herself up; and protesting she was not hurt, Miss Judd followed Venus and Phillis into the culinary region.

Here she went all round, examining everything; investigating the contents of the dresser-drawers; taking down the tins, &c., and neglecting to return them to their places; also looking into the store-closet, and inspecting the barrels and boxes. All this much discomfited Venus, and highly diverted Phillis. Then seating herself on a settle-bench near the sink, Miss Jonathina

Judd informed the colored women "that she was not proud."

"Very likely, ma'am"—said Venus. "There's five or six different sorts of pride. Which sort do you mean that you an't?"

"No sort"—replied Jonathina. "I have a perpetual thirst for knowledge; and I'm curious to know how you cook. So I will stay here to see you get breakfast. I expect to learn a great deal by seeing your process."

"I don't know what a process is"—said Venus. "It is a dish I'm not up to. I never could talk dick in my life."

"Dick! What language is that?"

"She means dicksonary—hard words"—explained Phillis. "We colored folks often say dick for shortness."

"Well, Venus"—pursued Jonathina—"when are you going to begin getting breakfast?"

"I'm very narvous"—was the reply—"and I can't cook if anybody's looking at me."

"Oh, you need not mind *me*"—said Miss Judd.

"Why not?"—inquired Venus.

At this juncture came in Zuby, who, seeing Miss Judd, exclaimed—"Well, now, if ever! Why, Miss Judd, what brought *you* down here? This is against all the laws of the land, and it won't do. Please go up stairs, and settle to something. We shall have no breakfast got this way."

Finally, Jonathina was induced to return to the parlor, which was now in order; but she soon disordered it. She rambled listlessly about both rooms, sat on all the chairs; again raised the window-blinds, and leaned out; saw the milkman leave milk and cream, and the baker leave bread and rolls; and inquired of the first if he watered his milk, and of the second if he adulterated his flour; and then told them she only asked for information. At last, seeing several persons pass by with baskets and butter-kettles, as if they were going to purchase their day's provision, she bethought herself of following some of them, till she found her way to the famous Philadelphia market. So she ran up for her bonnet; threw on a very hot and unsuitable shawl, and set off after a gentleman who (having sent on his servant man in advance) issued from the next house, himself carrying a small basket for fruit. This gentleman looked round several times to see what strange being seemed to be pursuing him.

When Mrs. Chesterwood came down, she inquired after Miss Judd; and Zuby told her, with great glee, that she had seen her "pacing full tilt, as hard as she could, after Mr. Allison, on his way to market."

"I fear she will lose herself"—said Mrs. Chesterwood.

"No danger"—answered Zuby. "I heard her say she could always find her way everywhere. And if she gets lost and never is found, so much the better."

An hour passed on—still Jonathina came not. Mr. Chesterwood took his breakfast alone, that he might hasten to his counting-house; but Mrs. Chesterwood was unwilling to sit down to hers before the return of their guest. Still there was no sign of Jonathina, though Vance went out repeatedly, and stood at the corner, looking up and down the street in quest of her—but all in vain.

Part Second

At last, Miss Jonathina Judd was descried in the act of turning the corner eating a huge ginger-cake, and with the other hand awkwardly holding on to the handle of a market-basket, which was carried by a tall, stout black boy of eighteen or nineteen, the hired servant of Mr. Allison. The boy looked much annoyed at the attention and wonderment attracted by his unusual assistant, as most of the people stared and laughed in passing. Vance immediately hastened forward, and, taking the basket himself, informed Miss Judd that Mrs. Chesterwood had long been waiting breakfast for her. The two servants then walked together, and the lady went before them.

"Samp"—said Vance, aside to his companion—"I thought you were a strong man like your namesake. How could you let a woman (lady, I mean) help you carry your basket? Such doings here in Philadelphia is a monstrosity."

"It ain't my fault"—replied Sampson, pouting—"the woman—the lady knows she came up and *pro*posed it herself. She said the basket was too heavy for me; which it ain't. I'm as strong as a black horse, be his color what it may. But she laid hold of the handle, and would subsist on helping me, for all I told her that ladies never help colored folks to carry baskets."

"More shame for them"—observed Jonathina, overhearing their talk. "I feel as if I had a mission to reform Philadelphia."

"Oh, please ma'am"—exclaimed Vance—"do take permission to deform some other place! Philadelphia is as stubborn as a mule in all its ways, and won't ever be better. There's no making a purse of handsome silk out of the rough, hairy ears of a large, old pig."

As soon as Miss Judd had got into the house, the two colored men, lagging behind, indulged in a laugh at her expense.

"If you'd only seen that strange woman"—said Samp—"following us about in the market, Mr. Allison dodging her all the time, and she keeping close behind, and stopping at the stalls wherever we stopped, and persuading the market people not to ask such high prices, and thereby affronting some of them, and setting a-laughing the people that was about. So Mr. Allison was glad to cut short his marketing, and slip out of the market-house, and run across to his store."

"I have it"—said Vance, pondering, and looking wise. "She is a woman of a very oncommon specie, and has a great notion of doing all the good she can, only she don't know how."

Meantime, Jonathina, seated at the breakfast-table, was descanting on the beauties of Philadelphia market, or rather of the marketing. After breakfast, Mrs. Chesterwood, well aware that the wardrobe of her guest required improvement, asked Miss Judd if she would like to visit some of the Philadelphia shops.

"Are you going shopping yourself?"—was Jonathina's answer. "If you are, and want a companion, I will cheerfully go with you. For my own part, I require nothing; always considering dress as below the dignity of woman."

"Not quite"—said her hostess. "If we live in the world, we must in some measure conform to its usages."

"That depends on what we understand by the world"—replied Jonathina. "As long as we do nothing morally wrong, I think we are not obliged, in dress or in anything else, to follow fashions that originate we do not know how, and are introduced by we do not know whom. What a pleasing variety there would be, if we all wore garments according to our taste and convenience, and if we did everything else in the same independent way."

"As to consulting nothing but our own convenience in our actions"—replied Mrs. Chesterwood—"we could not always do so without infringing on the comfort and convenience of others. Also, by dressing well, and in decided good taste, we present agreeable objects to the eyes of those who see us, and offer a pleasure to their sense of sight."

"Not if they are women"—replied Miss Judd. "Women are more likely to envy them that admire a well-dressed female. For my part, I have always been careful never to excite envy. Rather than do so, I would 'hide my lights under a bushel.' As to having a variety of dresses at once, what folly it is! Would it not be far more rational to get but one at a time, and wear that only, as long as it lasted? What a saving of money that might be better bestowed! Now, I became so tired of mantua-makers and milliners, that I long since resolved on making my own gowns, caps, and bonnets; and that without bestowing much time, thought, or pains on such idle work, or caring whether the things exactly fitted me or not; considering them only as coverings. I am always, when thus employed, anxious to get through, and return to the improvement of my mind, and the acquirement of knowledge. Sometimes, indeed, by way of exercising my inventive genius, I try new ways of constructing articles of raiment; but, if not successful, I wear them all the same, considering my looks as entirely my own affair."

"But things that are ill made are seldom comfortable"—observed Mrs. Chesterwood.

"Then it is our duty to accommodate ourselves to discomforts, and to be fastidious about nothing"—replied Jonathina. "For my part, I have serious thoughts of giving up all regular gowns and frocks, and making mine in the loose forms of wrappers or slips; and of nothing more expensive than calico; wearing always shoes the true shape of my feet; keeping my hair always cut closely to my head so as never to be more than an inch long; and covering it, when I go out, with a sun-bonnet or hood, having attached to it a long cape descending below my waist, so as to save the trouble of a shawl."

"A very sensible and convenient costume, no doubt"—said Mrs. Chesterwood—"but I hope you will not adopt it while in Philadelphia."

"Why not? Is there any danger of my being either prosecuted or persecuted for doing so? Would I be insulted, abused, fined, or imprisoned?"

"Neither; but you might be ridiculed. And it requires much courage to encounter 'the world's dread laugh.'"

"I have no fear of that, in a good cause"—was Jonathina's answer. "And I think I could convince even the Philadelphians that such a system of dress, if steadily pursued, would render their women both healthy and wealthy—ay, and wise also. Let me begin with you as my first pupil."

"There is much truth in your theory"—said Mrs. Chesterwood—"but I fear there will be great difficulty in reducing it to practice. I, for one, have not courage to begin. And yet I never conform so implicitly to the prevailing fashion, as to wear anything that I know to be unbecoming, or uncomfortable."

Mrs. Chesterwood had left the room to prepare for her shopping expedition, and Jonathina, as usual, was seeing the world from one of the front parlor windows, when Vance came in to clear away the table, and Zuby soon followed after.

"Miss Judd"—said he, with one of his second-best bows—"plenty to eat is as good as a great dinner-party; and some things may be reformed on Monday, some on Wednesday, and some on Saturday."

"Which means"—said Zuby—"that 'Enough's as good as a feast,' and 'There's a time for all things.'"

"Very true"—replied Jonathina—"but what have these proverbs to do with me?"

"Only this"—answered Zuby—"that there's been quite enough of your setting for ever at these here windows, and it's time you would quit practicing it."

"Excuse my resumption, ma'am, and Zuby's also"—said Vance, with his third-best bow—"but if you would only ingratify me so far as to allow the heat, the sun, and dust to be propelled from this room—if you'd only do me the honor to take the air in your own apartment, and let me shut the shutters."

"Miss Judd"—added Zuby—"don't be 'fronted—but all your ways is awful; and them that don't know nothing of human natur, ought to be learnt it till they do. Don't you understand yet that though mistress is too polite to say anything about it, we can't have the parlors heatened, and the furniture dustified, that you may sit at the windows looking out for prospects. Your own room's your castle, or your abbey, or your tower of strength, or whatever you choose to call it, and there you may do just as you choose about most things."

"There, you can take the privilege"—added Vance.

"Well, well"—replied Jonathina—"I see I am nothing more than a child in your hands—a mere nose of wax, to be moulded any way. But I don't know that I would let white people talk to me in this manner."

So saying, she rose and departed.

"What does she mean by a mouldy nose of wax?"—said Vance, looking perplexed.

"I am sure I don't pretend to fathom out half her meanings"—said Zuby—"and I neither know nor care. I suppose she's understood in New Haven, wherever that may be, or in that other place she calls Connecticut. As to her own nose, I looked at it when she spoke, and it seemed pretty much like other people's."

In passing the door of Mrs. Chesterwood's room, she saw her hostess equipping herself for walking, and Jonathina said to her—"Upon farther consideration, I think I had best see some of the Philadelphia stores. It will increase my stock of knowledge. I'll just put on my bonnet, and then I shall be ready to accompany you. Of course, this dress will do?"

Mrs. Chesterwood looked at the "suit of buckram," and knew that it would not do at all. She had supposed, when she invited Miss Judd to accompany her, that her guest would, of course, understand that such a costume was not admissible for a shopping expedition in a large city. However, before Mrs. Chesterwood had arranged a gentle and delicate reply, Miss Judd had entered her own apartment, put on her hideous bonnet, and was seeking her gloves, which were always lost.

Presently entered Zuby, with a plaid silk dress of Mrs. Chesterwood's on her arm, and in her hand a straw bonnet, trimmed with white.

"There now, Miss Judd"—said the girl—"see what it is to fall among quality! We are so very rich, that the mistress has plenty of everything; and so she lends you this purple and green plaid silk, and one of her own straw bonnets; for she has two, and could have two-and-twenty if she wanted them. I told her it was better to try and make you look decent than to go out with such an object as you are now. It ain't likely mistress's dress will fit you, but may be it can be managed somehow."

"I have concluded to be passive"—said Miss Judd.

"Best *for* you. There now—we've dragged it on, pretty harmonious. To be sure it's a great deal too long, but then it will cover your feet the better. The body won't meet, but any pulling or squeezing possible or probable; so it will have to go flying. But I can pin over the skirt-slit, so that *it* won't gape. And then, here's the cape to it; and large capes hides a multitude of sins—I mean in dress-bodies. There—finish with the pretty muslin-worked collar mistress gave you. And now, let me flatten down that hair of yours, and tie on the straw bonnet. Oh! mercy! mistress's pretty bonnet won't come down on you. It coggles right up on the top of your head. Let me give it another pull with both hands. Any how, it's better than that horror of your own. There, now, I've made the best of you I could. And how well you take mistress's lending you her clothes! You don't seem the least hurt about it."

"Why should I?"—answered Miss Judd. "All the kindnesses I receive I take as things of course, due from one human being to another. Our bounden duty is to do all the good we can to our fellow-creatures, and to accept without reluctance all favors that are offered to us. By so doing, we confer a favor on the givers and reward them for their generosity. This is my philosophy."

"I can't say I quite understand your sort of phosophy"—said Zuby. "But I can tell you the best way of paying mistress, and you may do it this day—try and behave yourself like other people; and don't disgrace her in the street, and make her ashamed of you in the shops."

Mrs. Chesterwood and her eccentric guest proceeded towards Chestnut street; Miss Judd frequently lagging behind, to look after things and people; and, in her thirst for knowledge, stopping at a corner where there was a fruit and candy-stall, and inquiring of its keeper if he paid any rent for the place, and what were his average profits. She ended by the purchase of some dry dates, all clodded into a lump, which she employed her fingers in separating, after she had overtaken Mrs. Chesterwood. While thus picking the dates apart, she was constrained to carry her parasol under her arm, from whence it slipped down and rolled towards the gutter; and, in running after and recovering it, she dropped her dates, which, to Mrs. Chesterwood's great regret, were picked up and restored to her by an over-honest chimney sweep. Miss Judd, with much praise of his integrity, generously rewarded the boy by a free gift of the aforesaid dates, with which, instead of crying "largesse," he walked away grinning.

After gazing a long time at the display in the windows, she followed Mrs. Chesterwood into one of the most fashionable and elegant stores in Chestnut street. That lady having soon selected a dress for herself, asked her companion, in a low voice, if she had any inclination to do the same.

"I do not want a dress"—replied Jonathina. "I have two already—three, indeed—two at your house, and one at home."

The attendants behind the counter looked down and bit their lips. Mrs. Chesterwood first blushed and then smiled.

"Perhaps, however"—proceeded Jonathina—"now that I am in Philadelphia, I may as well get another. But as I really want none, at present, I will not go beyond a dark muslin de laine."

"For warm summer weather?"—said Mrs. Chesterwood, deprecatingly.

"Oh no—I shall lay it by till fall."

Mrs. Chesterwood took her aside, and said to her—"Allow

me, Miss Judd, for the sake of your cousin, my husband's first love, to present you with a foulard."

"What is that?"—inquired Jonathina.

"A summer silk, printed in colors. There is always a handsome variety in this store. Permit me to select one for you."

"Just as you please"—replied Miss Judd. "To gratify *you*, I willingly accept it."

Mrs. Chesterwood chose for her a very pretty olive and pink foulard, and desired it to be sent immediately to a dressmaker's in the neighborhood, whom she indicated. She then conducted her guest to a milliner's; and, having purchased a morning cap for herself, she induced Miss Judd to try on several drawn or casing bonnets, till she found one of lavender-colored silk that fitted her, and which she was prevailed to take into immediate use, leaving the other to be sent home. Mrs. Chesterwood then conveyed her to the dressmaker's, and she was fitted for the foulard, which was promised to be completed by the next afternoon.

The morning tour was finished at a confectioner's, where they took ice cream and almond cake, and where Jonathina, ever anxious for knowledge, stayed behind Mrs. Chesterwood, to ask the ingredients of the various bonbons, or sugar things in the glass cases, and to inquire how they were made, of the girls at the counter, who, of course, knew no particulars of the composition.

The day passed on much as might be expected; Mr. Chesterwood, when at home, relieving his wife in the task of conversing with Miss Judd, who, at the desire of her hostess, continued to wear the plaid silk dress she had sent her, the cape concealing that the body could be fastened by only one hook.

Several days elapsed, developing new traits of singularity in Miss Jonathina Judd, who, meanwhile, was taken by the Chesterwoods to all the usual sights of Philadelphia. Her eccentricity would have been somewhat amusing to her entertainers, had it not also been so very inconvenient. If checked in one place, or rather in one thing, she was sure to break out in another. Yet, with scarcely a particle of common sense or practical knowledge, and with a total absence of good taste and judgment, she possessed some crude ideas that, if "licked into shape," might have produced some good results. Pride she had none, neither false pride nor proper pride; or rather, she was totally devoid of self-respect in most things that were not "morally wrong." She evinced no gratitude for favors bestowed on her, for she supposed the continual exercise of kindness a pleasurable duty, which all who had the means were bound to perform. She had not sufficient tact to perceive that what she called her independent way of acting might probably encroach upon the convenience of those about her, and that, in professing to be *above* the forms of polished society, she rather degraded than elevated herself. She understood nothing of the world, notwithstanding her perpetual pursuit of knowledge. She was full of theory, which she knew not how to bring into practice; and what she did practice, was either in ignorance, or in defiance of the observances that polish away the roughnesses of human nature, and render social intercourse smooth and agreeable.

"Vance"—said the mulatto girl Zuby—"if it wasn't for me and you, I don't know what would be done with Miss Judd. She minds nobody but us; and for my part, I have to be very sharp with her, for I can't trouble myself, like you, to be polite to all manner of geese and goobies; 'specially them that are phosophers. Well, thank fortune, she's now in her second week. I often wonder she don't get lost, in her wanderings and meanderings up town and down town, and even over Schuylkill. But no; like a bad penny, she is sure to come back to us."

"Her always returning to us like an impassable copper"—said Vance—"proves what I have long believed—that the streets of

Philadelphia are straight and regular, crossing one another by degrees of forty-five angles, and therefore easy to find your way round a square."

"She has often asked me to go out with her"—said Zuby—"but I know better than that. I ain't going to bemean myself in the street, as company for any such outlandish person, with her queer walk, and queer looks, and queer ways, and every body staring at her. Besides, I prefer going into public with my own color. It ain't fashionable to walk with white people."

It being summer, nearly all the friends of Mr. and Mrs. Chesterwood had left town, or were busily preparing to do so, therefore few visitors came to the house. Among those who, like the Chesterwoods, intended remaining in the city till July, were Mr. and Mrs. Penafield, who, living in the next street, came round to pass an evening with the host and hostess of our heroine. Mr. Penafield and Mr. Chesterwood sat together on an ottoman discussing the late news from Europe, and its probable effect on our own country; and Mrs. Penafield, who always brought her work, placed herself at a sofa-table, with Miss Judd (to whom she had been introduced) reclining beside her; and Mrs. Chesterwood sitting opposite with her netting. Presently a neighboring lady came in, who preferred being near a window, and Mrs. Chesterwood changed her seat, and left Jonathina and Mrs. Penafield to entertain each other, Miss Judd being that evening in a very eloquent disposition.

Mrs. Penafield was habitually taciturn, and like many other persons who had "a great genius for silence," she was said, by some of her acquaintances, to be a very sensible, shrewd woman, if you only knew her well. Others only allowed her the reputation of being a good hearer. And so she was, if good hearing consists in sitting perfectly mute during the longest discourse, never offering either objection or assent to anything, and rarely making the slightest comment. Also, her perpetually sewing was sufficiently interesting to keep her awake; and therefore she never shocked a determined talker by appearing sleepy or tired. But though she always heard passively, it was not so sure that she listened understandingly.

Miss Judd, that evening, was in a very loquacious, or rather a very declamatory humor, and, happy in securing such a hearer, held forth to Mrs. Penafield on fourierism, transcendentalism, millerism, and the whole circle of new isms, leaning towards all of them, but not quite a proselyte to any, and with very imperfect ideas of each.[1] At parting, she said to her new friend, as she termed her—"My dear Mrs. Penafield, I think it a privilege to have enjoyed so much of your society. Our conversation has given me great pleasure. I have met with no one whose ideas and feelings are so much after my own mind and heart. I hope soon to renew our interesting dialogue."

Mrs. Penafield, who did not know herself to be a silent woman, felt rather flattered at these compliments to her conversational powers; and told Miss Judd she should be very happy to see her at her own house, before she left town.

"Where do you live?"—asked Jonathina.

Mrs. Penafield, thus taken at her word, could do no less than designate the street and number; and Miss Judd assured her new friend that she might depend on seeing a great deal of her.

When the Penafields had gone—"Really"—said Jonathina—"that is a most charming little woman. We have enjoyed together 'the feast of reason, and the flow of soul.'[2] Her opinions on all subjects seem to correspond with mine."

The Chesterwoods smiled, but would not disturb her dream of delight by any remarks that might hint the possibility of her being mistaken.

Next morning, at the unseasonable hour of nine o'clock, Jonathina put on her new foulard dress, and, without notifying her intention, sallied forth to make a visit to Mrs. Penafield. It may be proper to mention, that, after the foulard came home, Zuby resolved that Miss Judd should wear no other while a guest at her mistress's house; and had, therefore, carried off and hidden the obnoxious grass-cloth, and the "still horrider brown stripe;" telling Jonathina that she would let her have them again when packing up to return home. "But till then"—said she—"I won't trust you with either of *them* two; for fear you should again disgrace us all by wearing the frights. No, no—I'm determined you shall stick to the foulard all the time you're here."

"I'm really under strange government"—said Jonathina.

"Be thankful, then, that you are"—replied Zuby. "Mistress don't know anything about managing queer folks, so I have taken the trouble off her hands—me and Vance."

To proceed—Mrs. Penafield was rather surprised to receive at so early an hour a visit from her new friend, who, when the street door was opened, had perceived that lady in the back porch or piazza, and therefore walked directly through, and presented herself. Supposing that this early visit would be merely a short call, Mrs. Penafield did not, on asking her to be seated, invite Miss Judd to take off her bonnet, but Jonathina removed it of her own accord. The porch was shaded by a trellis thickly overgrown with honeysuckles and climbing roses, and in summer was the favorite sitting and sewing place of Mrs. Penafield, the morning sun not shining in that direction. Her work-basket stood on the settee beside her, and she was earnestly engaged in making a patchwork chair-cover, according to the most approved and tedious honeycomb pattern. She resumed her sewing, and Miss Judd commenced a discourse on algebra, from whence she went to architecture, and afterwards to chemistry, and then again to mineralogy; Mrs. Penafield either not speaking at all, or, when her opinion was asked, replying in vague monosyllables, meaning anything, or nothing.

Miss Judd talked on, and sat on, till the cook came to take

orders for dinner. Mrs. Penafield rose, and begged her guest to excuse her while she attended to some business in the storeroom.

"Use no ceremony with me"—replied Jonathina—"only send one of your daughters to take your place, and I will pursue with her the last subject we have been discussing."

"I have no daughters"—answered Mrs. Penafield.

"One of your sons, then. I like the conversation of 'ingenuous youth.'"

"My sons are both at an academy, out of town. I fear I must leave you alone for a short time."

"Oh, never mind! Just let me have a book—always to me an interesting companion."

"Our books are all in the library"—replied Mrs. Penafield. "And my husband has the key away with him. I never read myself; having no time whatever."

"Surprising! How then did you acquire the vast fund of knowledge that I discover in your conversation? I have it! Your husband reads to you."

Mrs. Penafield did not say.

"Well, no matter. Go and attend to your household affairs, and I can sit here and meditate till your return. I will arrange some new perceptions on the subject of transcendentalism, and you shall have the benefit."

Mrs. Penafield gasped at the idea; but was still more annoyed when Jonathina, on second thoughts, proposed accompanying her to the storeroom to see how it was arranged, and what was in it, saying—"In the pursuit of knowledge, I think no investigation too humble—even that of sugar and soap, and coffee and candles."

To this proposal Mrs. Penafield, with all her suavity, would not consent, but could devise no better way of extricating herself from the embarrassment of a refusal than by saying—"Not today; the storeroom is not in perfect order—that is, to be sure—(I hope nothing in *my* house is ever out of order)—but still, I would rather the storeroom should not to-day be visited by a stranger."

"Oh, very well"—replied Jonathina. "I can see it some other time. I shall be often with you, while I remain in town."

"So much the worse"—thought her hostess.

When Mrs. Penafield returned, she found Miss Judd had gathered some of the honeysuckles that clustered over the pillars of the porch, and was separating their parts with a pair of little scissors from the work-basket, and examining their construction as she clipped them about the floor.

"You find me botanizing"—said she. "I was once devoted to that study, but have nearly given it up, finding the structure of the human mind of far more importance to a thinking being than the form of a flower. Of course, that is also your opinion."[2]

"Yes"—replied Mrs. Penafield.

"According to Dugald Stewart"[3]—proceeded Jonathina—and she then set sail on what she supposed the full stream of metaphysics; touching afterwards on the coasts of ancient history, antediluvian geography, and modern political economy—while, not to these, but to her patchwork, did the attention of her auditress "most seriously incline."

The dining hour approached; but still Miss Jonathina Judd sat on, and talked on. Mr. Penafield came home, and brought with him his partner, Mrs. William Wicklesby, a widower, whose wife was sister to Mrs. Penafield, and since her death he had continued to keep house as before.

Mr. Wicklesby had the character of being a prim, precise little man, and over-fastidious about everything. So Mr. Penafield, on seeing Miss Judd, regretted having asked his brother-in-law to come home with him to dinner. On being introduced to that remarkable personage, Mr. Wicklesby looked at her with as much evident wonder as civility would allow. She was then standing erect, and in the very act of smoothing down with both hands her disordered hair, having just remembered that she had forgotten to perform this highly judicious ceremony long ago, after removing her bonnet. Dinner being immediately announced, Mr. Penafield offered his arm to conduct her to the dinner-table; but she rejected it, saying—"No, no; give your arm to Mrs. Penafield. I never like to part man and wife." Mr. Wicklesby then presented his to Miss Judd; and she said—"Where is the necessity? Cannot I walk to the dinner table without assistance? I am trying to improve society, by setting my face against all useless ceremonies—including all fashions, and all follies."

Mr. Wicklesby could scarcely eat his dinner for looking at and listening to the fair Jonathina, while she held forth on various subjects. And Mr. and Mrs. Penafield could not forbear exchanging glances; expecting every moment to see their fastidious brother-in-law rise from his chair and make an excuse for leaving the house. But he did not.

A reasonable time had elapsed after dinner, and still Miss Judd evinced no symptoms of departure. So the weary Mrs. Penafield invited her guest up stairs, and offered her the loan of a loose dress, in which she might take a *siesta*. Jonathina declined; averring that she was not the least sleepy, that she felt quite comfortable in the dress she had on; and that all she desired was the key of the library. This was immediately obtained from Mr. Penafield; and his wife, conducting our heroine to this abode of books, left her there, and retired to her own room.

As the two gentlemen walked down to their place of business, Mr. Penafield spoke of Miss Judd, and her peculiarities.

"She is certainly a very strange woman"—replied Mr. Wicklesby—"quite a curiosity. I should really like to see some more of her. Most women are so much alike, that it is quite refreshing to meet with one a little different from the general character of the sex."

"Then come back with me to tea"—said Mr. Penafield—"for doubtless we shall still find her there. I will guarantee your seeing enough of her."

"'Tis a sign she likes your house, and its society"—observed Wicklesby.

They did find her there.

When tea was over, Miss Judd still said nothing that savored of her concluding her long, long morning call. Establishing herself at a window, whither Mr. Wicklesby followed, and seated himself near her, she talked, and talked, and talked; but not now to a regardless auditor; for the attentive ears of the gentleman drank in every word she said; and he came to the conclusion that she had more mind, and more knowledge, than any woman he had ever heard. Neither did he listen in entire silence; but whenever he could catch an opportunity, he uttered something expressive of approbation. Meanwhile, Mrs. Penafield sat at the sofa-table, assiduously plying her needle; and her husband amused himself with a new book.

But no visit is quite interminable, and the very longest must at last have an end. It is true we have heard of a lady in our native city, who made a morning call, and stayed eleven years; but that case is the only one on record, and therefore deserves a place in the Annals of Philadelphia.

When indications were heard and seen, of the servants going round to shut up the house, Jonathina arose, and began to talk about her bonnet. It was brought to her, with great alacrity; and she took leave of the Penafields; telling them that she had derived so much pleasure and improvement, and so many new ideas, from her visit, that she should very soon repeat it.

Mr. Wicklesby formally requested the honor of escorting her home; and she informally replied, that the honor would be mutual. Mr. Wicklesby felt himself flattered—or, rather, he wished in his mind that all women were equally sincere.

He gallanted her to the door of the Chesterwoods, and, as soon as it was opened, made his bow and went home; his thoughts full of this extraordinary woman, the like of whom he had never seen.

"La! Miss Judd"—exclaimed Zuby, who had followed Vance when he answered the door-bell—"where *have* you been all this blessed day? You've westigated the whole city, long ago; so I concluded you must have been pirating about Manayunk, or Passyunk, or some other of them unks, wherever they are. Vance thought, may be you'd been 'ploring the wharves, and was carried off in a steamboat, either up the river or down, or clear over to New York and Albany."

"I've only been calling on Mrs. Penafield"—said Jonathina to Mr. and Mrs. Chesterwood, whom she found in the parlor—"and I've been enjoying in her society the delights of a congenial mind."

That night, Mr. William Wicklesby slept not as soundly as usual. In truth, he was strangely smitten with the strange woman. An old song most truly says—"What has love to do with reason?" And who can live in the world, and not be astonished at the variety of incomprehensible love fancies, and unsuitable matches, that are continually taking place? Nay, some casuists aver that, "if you can give a reason for loving, it is a proof that you *do not* love." However that may be, it is a fact the nice, neat, over-scrupulous, over-particular, over-polite (but not over-sensible) Mr. William Wicklesby, had become suddenly and thoroughly enamored of the careless, unmannered, unbeautiful, uncouth, and ill-dressed Miss Jonathina Judd. Yet so it was, and such things are.

It is true his late wife was a very commonplace, silly woman, fatiguingly devoted to dress and fashion, and as deficient in conversational powers as her sister, Mrs. Penafield; but without that lady's kindness of heart, and patience of temper. His three children had died in infancy, and Mr. Wicklesby was not alone in the world, with a handsome and well-furnished house all to himself and his servants; for he prudently retained his establishment, in case he should be induced to marry again; for, though scrupulous to the letter in going through all the observances of "decent sorrow," he was by no means a disconsolate widower. Many caps had been set at him, and were still setting, but as yet without success; Mr. Wicklesby, after his experience of a silly, insipid wife, having a secret inclination to try a sensible woman next time. And having had but small experience in that species, he believed Miss Judd to belong to it. As to her faults and foibles, they either did not strike him as vividly as they appeared to others, or else he was willing to compound for them in favor of her better qualities. As to her want of beauty, he either did not perceive it, or was magnanimously resolved to dispense with that qualification, having had too much of it, and its usual appendages, in his former partner. Perhaps, after all, Mr. Wicklesby did *not* fall into the above train of reasoning, or any other. But, the fact was certain, that he liked Miss Judd.

Next morning, about eleven o'clock, Jonathina came home, her arms laden and piled with books, which she had bought at a cheap shop, and had insisted on carrying herself, asserting that she was quite as able to do this as a shop-boy, and even more so. And having tumbled the others on the floor of her room, she selected two, and sat down to reading them.

Suddenly the girl Zuby ran into the room, exclaiming—"Oh! Miss Judd! quit them books, and make yourself decent—now, right away. A beau is come! Only think—a beau for you, yourself. Wonders won't never cease! Here's his card. He's waiting in the back parlor. He didn't ask for a creature but you. Only think of *your* having a sweetheart!"

Miss Judd took the card, read the name of William Wicklesby, and looked as she had never looked before.

"Here! here!"—proceeded Zuby—"make haste, and fix up. Go and wash your hands, after them dusty books; and let me put you in some sort of order. Head first—hair first! That hair's always my horror! Where's the comb? Where's the brush? I'm in such a flurry for you. Don't keep him waiting, or he may get tired and go off. Now put that book out of your hand. But you needn't have plumped it down into that puddle of slop you always keep on the washstand."

"I forgot"—apologized Miss Judd.

"Never mind—let it lay"—hurried Zuby—"'tis only a book. I'll wipe and dry it myself, after awhile. Come, now; on with the foulard, and the new collar. There, now; I've dressed you by sleight of hand. I must hurry to mistress, and tell her not to come down and disturb the courting, as I often say to Venus and Phillis."

Jonathina went down, and paused near the parlor door, and raised her eyes to the ceiling, and made a resolution not to accept Mr. Wicklesby, preferring to live on as she was, under no government but her own.

Mr. Wicklesby, however, did not offer; so the question remained unpopped; though he thought she looked much better than on the preceding day. And so she did; thanks to Zuby, and her sleight of hand.

He informed Miss Judd that, having heard her last evening on the subject of manufactures, he had come to offer his services in escorting her to a cotton factory over Schuylkill; a large establishment, well worth her inspection. She consented, eagerly. It was then arranged that he was to be at Mr. Chesterwood's door at four in the afternoon, with his chaise. As soon as Jonathina had delivered a speech on the causes of crime, Mr. Wicklesby took his leave for that time. When going up to her room, she met Zuby on the landing-place of the stairs.

"I guess"—said the girl—"he didn't ask you, after all. You don't look as if you was engaged. Men is so onsartain, as I often say to Vance."

Miss Judd came down to dinner with a very peculiar face, that continued on her all the time she remained at the table, which she left unusually early. During the repast, she gave no dissertation, advanced no theories, and suggested no improvements in the social or any other system. And when Mr. and Mrs. Chesterwood addressed any part of their conversation to her, she answered slightly and irrelevantly. No allusion whatever was made to Mr. Wicklesby.

Punctually at four, he drove up to the door in a very neat chaise, or gig; and Zuby having made an entire refixing of Miss Judd, and complimenting her by saying—"Well, I declare now, you don't look quite as bad as usual," the lady (awkwardly and confusedly on her part) was put into the vehicle, and they drove towards the Schuylkill.

It was after sunset before they returned. As soon as the gig was heard to stop, all the servants looked out at the kitchen windows, and were unanimous in the opinion that Miss Judd and her beau had come home engaged; their present faces being now very superior to those of the forenoon; also, they evinced considerable alacrity in alighting from the chaise, and running up the doorsteps.

Mr. Wicklesby, after taking home the vehicle, passed the evening at the Chesterwood house; and so he did every evening for two weeks; at the end of which time he was united to Miss Judd, one morning, in church, in the presence of the Chesterwoods, near the altar, and the servants not far behind. The Penafields, disapproving the match, did not appear. The bride was attired in a new and proper-looking traveling costume; and from the church door they departed for Connecticut, from whence, after a few weeks' sojourn, they were to return and take possession of Mr. Wicklesby's house in Philadelphia.

"If I had not taken her in charge"—said Zuby—"and worked hard for her civilizement, she never would have got a husband."

"And I"—said Vance—"I helped her on, in my own undirect way, as far as I could. Well, she's married, after all. When a fenced road is too long, it must always come to a turn at the last."

By the bye, Zuby became Mrs. Vance, in less than a year.

When their eccentric guest was fairly off, Mr. Chesterwood said to his wife—"Who would have supposed, my dear, when this curiosity of a woman first billeted herself upon us, that, in a few weeks, she would depart as the bride of a respectable man, to return as mistress of a handsome establishment?"

"And I hope and believe"—replied Mrs. Chesterwood—"that the match, strange and unsuitable as it now seems, may yet turn out well; for certainly, with all her awkward and inconvenient ways, and her entire want of tact and of common sense, she is far from stupid; and truly, in her whole heterogeneous composition, there is nothing morally wrong."

NONFICTION

Seventy-Five Receipts for Pastry, Cakes, and Sweetmeats

AN EXCERPT

BLACK CAKE, OR PLUM CAKE

One pound of flour, sifted.
One pound of fresh butter.
One pound of powdered white sugar.
Twelve eggs.
Two pounds of the best raisins.
Two pounds of currants.
Two table-spoonfuls of mixed spice, mace and cinnamon.
Two nutmegs, powered.
A large glass of wine }
A large glass of brandy } mixed together
Half a glass of rose-water }
A pound of citron.

Pick the currants very clean, and wash them, draining them through a cullender. Wipe them in a towel. Spread them out on a large dish, and set them near the fire or in the hot sun to dry, placing the dish in a slanting position. Having stoned the raisins,[1] cut them in half, and when all are done, sprinkle them well with sifted flour, to prevent their sinking to the bottom of the cake. When the currants are dry, sprinkle them also with flour.

Pound the spice, allowing twice as much cinnamon as mace. Sift it, and mix the mace, nutmeg, and cinnamon together. Mix also the liquor and rose-water, in a tumbler or cup. Cut the citron in slips. Sift the flour into a broad dish. Sift the sugar into a deep earthen pan, and cut the butter into it. Warm it near the fire, if the weather is too cold for it to mix easily. Stir the butter and sugar to a cream.

Beat the eggs as light as possible. Stir them into the butter and sugar alternately with the flour. Stir very hard. Add, gradually, the spice and liquor. Stir the raisins and currants alternately into the mixture, taking care that they are well floured. Stir the whole as hard as possible, for ten minutes after all the ingredients are in.

Cover the bottom and sides of a large tin or earthen pan, with sheets of white paper well buttered, and put into it some of the mixture. Then spread on it some of the citron, which must not be cut too small. Next put a layer of the mixture, and then a layer of citron, and so on till it is all in, having a layer of the mixture at the top.

This cake is always best baked in a baker's oven, and will require four or five hours in proportion to its thickness.

Ice it, next day.

SPUNGE CAKE

Twelve eggs.
Ten ounces of sifted flour, dried near the fire.
A pound of loaf-sugar, powered and sifted.
Twelve drops of essence of lemon.
A grated nutmeg.
A tea-spoonful of powered cinnamon and mace, mixed.

Beat the eggs as light as possible. Eggs for spunge or almond-cakes require more beating than for any other purpose. Beat the sugar, by degrees, into the eggs. Beat very hard, and continue to beat some time after the sugar is all in.

No sort of sugar but loaf, will make light spunge-cake. Stir in, gradually, the spice and essence of lemon. Then, by degrees put in the flour, a little at a time, stirring round the mixture very slowly with a knife. If the flour is stirred too hard, the cake will be tough. It must be done lightly and gently, so that the top of the mixture will be covered with bubbles. As soon as the flour is all in, begin to bake it, as setting will injure it.

Put it in small tins, well buttered, or in one large tin pan. The thinner the pans, the better for spunge-cake. Fill the small tins about half full. Grate loaf-sugar over the top of each, before you set them in the oven.

Spunge-cake requires a very quick oven, particularly at the bottom. It should be baked as fast as possible, or it will be tough and heavy, however light it may have been before it went into the oven. It is of all cakes the most liable to be spoiled in baking. When taken out of the tins, the cakes should be spread on a sieve to cool. If baked in one large cake, it should be iced.

A large cake of twelve eggs, should be baked at least an hour in a quick oven.

For small cakes, ten minutes is generally sufficient. If they get very much out of shape in baking, it is a sign that the oven is too slow.

Some think that spunge-cake and almond cakes are lighter, when the yolks and whites of the eggs are beaten in separate pans, and mixed gently together before the sugar is beaten into them.

If done separately from the yolks, the whites should be beaten till they stand alone.

ALMOND CAKE

Two ounces of blanched bitter almonds, pounded very fine.
Seven ounces of flour, sifted and dried.
Ten eggs.
A pound of loaf-sugar, powdered and sifted.
Two table-spoonfuls of rose-water.

Take two ounces of shelled bitter almonds, or peach-kernels. Scald them in hot water, and as you peel them, throw them into a bowl of cold water. Then wipe them dry, and pound them one by one in a mortar, till they are quite fine and smooth.

Break ten eggs, putting the yolks in one pan and the whites in another. Beat them separately as light as possible, the whites first, and then the yolks.

Add the sugar, gradually, to the yolks, beating it in very hard. Then, by degrees, beat in the almonds, and then add the rose-water.

Stir half the whites of eggs, into the yolks and sugar. Divide the flour into two equal parts, and stir in one half, slowly and lightly, till it bubbles on the top. Then the other half of the white of egg, and then the remainder of the flour, very lightly.

Butter a large square tin pan, or one made of paste-board, which will be better. Put in the mixture, and set immediately in a quick oven, which must be rather hotter at the bottom than at the top. Bake it according to the thickness. If you allow the oven to get slack, the cake will be spoiled.

Make an icing with the whites of three eggs, twenty-four tea-spoonfuls of loaf-sugar, and eight drops of essence of lemon.

When the cake is cool, mark in it small squares with a knife. Cover it with icing, and ornament it while wet, with nonpareils dropped on in borders, round each square of the cake.[2] When the icing is dry, cut the cake in squares, cutting through the icing very carefully with a penknife. Or you may cut it in squares first, and then ice and ornament each square separately.

FRENCH ALMOND CAKE

Six ounces of shelled sweet almonds.
Three ounces of shelled bitter almonds, or peach kernels.
Three ounces of sifted flour, dried near the fire.
Fourteen eggs.
One pound of powdered loaf-sugar.
Twelve drops of essence of lemon.

Blanch the almonds, by scalding them in hot water. Put them in a bowl of cold water, and wipe them dry, when you take them out. Pound them, one at a time, in a mortar, till they are perfectly smooth. Mix the sweet and bitter almonds together. Prepare them, if possible, the day before the cake is made.

Put the whites and yolks of the eggs, into separate pans. Beat the whites till they stand alone, and then the yolks till they are very thick.

Put the sugar, gradually, to the yolks, beating it in very hard. Add, by degrees, the almonds, still beating very hard. Then put in the essence of lemon. Next, beat in, gradually, the whites of the eggs, continuing to beat for some time after they are all in. Lastly, stir in the flour, as slowly and lightly, as possible.

Butter a large tin mould or pan. Put the cake in, and bake it in a very quick oven, an hour or more, according to its thickness.

The oven must on no account be hotter at the top, than at the bottom.

When done, set it on a sieve to cool.

Ice it, and ornament it with nonpareils.

These almond cakes are generally baked in a turban-shaped mould, and the nonpareils put on, in spots or sprigs.

A pound of almonds in the shells (if the shells are soft and thin,) will generally yield half a pound when shelled. Hard, thick-shelled almonds, seldom yield much more than a quarter of a pound, and should therefore never be bought for cakes or puddings.

Bitter almonds and peach-kernels can always be purchased with the shells off.

Families should always save their peach-kernels, as they can be used in cakes, puddings and custards.

MACCAROONS

Half a pound of shelled sweet almonds.
A quarter of a pound of shelled bitter almonds.
The whites of three eggs.
Twenty-four large tea-spoonfuls of powdered loaf-sugar.
A tea-spoonful of rose-water.
A large tea-spoonful of mixed spice, nutmeg, mace and cinnamon.

Blanch and pound your almonds, beat them very smooth, and mix the sweet and bitter together; do them, if you can, the day before you make the maccaroons. Pound and sift your spice. Beat the whites of three eggs till they stand alone; add to them, very gradually, the powdered sugar, a spoonful at a time, beat it in very hard, and put in, by degrees, the rose-water and spice. Then stir in, gradually, the almonds. The mixture must be like a soft dough; if too thick, it will be heavy; if too thin, it will run out of shape. If you find your almonds not sufficient, prepare a few more, and stir them in. When it is all well mixed and stirred, put some flour in the palm of your hand, and taking up a lump of the mixture with a knife, roll it on your hand with the flour into a small round ball; have ready an iron or tin pan, buttered, and lay the maccaroons in it, as you make them up. Place them about two inches apart, in case of their spreading. Bake them about eight or ten minutes in a moderate oven; they should be of a pale brownish colour. If too much baked, they will lose their flavor; if too little, they will be heavy. They should rise high in the middle, and crack on the surface. You may, if you choose, put a larger proportion of spice.

Domestic French Cookery

AN EXCERPT

Preface

The design of the following little book is to furnish receipts for a select variety of French dishes, explained and described in such a manner as to make them intelligible to American cooks, and practicable with American utensils and American fuel. Those that (according to the original work) cannot be prepared without an unusual and foreign apparatus have been omitted; and also such as can only be accomplished by the consummate skill and long practice of native French cooks.

Many dishes have been left out, as useless in a country where provisions are abundant. On this side of the Atlantic all persons in respectable life can obtain better articles of food than sheeps' tails, calves' ears, &c. and the preparation of these articles (according to the European receipts) is too tedious and complicated to be of any use to the indigent, or to those who can spare but little time for their cookery.

Also, the translator has inserted no receipts which contain nothing different from the usual American mode of preparing the same dishes.

Most of the French Cookery Books introduced into this country have failed in their object, from the evident deficiency of the translators in a competent knowledge of the technical terms of cookery and from the multitude of French words interspersed through the directions, and which cannot, in general, be comprehended without an incessant and troublesome reference to the glossary.

The translator of the following pages has endeavored, according to the best of her ability, to avoid these defects, and has aimed at making a book of practical utility to all those who may have a desire to introduce occasionally at their tables good specimens of French culinary art.

From these receipts she believes that many advantageous hints may be taken for improvements in American cookery; and she hopes that, upon trial, this little work may be found equally useful in private families, hotels, and boarding-houses.

Philadelphia, September, 1832

Miscellaneous Receipts

French Coffee

Let the coffee be roasted immediately before you want to use it, as it loses much of its strength by keeping. Its color, when done, should be a fine, bright brown; but by no means allow it to scorch. A cylindrical coffee-roaster that can be turned by a handle, and sets before the fire, is far preferable to a pot or a pan. Grind the coffee while warm.

If you intend to make half a dozen cups of coffee for drinking, measure six cups of water into the coffee-pot. Set it on hot coals, and when the water boils, put in two or three chips of isinglass, or the white of an egg. Then throw in six large teaspoonfuls of ground coffee. Stir it several times while boiling, and set it several times back from the fire to diminish the boiling gradually. When it has boiled sufficiently, remove it entirely from the coals, pour in a cup of cold water, and then put it in a corner and let it settle for half an hour. Afterwards pour it off from the grounds into another pot (which must first be scalded), and set it close to the fire, but do not let it boil again.

If you intend to serve it up with hot cream, you must make the coffee stronger. While the coffee is clearing, boil your cream or milk, and pour some of it hot into each cup of coffee.

Coffee without Boiling

Coffee made without boiling is much stronger, more economical, and less troublesome than the usual way; but it requires a pot of particular construction. The best sort of pot for this purpose is called in French a Grecque (Greek). It must be made of the best black-tin, and of a tall cylindrical shape, with the spout very near the bottom. The receptacle for the coffee-powder fits into the upper part of the coffee-pot, and must be taken out when washed. The bottom of this receiver is pierced with very small holes, and there are two other strainers, made of movable plates of tin, also covered with fine holes. These two strainers fit into the receivers. The powdered coffee is to be placed between them, so that it may filter through the lower strainer, and also through the holes at the bottom of the receiver. Having scalded the pot, put the coffee into the receiver between the two movable strainers, and pour in some water which must be boiling hard at the time. The coffee will then drain through into the lower part of the pot where the spout is, and will clear itself in pouring through the holes. Shut down the lid, place the pot near the fire, and the coffee will be ready for use as soon as it has done draining through.

Allow a large tea-spoonful of the powder for each cup that you intend to have.

This mode of preparing coffee is very expeditious, and requires neither isinglass nor white of egg.

Chocolate

Never boil chocolate in milk, as that spoils the flavor; and do not scrape it, but merely cut it into pieces. To an ounce of chocolate allow a cup of boiling water.

Having first scalded the pot, put in the chocolate, pour the water on it, and boil it till one third has evaporated. Then supply that third with cream or milk, and take it immediately from the fire.

You need not stir it more than two or three minutes.

Fine Lemonade

Allow a whole lemon and four or five lumps of loaf-sugar to half a pint of cold water. Roll the lemons hard on a table to make them more juicy. Cut them in half, and squeeze them over the sugar. Then pour on the water, and stir till the sugar is dissolved. Take out whatever seeds may have fallen in. In warm weather, put a lump of ice into each glass.

Punch

Take three large lemons, and roll them very hard on the table to make them more juicy. Then pare them as thin as possible. Cut out the pulp and throw away the seeds and the white part of the rind. Put the yellow rind and the pulp into a pint of boiling water; set it on the fire, and let it boil two or three minutes. Take it off, and throw in a tea-spoonful of raw green tea of the best sort, and let it infuse about five minutes. Then strain it through linen. Stir into it three quarters of a pound of loaf-sugar, and a pint of brandy, or any other suitable liquor. Set it again over the fire, and when it is just ready to boil, remove it, and pour it into a china bowl or pitcher.

Convenient Lemonade

Take four ounces of powdered tartaric acid, and two drachms of essential oil of lemon. Mix them together, and keep them in a well-corked phial. A table-spoonful mixed with sugar and water, will make six or eight glasses of lemonade.

It will keep about a month, but not longer, as it will then lose its strength.

French Mustard

Put on a plate an ounce of the very best mustard powder, with a salt-spoon of salt, a few leaves of tarragon, and a clove of garlic minced fine. Pour on by degrees sufficient vinegar to dilute it in the proper consistence (about a wine-glassful), and mix it well with a wooden spoon. Do not use it in less than twenty-four hours after it is mixed.

Potato Flour

Potato flour is excellent for sponge-cake, and other things which require extraordinary lightness. It is also good for young children, and for convalescent sick persons.

Take the best and most mealy potatoes; pare them, and wash them through several waters. Then rasp or grate them over a tureen half full of cold water. Continue to grate the potatoes till the lower half of the tureen is filled with the pulp, so that the water may rise to the top. The mealy part of the potatoes will sink to the bottom, while the remainder or the useless part will rise to the surface. When nothing more rises, pour off the water carefully, and dry the flour which you find at the bottom. When quite dry, pound it in a mortar to a fine powder, and sift it through a sieve.

Potato flour is much lighter than that of wheat.

Cold Pickles

Season some of the best vinegar with a little garlic, a little tarragon, and a little sweet-oil. Put it into a glass jar, and keep it well covered. You may throw into it the green seeds of nasturtiums, morella cherries, little onions, small young carrots when but a finger long, radish pods, and various other things. Keep the jar well closed, and the pickles will be as good and keep as long as if they had been boiled.

Nasturtiums and cherries will keep in plain vinegar without any seasoning.

Cornichons, or French Cucumber Pickles

Take ten pounds of very small cucumbers. Brush them all over to clean them well, and cut off the stems. Put them into an earthen pan with two handfuls of salt. Let them rest twenty-four hours, and then dress them. When they are well drained, put them back into the same pan, and pour in a quantity of boiling hot white wine vinegar, sufficient to cover them. Then cover the pan carefully with a lid or dish, and let the cucumbers set in the vinegar twenty-four hours. They will then be yellow. Pour the vinegar from them, and cover them with vine-leaves. Boil the vinegar again, and when it boils throw it over the cucumbers, stirring them well.

When the vinegar is cold, pour it from the cucumbers, and boil it again. Then pour it over them, and proceed in this manner four or five times, till they become of a fine green. Keep them in the interval always covered with a layer of vine-leaves, fresh each time, and also with a cloth kept down by a large dish. This, by keeping in the steam, will assist them in greening.

Then drain them on a sieve, and put them into glass jars.

Afterwards, boil some fresh white wine vinegar, first mixing in it the following seasoning. To every quart of vinegar allow half an ounce of mace, half an ounce of sliced ginger, half an ounce of whole black pepper, six cloves, a few sprigs of tarragon, and half a clove of garlic.

Boil the vinegar with these ingredients for five minutes, and then pour it hot on the pickles. Tie them up carefully. They may be used in a week.

The generality of French pickles are made in a manner similar to those of England and America.

Fine Cologne Water

Procure in an apothecary's the following oils, and have them all put into the same phial:—Oil of lemons, 2 drams; oil of rosemary, 2 drams; oil of lavender, 1 dram; oil of bergamot, 2 drams; oil of cinnamon, 10 drops; oil of cloves, 10 drops; oil of roses, 2 drops; tincture of musk, 8 drops.

Put a pint of highly rectified spirits of wine into a bottle, and pour the oils into it. Shake it hard for a few minutes, having corked it tightly. It will be fit for immediate use, but it improves by keeping.

If you wish it stronger, double the quantity of all the oils, but have only a pint of spirits of wine.

American Girl's Book, or Occupation for Play Hours

AN EXCERPT FROM PART III, "AMUSING WORK—PINCUSHIONS"

A Strawberry

This pincushion is made of a piece of coarse linen, about half a quarter square, cut into two triangular or three-cornered halves, stuffed with bran and covered with scarlet cloth; which cover must be sewed neatly on the wrong side, and then turned. The top or broad part must be gathered so as to meet all round, and concealed by sewing on a small round piece of green velvet, scolloped in imitation of the cap of green leaves that surround the stem where it joins the strawberry. The stem must be imitated by sewing on a small green silk cord. To represent the seeds, the strawberry must be dotted over with small stitches, made at regular distances with a needle-full of yellow silk, and close to each yellow stitch must be a stitch of black.

Emery bags are often made in this manner, but of course much smaller; not exceeding the size of a large real strawberry.

A Basket Pincushion

Get a very small round basket, with or without a handle. It must be closely woven, so that nothing can be seen through its sides. Make of coarse linen, stuffed with wool or bran, a round pincushion exactly to fit the basket. Cover the top of it with velvet or silk, and put it into the basket, sewing it firmly to the inside of the rim. This is for a toilet-table.

A Bunch of Hearts

Cut out ten or twelve small hearts of double pasteboard; that is, two pieces of pasteboard for each heart. Cover them with different shades of red silk, crimson, scarlet, and pink, sewing them very neatly at the edges. Sew a string of narrow ribbon to the top of each, and tie the ends of all the strings together. Stick pins round the edge of each pincushion where the two sides unite. These bunches of hearts look very pretty when hung on a toilet-glass.

The Elephant

The Elephant is the most sagacious and intelligent of all quadrupeds, and the nearest in its approach to human reason. Its enormous size and immense strength render it a formidable enemy when provoked, but even in a wild state it is not ferocious. It is easily tamed by kindness and caresses, and when properly treated it is obedient, grateful, and discriminating to a degree that proves it to be endued with a portion of something very similar to rationality. Elephants, even when wild, evince signs of great ingenuity, forethought, and memory; and show much regard and consideration for each other. They generally go in herds or companies; sometimes carrying in their trunks branches of trees which they use as fans to cool themselves. If one of them gets hurt, the others take care of him, bringing him food and nursing him till he recovers. In crossing a river the old ones swim over first, to seek a proper landing place: and when safe on the other side, give a signal by a sort of cry or shout for the young ones to follow. The little elephants then venture across, supporting each other by interlacing or locking their trunks together. The old elephants sometimes carry the very small ones laid high across their tusks, twining their trunks round them to prevent their falling. If they find a dead elephant in the woods, they stop and cover him with grass or with the boughs of trees. The elephant will eat almost every sort of vegetable food, and is extravagantly fond of confectionary, but abhors flesh and fish. I have seen them drink wine and porter, taking the bottle in their trunk which they bend under to the mouth, holding back the head so as to let the liquor run down their throat. In India the tame elephant is used for various services. He will perform more work, and carry or draw greater burthens, than six horses: but he must be well fed and properly taken care of. It is said that he will eat a hundred pounds of rice in a day, drinking forty gallons of water: but his diet should be varied with fruit and herbage, and he must be led to the river twice a day for the purpose of bathing.

There is a story of an elephant becoming so fond of his keeper's child that he could scarcely bear to have it taken out of his sight. At last he would not eat his food unless the infant's cradle was placed between his feet, and as soon as this was done he ate heartily. If the child awoke and cried, the elephant frequently put it to sleep again by rocking the cradle with his trunk.

The duke of Devonshire had a very fine elephant which he kept in the grounds of his villa at Chiswick, near London, in a handsome stone building of one story erected purposely for the accommodation of the animal, who went in and out on a slanting platform or inclined plane. Some relatives of mine saw it there a few years since. The elephant was walking about under the trees. He seemed very proud of a rich mantle or pall of blue and crimson which was thrown over him. At the desire of his keeper he took it off with his trunk, spread it evenly on the grass, carefully smoothing every wrinkle, then folded it square and neatly, and laying it on his back carried it into his house and put it away.

A gentleman who came from India in the ship which brought the elephant Caroline, told me that the tediousness of the long passage was much relieved by the interest they all took in this animal, and the constant amusement she afforded them. There was great friendship between her and a dog who stayed about her almost continually. At the commencement of the voyage she was provided with a covering, lest she should be chilled by the sea-air. But being still in the warm climate of the torrid zone, she did not then feel the want of clothing, and immediately stripped off the garment and threw it aside. Afterwards when they proceeded into a cooler latitude and the covering was again put on, she seemed very glad to have it, and wore it without any further objection. At the termination of the voyage the vessel encountered a violent storm, and was wrecked near the mouth of the Delaware. The crew and passengers saved themselves in the long boat. When they reached the shore, they grieved exceedingly at having left the poor elephant in the ship abandoned to her fate. Some of the men volunteered to go back for her in the boat, notwithstanding the terrors of the storm and the imminent risk, of their own lives. When they reached the ship, they found the elephant in great tribulation; but they could not prevail on her to come away with them till she had provided for the safety of her friend the dog by taking him in her trunk and handing him down to the boat. This done, she gladly allowed the men to make her fast by a rope to the stern of the boat, and thus she swam after them to the shore. The elephant Caroline was afterwards exhibited in Philadelphia.

Once, when on a visit to some friends in the interior of Pennsylvania, I was told by them of an elephant that the preceding summer had been taken through that part of the country as a show, his conductors generally travelling with him at night. On one occasion, they lost their way in the woods and their lantern went out. Chaining the elephant to a tree, the men set off in different directions in search of a house where they might replenish their light and inquire the road. Two of them came to the farm of one of my kinsmen, who gave them what they wanted and offered to guide them through the intricacies of the wood paths. When they arrived at the place where they had left the elephant, they found the animal gone. He had torn up the tree (which was a sapling and less strong than they supposed it) and rambled off, dragging it after him by the chain. They spent the remainder of the night in search of him. At daylight in the morning, the elephant wandered to a fence which ran along a wheat-field on the edge of the woods. The reapers (for it was harvest time) happened to be stooping down at their work with their backs toward the forest, and on turning their heads were much amazed to see an elephant looking over the fence. In a few minutes his conductors came up, and were very glad to find him. He was afterwards exhibited for some days in a barn in the neighbourhood of the nearest village, and crowds from all parts of the country came to see him; many persons making him daily visits and bringing him fruit and cakes. Once when he was thrusting his trunk about among the spectators in search of something good to eat, a young man mischievously gave him some tobacco, which the elephant (not knowing what it was) conveyed immediately to his mouth, but instantly put it out again with signs of the greatest disgust, in which he showed his sense. A few days afterwards, the same young man was there again. The elephant directly remembered him, and singling him out from the crowd, put forth his trunk and seizing the offender's hand squeezed and pinched it so hard as to make him cry out with pain.

The tusks of the elephant supply the whole world with ivory. It is valued for its whiteness, hardness, and the fine polish of which it is susceptible. There is a small insect, invisible to the naked eye, which sometimes gets into articles made of ivory and eats holes in them in a very ingenious manner. I have a fan entirely of ivory, which is almost as thin as the best white paper, and is carved all over in a sort of delicate lace or open work. It was made for me in Canton when a girl, and has in the center the initials of my name elegantly cut. In a few years the unseen worm commenced his depredations, and my beautiful fan is now eaten in small square holes of so regular a form that they look as if made purposely with an instrument. One of my sisters had a fine set of ivory chessmen that came from China, and after awhile they were found perforated with small holes not larger than if pierced by a small needle. The chess-king was drilled completely through, from his crown down to his feet. It is probably a similar invisible insect that eats off the points of camel's hair pencils as they lie in the boxes at the stationers, making them square at the ends and therefore useless.

The spirited engraving which is put for a frontispiece, represents a scene which took place in India, at a hunting-party, and is related by Capt. Mundy in his Sketches of India, in the following narrative.[1]

"A gentleman of our party had, perhaps, as perilous an adventure with a lion as any one; he having enjoyed the singular distinction of laying for some moments in the very clutches of the royal quadruped. Though I have heard him recount the incident more than once, and have myself sketched the scene, yet I am not sure that I relate it correctly. The main feature however of the anecdote, affording so striking an illustration of the sagacity of the elephant, may be strictly depended upon.

"A lion charged my friend's elephant, and he [the friend], having wounded him [the lion], was in the act of leaning forward in order to fire another shot, when the howdah (which is the box upon the elephant's back) suddenly gave way, and he was thrown over the head of the elephant into the very jaws of the furious beast. The lion, though severely hurt, immediately seized him, and would shortly have put a fatal termination to the conflict, had not the elephant, urged by his mahout, or driver, stepped forward, though greatly alarmed, and grasping in her trunk the top of a young tree, bent it down across the back and loins of the lion, and thus forced the tortured animal to quit his hold! My friend's life was thus saved, but his arm was broken in two places, and he was severely clawed on the breast and shoulders."

The Ladies' Guide to True Politeness and Perfect Manners, or Miss Leslie's Behavior Book

AN EXCERPT

Chapter XIII

Letters

The practice of inclosing letters in envelopes is now universal; particularly as when the letter is single no additional postage is charged for the cover. The postage now is in almost every instance pre-paid, it being but three cents when paid by the writer, and five if left to the receiver. Therefore, none but very poor or very mean people send unpaid letters. Letter-stamps for the United States post should be kept in a little box on your writing-table. You can get them always by sending to the post-office—from a dollar's worth or more, down to fifty or twenty-five cents' worth, at a time. In a second box, keep stamps for the city or penny post, which transmits notes from one part of the town to another. And in a third, stamps to go on the covers of newspapers.

Sealing with wax is found to be very insecure for letters that are carried by steamers into warm climates—the wax melting with the heat, and sticking the letters to each other, so that they cannot be separated without tearing. Wafers are better.

It would be very convenient to use the post-office stamp as a seal, but the clerks in that establishment charge extra postage for the trouble of turning the letter to mark the stamp. This subjects the receiver to the payment of two additional cents.

In writing upon business exclusively your own, for instance to make a request, to ask for information, to petition for a favour, or to solicit an autograph, it is but right not only to pay the postage of your own letter, but to enclose a stamp for the answer. This is always done by really polite and considerate people. You have no right, when the benefit is entirely your own, to cause any extra expense to the receiver of the letter—not even the cost of three cents to pay the postage back again. It is enough to tax their time by requiring them to write to you and send off the reply. Also, in corresponding with a relative, or very intimate friend, to whom even a small expense is of more importance than to yourself, you may enclose a stamp for the answer. Do so always in writing to poor people. Be careful not to allow yourself to get entirely out of post-office stamps. Replenish your stock in time. If the gum on the back seems too weak, go over it afresh with that excellent cement, "Perpetual Paste." Embossed or bordered envelopes are not often used except in notes of ceremony—or when the acquaintance is slight. The same with ornamented note-paper. Intimate friends and relatives use paper that is handsome, but plain. Letters of business are generally enclosed in yellow or buff-coloured envelopes. Some of these yellow envelopes are large enough to contain a folio sheet when folded. Notes *not* to be sent by post, are usually sealed with wax—the seal very small. But a *small* wafer is admissible—a white one looks best for a note. In folding your note or letter, see that it is not too large to go into the envelope. It is customary to write the direction on the envelope only. Nevertheless, if the letter is to go a long distance by post, the envelope may be worn off, or torn off accidentally, or get so damaged in the letter-bag as to be rendered illegible. The surest and safest way is to put the address on the letter also; or if the sheet is full, to find a corner for the direction, either at the beginning or end.

We have seen no *good* letter-paper at less price than twenty-five cents per quire; and for that it ought to be *very* good. If of lower cost, you may find it soft and fuzzy, so that the pen will not move freely, (the nib wearing out directly,) or so thin that you cannot write on both sides of the sheet. In paper, as in most other things, the best is the cheapest. If the tint is bluish, the writing will not be so legible as on a pure white. The surface should be smooth and glossy. For letter writing *ruled* paper is rarely used, except by children. In writing for the press, no other is so convenient. A page of ruled lines to slip beneath, is indispensable to those who cannot otherwise write straight. They are to be had for a few cents at every stationer's. It is well to get three different sizes. If you write a small hand, the lines should be closer together than if your writing is large. If you are addressing a friend and have much to say, and expect to fill a sheet, begin very near the top of the first page. But if your letter is to be a short one, commence lower down, several inches from the top. If a *very* short letter of only a few lines, begin but a little above the middle of the page. Crossing a letter all over with transverse lines is obsolete. It is intolerable to read, and there is no excuse for it now, when postage is so low, and every body pays their own.

Write the date near the right-hand side of the first page, and place it about two lines higher than the two or three words of greeting or accosting with which letters usually commence. Begin the first sentence a little below those words, and farther toward the right than the lines that are to follow. It is well in dating *every* letter to give always your exact residence—that is, not only the town you live in, but the number and street. If your correspondent has had *but one* notification of your present place of abode, she may have forgotten the number, and even the street. Your letter containing it may not be at hand as a reference, and the answer may, in consequence, be misdirected—or directed in so vague a manner that it will never reach you. We have known much inconvenience (and indeed loss) ensues from not specifying with the date of *each* letter the exact dwelling-place of the writer. But if it is *always* indicated at the top of *every one*, a reference to *any* one of your letters will furnish your proper address. If you are in the country, where there are no streets or numbered houses, give the name of the estate and that of the nearest post-town; also the county and state. All this will occupy a long line, but you will find the advantage. If your letter fills more than one sheet, number each page. Should you have no envelope, leave, on the inside of the third page, two blank spaces where the seal is to come. These spaces should be left rather too large than too small. Lest you should tear the letter in *breaking* it open, it is best to *cut* round the seal. We have seen letters that were actually illegible from the paleness of the ink. If you write from your own house this is inexcusable, as you ought always to be *well* supplied with that indispensable article; and in a city you can easily send to a stationer's and buy it. It is still better to make it yourself; than which nothing is more easy. The following receipt *we know, by experience, to be superlative.* Try it.

Buy at a druggist's four ounces of the best blue Aleppo nutgalls; half an ounce of green copperas; and half an ounce of clean, white gum-arabic. These three articles must be pulverized in a mortar. Put them into a large, clean, white-ware pitcher, and pour on a quart of boiling water. Stir the whole with a stick that will reach to the bottom, and set the pitcher in a warm place; covering it lightly with a folded newspaper. In about an hour, stir it again very hard; and repeat the stirring several times during the day. Let it remain in the pitcher several days, or a week, till it becomes an excellent black; the blackening will be accelerated by keeping the pitcher in the sun; for instance, in a sunny balcony. Stir it, down to the bottom, two or three times a day—always with a stick. Use nothing of metal in making this ink. When it is very black, and writes well, pour it off carefully from the bottom, (which must have rested undisturbed for two or three hours previous,) passing it through a funnel into pint-bottles. Before you cork them, put into each a large tea-spoonful of brandy, to prevent moulding, or a few drops of lavender. A small tea-spoonful of cloves (slightly broken), placed in the bottom of each bottle, before the ink is poured in, will answer the same purpose. Scouring the pitcher with soap and sand, after throwing away the dregs of the ink, will completely clear off the stains.

Ink-stands should be washed out, before they are filled anew.

There is no ink superior to this in blackness or smoothness. You can make it at less than half the cost of that which you buy in the shops. It looks blacker the next day after using, and never fades. If it becomes rather too thick, dilute it slightly with water, and stir it down to the bottom.

Never use *blue* ink. If a letter chances to get wet, the writing will be effaced. Serious losses have resulted from business letters being written in blue ink.

If you make a mistake in a word, draw your pen through it, or score it so as to be quite illegible, and then interline the correction, placing a caret beneath. This will be better than scratching out the error with your penknife, and afterward trying to write a new word in the identical place; an attempt which rarely succeeds, even with the aid of pounce-powder, which is pulverized gum-sandarac.

At the end of the letter, somewhat lower than your signature, (which should be very near the right-hand edge of the page,) add the name and address of the person for whom the letter is designated, and to whom it will thus find its way, even if the envelope should be defaced, or torn off and lost. Write your own name rather larger than your usual hand, and put a dot or dash after it.

Some of the ensuing paragraphs are taken (with permission of the publisher) from a former work of the author's.

In folding a letter, let the breadth (from left to right) far exceed the height. A letter folded tall is ridiculous, and one verging towards squareness looks very awkward. It is well to use a folder (or paperknife) to press along the edges of the folds, that they may be smooth and straight. If one is looser than another, or if there is the slightest narrowing in, or widening out, toward the edge of the turn-over, the letter will have an irregular, unsightly appearance. Pieces of ruled lines may be so cut that you can slip them under the back of a letter after it is folded, and then you will be in no danger of writing the direction crooked, or uneven.

Write the name of your correspondent about the middle of the back, and very clearly and distinctly. Then give the number and street on the next line, a little nearer to the right. Then the town in *large* letters, extending still nearer to the right. If a country-town, give next (in letters a little smaller) the name of the *county* in which it is situated. This is very necessary, as in some of our states there is more than one town of the same name, and "Washingtons" all over the Union. Lastly, at the very bottom, and close to the right, indicate the state or district by its usual abbreviation,— for instance, *Me.* for Maine[1]—*N.H.* New Hampshire—*Vt.* Vermont—*Mass.* Massachusetts—*R.I.* Rhode Island—*Ct.* or *Conn.* Connecticut—*N.Y.* New York—*N.J.* New Jersey—*Pa.* or *Penna.* Pennsylvania—*Del.* Delaware—*Md.* Maryland—*Va.* Virginia—*N.C.* North Carolina—*S.C.* South Carolina—*Ga.* or *Geo.* Georgia—*Ala.* Alabama—*Miss.* Mississippi—*Mo.* Missouri—*La.* Louisiana—*Tenn.* Tennessee—*Ky.* Kentucky—*O.* Ohio—*Ind.* Indiana—*Ill.* Illinois—*Mich.* Michigan—*Ark.* Arkansas—*Wis.* Wisconsin—*Io.* Iowa—*Tex.* Texas—*Flo.* Florida—*Cal.* California—*Or.* Oregon—*Minn.* Minnesota—*Utah*—*D.C.* District of Columbia.

To these may be added the abbreviations of the British possessions in North America: *U.C.* Upper Canada—*L.C.* Lower Canada—*N.S.* Nova Scotia—*N.B.* New Brunswick—*N.P.* New Providence.

In directing a letter to a foreign country, give the whole name, as France, Spain, Belgium, England, Ireland, Scotland, &c. We have towns in America called after all manner of European towns. For instance, a letter directed to our Havre-de-Grace, might, if Maryland was not designated, find its way to Havre-de-Grace in France; Rome in the state of New York might be taken to Rome in Italy,—York in Pennsylvania to York in England, &c. We know an instance of a gentleman directing an important letter to Boston, and, forgetting to add *Mass.* (for Massachusetts) at the bottom, the letter actually went from Philadelphia to the small town of Boston in Lincolnshire, England. In writing *from* Europe, finish the direction with the words *United States of America.*

When you send a letter by private opportunity, (a thing which is already almost obsolete since the days of cheap postage,) it will be sufficient to introduce very near the lower edge of the left-hand corner of the back, simply the name of the gentleman who carries it, written small. It is now considered old-fashioned to insert on the back of such a letter—"Politeness of Mr. Smith"—"Favoured by Mr. Jones"—"Honoured by Mr. Brown." If the letter is to cross the sea, by mail or otherwise, write the name of the vessel on the left-hand corner of the outside.

When a letter is to go to New York city, always put the words New York *in full,* (and not N.Y.,) written large. Much confusion is caused by the name of this state and its metropolis being the same. It has been well-suggested that the name of the state of New York should be changed to Ontario—a beautiful change. In directing to any of the towns in the state of New

York, then put N.Y. after the name of the town, as Hudson, N.Y.,—Syracuse, N.Y., &c.

In sending a letter to the metropolis of the Union, direct for Washington, D.C.

In directing to a clergyman, put *Rev.* (Reverend) before his name. If a bishop, *Right Reverend.* To an officer, immediately after his name put U.S.A. for United States Army, or U.S.N. for United States Navy—having preceded his name with *Gen.*, *Col.*, *Capt.*, *Lieut.*, according to his rank.

The title *Hon.* (Honourable) is always used in directing to a member of congress, a member of the cabinet, a judge of the supreme court, an ambassador, or the governor of a state. For the Chief Magistrate of the Union, you may direct simply to the President of the United States. The term "Excellency" is now but little used.

For a gentleman holding a professorship in a university, preface his name with *Prof.* or *Professor.* The title of "Professor" does not really belong to all men who teach any thing, or to every man that exhibits a show—or to mesmerists, and spiritual knockers. Do not give it to them.

For sealing letters no light is so convenient as a wax taper in a low stand. A lamp, or candle, may smoke or blacken the wax. To seal well, your wax should be of the finest quality. Red wax of a bright scarlet colour is the best. Low-priced wax consumes very fast; and when melted, looks purplish or brownish. When going to melt sealing-wax, rest your elbow on the table to keep your hand steady. Take the stick of wax between your thumb and finger, and hold it little above the light, so that it barely touches the point of the flame. Turn the stick round till it is equally softened on all sides. Then insert a little of the melted wax *under* the turn-over part of the letter, just where the seal is to come. This will render it more secure than if the sole dependence was on the outside seal. Or instead of this little touch of wax, you may slip beneath the turn-over a small wafer, either white or of the same colour as the wax. Then begin at the outer edge of the place you intend for the seal; and move the wax in a circle, which must gradually diminish till it terminates in the centre. Put the seal exactly to the middle of the soft wax, and press it down hard, but do not screw it round. Then withdraw it suddenly. Do not use motto seals unless writing to a member of your own family, or to an intimate friend. For common service, (and particularly for letters of business,) a plain seal, with simply your initials, is best.

For a note always use a very small seal. In addressing one of your own family, it is not necessary to follow scrupulously all these observances. In writing to persons decidedly your inferiors in station, avoid the probability of mortifying them by sending mean, ill-looking notes.

Remember also (what, strange to say, some people calling themselves ladies seem not to know) that a note commenced in the first person must continue in the first person all through. The same when it begins in the third person. We have heard of invitations to a party being worded thus:—

> Mrs. Welford's compliments to Mrs. Marley, and requests the pleasure of her company on Thursday evening.
>
> Yours sincerely,
> E. WELLFORD

Notes of invitation should always designate both the day of the week and that of the month. If that of *the month only* is specified, one figure may perhaps be mistaken for another; for instance, the 13th may look like the 18th, or the 25th like the 26th. We know instances where, from this cause, some of the guests did not come till the night *after* the party.

There are some very sensible people who, in their invitations, tell frankly what is to be expected, and if they really ask but *a few* friends, they at once give the names of those friends, so that you may know whom you are to see. If you are to meet no more than can sit round the tea-table, they signify the same. If they expect twenty, thirty, or forty persons, they say so—and do not leave you in doubt whether to dress for something very like a party, or for a mere family tea-drinking.

If it is a decided music-party, by all means specify the same, that those who have no enjoyment of what is considered fashionable music, may stay away.

Always reply to a note of invitation the day after you have received it. To a note on business send an answer the same day. After accepting an invitation, should any thing occur to prevent your going, send a second note in due time.

Do not take offence at a friend because she does not invite you every time she has company. Her regard for you may be as warm as ever, but it is probably inconvenient for her to have more than a certain number at a time. Believe that the omission is no evidence of neglect, or of a desire to offend you; but rest assured that you are to be invited on other occasions. If you are *not*, then indeed you may take it as a hint that she is no longer desirous of continuing the acquaintance. Be dignified enough not to call her to account; but cease visiting her, without taking her to task and bringing on a quarrel. But if you *must* quarrel, let it not be in writing. A paper war is always carried too far, and produces bitterness of feeling which is seldom entirely eradicated, even after apologies have been made and accepted. Still, when an offence has been given in writing, the atonement should be made in writing also.

Much time is wasted (particularly by young ladies) in writing and answering such epistles as are termed "letters of friendship,"—meaning long documents (frequently with crossed lines) filled with regrets at absence, asseverations of eternal affection, modest deprecations of your humble self, and enthusiastic glorifying of your exalted correspondent; or else wonderments at both of you being so much alike, and so very congenial; and anticipations of rapture at meeting again, and lamentations at the slow progress of time, till the extatic hour of re-union shall arrive—the *postscript* usually containing some confidential allusion to a lover, (either real or supposed,) and perhaps a kind enquiry about a real or supposed lover of your friend's.

Now such letters as these are of no manner of use but to foster a sickly, morbid feeling, (very often a fictitious one,) and to encourage nonsense, and destroy all relish for such true friendship as is good and wholesome.

A still worse species of voluminous female correspondence is that which turns *entirely* upon love, or rather on what are called "beaux;" or entirely on hate—for instance, hatred of step-mothers. This topic is considered the more *piquant* from its impropriety, and from its being carried on in secret.

Then there are young ladies born with the organ of letter-writing amazingly developed, and increased by perpetual practice, who can scarcely become acquainted with a gentleman possessing brains, without volunteering a correspondence with him. And then ensues a long epistolary dialogue about nothing, or at least nothing worth reading or remembering; trenching closely on gallantry, but still not quite *that*; affected flippancy on the part of the lady; and unaffected impertinence on that of the gentleman, "which serves her right"—alternating with pretended poutings on her side, and half or whole-laughing apologies on his. Sometimes there are attempts at moralizing, or criticising, or sentimentalizing—but nothing is ever elicited that, to a third person, can afford the least amusement or improvement, or excite the least interest. Yet, strange to say, gentleman have been inveigled into this sort of correspondence, even by ladies who have made a business of afterward selling the letters for publication, and making money out of them. And such epistles have actually been printed. We do not suppose they have been read. The public is very stubborn in refusing to read what neither amuses, interests, or improves—even when a publisher is actually so weak as to print such things.

No young lady ever engages in a correspondence with a gentleman that is neither her relative or her betrothed, without eventually lessening herself in his eyes. Of this she may rest assured. With some men, it is even dangerous for a lady to write a note on the commonest subject. He may show the superscription, or the signature, or both, to his idle companions, and make insinuations much to her disadvantage, which his comrades will be sure to circulate and exaggerate.

Above all, let no lady correspond with a married man, unless she is obliged to consult him on business; and from that plain, straight path let her not diverge. Even if the wife sees and reads every letter, she will, in all probability, feel a touch of jealousy, (or more than a touch,) if she finds that they excite interest in her husband, or give him pleasure. This will inevitably be the case if the married lady is inferior in intellect to the single one, and has a lurking consciousness that she is so.

Having hinted what the correspondence of young ladies ought *not* to be, we will try to convey some idea of what it ought. Let us premise that there is no danger of *any* errors in grammar or spelling, and but few faults of punctuation, and that the fair writers are aware that a sentence should always conclude with a period or full stop, to be followed by a capital letter beginning the next sentence; and that a new paragraph should be allotted to every change of subject, provided that there is room on the sheet of paper. And still, it is well to have always at hand a dictionary and a grammar, in case of unaccountable lapses of memory. However, persons who have read much, and read to advantage, generally find themselves at no loss in orthography, grammar, and punctuation. To spell badly is disgraceful in a lady or gentleman, and it looks as if they had quitted reading as soon as they quitted school.

To write a legible and handsome hand is an accomplishment not sufficiently valued. And yet of what importance it is! We are always vexed when we hear people of talent making a sort of boast of the illegibility of their writing, and relating anecdotes of the difficulty with which it has been read, and the mistakes made by its decipherers. There are persons who affect bad writing, and boast of it, because the worst signatures extant are those of Shakespeare, Bonaparte, and Byron. These men were great in spite of their autographs, not because of them. The caliph Haroun Alraschid, who was well imbued with Arabic learning, sent an elegantly written letter to Charlemagne, with a splendid cover and seals; not being aware that the European emperor's signature was made by dipping his thumb into the ink and giving a smear—sealing with the hilt of his dagger.

The "wording" of your letter should be as much like conversation as possible, containing (in a condensed form) just what you would be most likely to talk about if you saw your friend. A letter is of no use unless it conveys some information, excites some interest, or affords some improvement. It may be handsomely written, correct in spelling, punctuation, and grammar, and yet stiff and formal in style—affectedly didactic, and therefore tiresome—or mawkishly sentimental, and therefore foolish. It may be refined, or high-flown in words, but flat and barren in ideas, containing nothing that a correspondent cares to know.

Read over each page of your letter, as you finish it, to see that there are no errors. If you find any, correct them carefully. In writing a familiar letter, a very common fault is tautology, or a too frequent repetition of the same word—for instance, "Yesterday I received a letter from sister Mary, which was the first letter I have received from sister since she left." The sentence should be, "Yesterday I received a letter from my sister Mary, the first since she left us."

Unless you are writing to one of your own family, put always the pronoun "*my*" before the word "sister." Say also—"my father," "my mother," and not "father," "mother," as if they were also the parents of your correspondent.

To end the sentence with the word "left," (for departed,) is awkward and unsatisfactory—for instance, "It is two days since he left." Left what? It is one of the absurd innovations that have crept in among us of late years, and are supposed to be fashionable. Another is the ridiculous way of omitting the possessive S in words ending with that letter; for instance, "Sims' Hotel" instead of "Sims's Hotel"—"Jenkins' Bakery" for "Jenkins's Bakery." Would any one, in talking, say they had stayed at Sims' Hotel, or that they bought their bread at Jenkins' Bakery. This is ungrammatical, as it obliterates the possessive case, and is therefore indefinite; and moreover, it looks and sounds awkwardly.

Many persons who think themselves good grammarians put on their cards "The Misses Brown,"—"The Misses Smith." Those who *really* are so, write "The Miss Browns"—"The Miss Smiths"—the plural being always on the substantive, and never on the adjective. Would we say, "the whites glove" instead of "the white gloves"—or the "blues ribbon" for the "blue ribbons." Does any lady in talking say, "The two Misses Brown called to see me?"

It is also wrong to say "two *spoons*ful," instead of two *spoon*fuls. Thus, "two spoonsful of milk" seems to imply two separate spoons with milk in each; while "two spoonfuls of milk" gives the true idea—one spoon twice filled.

Avoid in writing, as in talking, all words that do not express the true meaning. We are sorry to say that sometimes even among educated people, when attempting smartness or wit, we find a sort of conventional slang that has, in truth, a strong tinge of vulgarity, being the willful substitution of bad words or bad phrases for good ones. When we find them issuing from the lips or the pen of a *lady*, we fear she is unfortunate in a reprobate husband, or brother, from whom she must have learnt them. Yet even reprobates dislike to hear their wives and sisters talking coarsely.

Unless you know that your correspondent is well versed in French, refrain from interlarding your letters with Gallic words or phrases.

Do not introduce long quotations from poetry. Three or four lines of verse are sufficient. One line, or two, are better still. Write them rather smaller than your usual hand, and leave a space at the beginning and end; marking their commencement and termination with inverted commas, thus " ".

One of our young relatives when seven or eight years old, tried her hand at story-writing. In finishing the history of a naughty girl, much addicted to falsehood, the terminating sentence ran thus:—

"Arabella did not cure herself of this fault; but when she grew up, and became an authoress, she never marked her quotations."

If your letter is longer than can be comprised in one sheet, number the pages, placing the number near the upper corner. If engaged in a regular correspondence on business or other things, or in writing from a foreign country to your family at home, number not only the pages, but the letter itself, putting that figure in the centre at the top of the first page. Thus, if your friend, having received No. 10, finds the next letter that comes to hand is No. 12, she will know that No. 11 is missing, and will tell you so in her reply. Keep a memorandum of the letters you have sent, that you may know how to number the next. Before commencing a long letter, it is well to put down on a slip of paper, a list of the subjects you intend to write on.

Unless to persons living in the same house, do not inclose one letter in another. And even then, it is not always safe to do so. Let each letter be transmitted on its own account, by mail, with its own full direction, and its own post-office stamp. We know an instance where the peace of a family was entirely ruined by one of its members suppressing enclosed letters. Confide to no one the delivery of an important letter intended for another person. It is better to trust the mail, and send a duplicate by the next post.

To break the seal of a letter directed to another person is punishable by law. To read *secretly* the letter of another is morally as felonious. A woman who would act thus meanly is worse than those who apply their eyes or ears to key-holes, or door-cracks, or who listen under windows, or look down from attics upon their neighbours; or who, in a dusky parlour, before the lamps are lighted, ensconce themselves in a corner, and give no note of their presence while listening to a conversation not intended for them to hear.

We do not conceive that, unless he authorizes her to do so, (which he had best not,) a wife is justifiable in opening her husband's letters, or he in reading hers. Neither wife nor husband has any right to entrust to the other the secrets of their friends; and letters may contain such secrets. Unless under extraordinary circumstances, parents should not consider themselves privileged to inspect the correspondence of grown-up children. Brothers and sisters always take care that their epistles shall not be unceremoniously opened by each other. In short, a letter is the property of the person to whom it is addressed, and nobody has a right to read it without permission.

If you are shown an autograph signature at the bottom of a

letter, be satisfied to look at *that only*; and do not open out, and read the whole—unless desired.

Some years ago, in one of our most popular magazines, were several pages containing fac-simile signatures of a number of distinguished literary women—chiefly English. We saw an original letter, from a lady, who complained that some mischievous person had taken *her* magazine out of the post-office before it reached her, and shamefully *scribbled women's names* in it, disfiguring it so as to render it unfit for binding; therefore she desired the publisher to send her a clean copy in place of it.

In putting up packets to send away, either tie them round and across, with red tape, (sealing them also where the tape crosses,) or seal them without any tape. If the paper is strong, the wax good, and the contents of the parcel not too heavy, sealing will in most cases be sufficient. Twine or cord may cut the paper, and therefore is best omitted. Never put up a parcel in newspaper. It looks mean and disrespectful, and will soil the articles inside.

Keep yourself provided with different sorts and sizes of wrapping-paper.

A large packet requires more than one seal; the seals rather larger than for a letter.

Put up newspapers, for transmission, in thin whitish or brownish paper, pasting the cover, and leaving one end open. Newspaper-stamps cost but one cent, and are indispensable to the transmission of the paper.

Avoid giving letters of introduction to people whose acquaintance cannot possibly afford any pleasure or advantage to those whose civilities are desired for them, or who have no leisure to attend to strangers. Artists, authors, and all other persons to whom "time is money," and whose income stops whenever their hands and eyes are unemployed, are peculiarly annoyed by the frequency of introductory letters, brought by people with whom they can feel no congeniality, and whom they never would have sought for. Among the children of genius, but few are in a situation to entertain strangers *handsomely*, as it is called, which means, *expensively*. Many are kept always in straitened circumstances, from the incessant demands on their time and attention. And in numerous instances, letters are asked and given with no better motive than the gratification of idle curiosity.

We advise all persons obtaining an introductory letter to a painter, to ascertain, before presenting it, what branch of the art he professes. We have been asked whether a certain artist (one of the most distinguished in London) painted "figures, flowers, or landscapes." Also, no one should presume to request an introduction to an authoress, if they are ignorant whether she writes prose or verse. Not that they are expected to talk to her, immediately, on literary subjects. Far from it; but if they know nothing of her works, they deserve no letter. In America, books, or at least newspapers, are accessible to all who can read.

Bores are particularly addicted to asking letters of introduction, in accordance with their system of "bestowing their tediousness" upon as many people as possible. We pity the kind friends from whom these missives are required, and who have not courage to refuse, or address enough to excuse themselves plausibly from complying.

We have known instances of stupid, vulgar persons, on preparing to visit another city, obtaining letters to families of the really highest class, and receiving from them the usual civilities, which they knew not how to appreciate.

On the other hand, how pleasant it is, by means of an introductory letter, to bring together two kindred spirits, whose personal intercourse must inevitably produce mutual satisfaction, who are glad to know each other, glad to meet frequently, and grateful to the friend who has made them acquainted.

Letters of introduction should not be sealed. To do so is rude, and mean. If you wish to write on the same day to the same person, take another sheet, write as long an epistle as you please, seal it, and send it *by mail.*

It is best to deliver an introductory letter in person, as the lady or gentleman whose civilities have been requested in your behalf, may thus be spared the trouble of calling at your lodgings, with the risk of not finding you at home. This is very likely to happen, if you *send* instead of taking it yourself. If you *do* send it, enclose a card with your residence. Also, it is more respectful to go yourself, than to expect them to come to you.

As soon as you are shown into the parlour, send up the letter, and wait till the receiver comes to you.

When a letter is brought to you by a private hand, the usual ceremony is to defer reading it till the bringer had departed, unless he desires you to read it at once, which he will, if it is evidently a short letter. If a long one, request him to excuse you a moment while you look at the beginning, to see if your correspondent is well.

On farewell cards, it is usual to write with a pencil the letters "t.t.l.," "to take leave"—or "p.p.c.," "*pour prendre congé.*" A lady complained to us that an acquaintance of hers, about to leave town, had left a card for her with "p.d.a." upon it. Not understanding the meaning of these letters, she had applied to a friend for explanation, who told her they meant "poor dear adieu." "Now," continued she—"I cannot understand why a mere acquaintance should be so familiar as to call me 'poor dear;' why am I a poor dear to her?" We relieved her by explaining that "pour dire adieu" was French for "to bid adieu."

To conclude—let nothing induce you to give a letter of introduction to any person whose moral character is disreputable.

Chapter XX

Conduct to Literary Women

On being introduced to a female writer, it is rude to say that "you have long had a great *curiosity* to see her." Curiosity is not the right word. It is polite to imply that, "knowing her well by reputation, you are glad to have an opportunity of making her personal acquaintance." Say nothing concerning her writings, unless you chance to be alone with her. Take care not to speak of her first work as being her best; for if it is really so, she must have been retrograding from that time; a falling off that she will not like to hear of. Perhaps the truth may be, that you yourself have read only her *first* work; and if you tell her this, she will not be much flattered in supposing that you, in reality, cared so little for her first book, as to feel no desire to try a second. But she will be really gratified to learn that you are acquainted with most of her writings; and, in the course of conversation, it will be very pleasant for her to hear you quote something from them.

If she is a writer of fiction, and you presume to take the liberty of criticising her works, (as you may at her own request, or if you are her intimate friend,) refrain from urging that certain incidents are *improbable*, and certain characters *unnatural*. Of this it is impossible for you to judge, unless you could have lived the very same life that she has; known exactly the same people; and inhabited with her the same places. Remember always that "Truth is stranger than fiction." The French say—"Le vrai n'est pas toujours le plus vraisemblable,"—which, literally translated, means that "Truth is not always the most truth-like." Also, be it understood that a woman of quick perception and good memory can see and recollect a thousand things which would never be noticed or remembered by an obtuse or shallow, common-place capacity. And the intellect of a good writer of fiction is always brightened by the practice of taking in and laying up ideas with a view toward turning them to professional use. Trust in her, and believe that she *has* painted from life. A sensible fictionist always does. At the same time, be not too curious in questioning her as to the identity of her personages and the reality of her incidents. You have no right to expect that she will expose to you, or to any one else, her process of arranging the story, bringing out the characters, or concocting the dialogue. The machinery of her work, and the hidden springs which set it in motion, she naturally wishes to keep to herself; and she cannot be expected to lay them bare for the gratification of impertinent curiosity, letting them become subjects of idle gossip. Be satisfied to take her works as you find them. If you like them, read and commend them; but do not ask her to conduct you behind the scenes, and show you the mysteries of her art—for writing is really an art, and one that cannot be acquired, to any advantage, without a certain amount of talent, taste, and cultivation, to say nothing of genius. What right have you to expect that your literary friend will trust you with "the secrets of her prison-house," and put it into your power to betray her confidence by acquainting the world that a certain popular novelist has informed you with her own lips ("but it must on no account be mentioned, as the disclosure would give mortal offence, and create for her hosts of enemies,") that by her character of Fanny Gadfly she really means Lucy Giddings; that Mr. Hardcastle signifies Mr. Stone; that Old Wigmore was modelled on no less a person than Isaac Baldwin; that Mrs. Baskings was taken from Mrs. Sunning; and Mrs. Babes from Mrs. Childers—&c. &c. Also, do not expect her to tell you on what facts her incidents were founded, and whether there was any truth in them, or if they were mere invention.

Be not inquisitive as to the length of time consumed in

writing this book or that—or how soon the work now on hand will be finished. It can scarcely be any concern of yours, and the writer may have reasons for keeping back the information. Rest assured that whenever a public announcement of a new book is expedient, it will certainly be made in print.

There are persons so rude as to question a literary woman (even on a slight acquaintance) as to the remuneration she receives for her writings—in plain terms, "How much did you get for that? And how much are you to have for this? And how much do you make in the course of a year? And how much a page do you get? And how many pages can you write in a day?"

To any impertinent questions from a stranger-lady concerning the profits of your pen, reply concisely, that these things are secrets between yourself and your publishers. If you kindly condescend to answer without evasion, these polite enquiries, you will probably hear such exclamations as, "Why, really—you must be coining money. I think I'll write books myself! There can't be a better trade," &c.

Ignorant people always suppose that popular writers are wonderfully well-paid—and must be making rapid fortunes—because they neither starve in garrets, nor wear rags—at least in America.

Never ask one writer what is her *real* opinion of a contemporary author. She may be unwilling to entrust it to you, as she can have no guarantee that you will not whisper it round till it gets into print. If she voluntarily expresses her own opinion of another writer, and it *is* unfavourable, be honourable enough not to repeat it; but guard it sedulously from betrayal, and avoid mentioning it to any one.

When in company with literary women, make no allusions to "learned ladies," or "blue stockings," or express surprise that they should have any knowledge of housewifery, or needlework, or dress; or that they are able to talk on "common things."

It is rude and foolish, and shows that you really know nothing about them, either as a class or as individuals.

Never tell an authoress that "you are afraid of her"—or entreat her "not to put you into a book." Be assured there is no danger.

An authoress has seldom leisure to entertain morning visiters; so much of her time being professionally occupied either in writing, or in reading what will prepare her for writing. She should apprize all her friends of the hours in which she is usually engaged; and then none who are really her friends and well-wishers, will encroach upon her convenience for any purpose of their own; unless under extraordinary circumstances. To tell her that you were "just passing by," or "just in the neighbourhood," and "just thought you would stop in," is a very selfish, or at least a very inconsiderate excuse. Is she to suppose that you do not consider her conversation worthy of a visit made on purpose?

Recollect that to a woman who gets her living by her pen, "time is money," as it is to an artist. Therefore, encroaching on her time is lessening her income. And yet how often is this done (either heedlessly or selfishly) by persons professing to be her friends, and who are habitually in the practice of interrupting her in her writing hours, which should always be in the morning, if possible. They think it sufficient to say, like Paul Pry, "I hope I don't intrude"—knowing all the time that they *do*, and pretending to believe her when civility obliges her to tell them they do *not*.[2] Even if the visit is not a long one, it is still an interruption. In one minute it may break a chain of ideas which cannot be reunited, dispel thoughts that can never be recalled, disturb the construction of a sentence, and obliterate a recollection that will not return. And to all this the literary lady must submit, because her so-called friend "chanced to be out that morning shopping"—or "happened to be visiting in that part of the town"—and therefore has called on *her* by way of "killing two birds with one stone." Very likely, the visitor will say to the unfortunate visited, "I know it is inconvenient to you to see your friends in the morning, but I never feel like going out in the afternoon. As soon as dinner is over I must have my nap; and by the time that is finished, it is too late for any thing else."

In consequence of these ill-timed visits, the printer may have to send in vain for "copy" that is not yet ready; and an article written expressly for a magazine may arrive too late for the next month, and be therefore deferred a month later, which may subject her not only to inconvenience, but to actual pecuniary loss—loss of money. Or, at least, the interruption may compel her to the painful effort of trying to finish it even by sitting up late at night, and straining her weary eyes by lamp-light. Yet this she must endure because it suits an idle and thoughtless *friend* to make her a long and inopportune visit. The children of the pen and the pencil might say to these intruders, like the frogs in the pond when the boys were pelting them with stones—"This may be sport to you, but it is death to us."

If, when admitted into her study, you should find her writing-table in what appears to you like great confusion, recollect that there is really no wit in a remark too common on such occasions,—"Why, you look quite *littery*,"—a poor play on the words *literary* and *litter*. In all probability, she knows precisely where to lay her hand upon every paper on the table: having in reality placed them exactly to suit her convenience. Though their arrangement may be quite unintelligible to the uninitiated, there is no doubt method (her own method, at least) in their apparent disorder. It is not likely she may have time to put her writing table in nice-looking order every day. To have it done by servants is out of the question, as *they* would make "confusion worse confounded;" being of course unable to comprehend how *such a table* should be arranged.

If you chance to find an authoress occupied with her needle, express no astonishment, and refrain from exclaiming, "What! can *you* sew?" or, "I never supposed a literary lady could even hem a handkerchief!"

This is a false, and if expressed in words, an insulting idea. A large number of literary females are excellent needle-women, and good housewives; and there is no reason why they should not be. The same vigour of character and activity of intellect which renders a woman a *good* writer, will also enable her to acquire with a quickness, almost intuitive, a competent knowledge of household affairs, and of the art of needle-work. And she will find, upon making the attempt, that, with a little time and a little perseverance, she may become as notable a personage (both in theory and practice) as if she had never read a book, or written a page.

The Dora of David Copperfield is an admirable illustration of the fact that a silly, illiterate woman may be the worst of housewives. Dickens has unquestionably painted this character exactly from life. But that he always does. He must have known a Dora. And who has not?

If you find your literary friend in dishabille, and she apologizes for it—(she had best *not* apologize)—tell her not that "authoresses are privileged persons, and are never expected to pay any attention to dress." Now, literary slatterns are not more frequent than slatterns who are not literary. It is true that women of enlarged minds, and really good taste, do not think it necessary to follow closely all the changes and follies of fashion, and to wear things that are inconvenient, uncomfortable, and unbecoming, merely because milliners, dress-makers, &c. have pronounced them "the last new style."

It is ill-manners to refer in any way to the profession of the person to whom you are talking, unless that person is an intimate friend, and you are alone with her; and unless she herself begins the subject. Still worse, to allude to their profession as if you supposed it rendered them different from the rest of the world, and marked them with peculiarities from which other people are exempt.

It is true that authorlings and poetizers are apt to affect eccentricity. Real authors, and even real poets, (by real we mean good ones,) have generally a large portion of common sense to balance their genius, and are therefore seldom guilty of the queernesses unjustly imputed to the whole fraternity.

When in company with a literary lady with whom you are not on very confidential terms, it is bad taste to talk to her exclusively of books, and to endeavour to draw out her opinion of authors with whom she is personally acquainted—and whom she will, of course, be unwilling to criticise, (at least in miscellaneous society,) lest her remarks should be invidiously or imprudently repeated, and even get into print. "Anything new in the literary world?" is a question by which some people always commence conversation with an author. Why should it be supposed that they always "carry the shop along with them," or that they take no interest or pleasure in things not connected with books. On the contrary, they are glad to be allowed the privilege of unbending like other people. And a good writer is almost always a good talker, and fully capable of conversing well on various subjects. Try her.

It was beautifully said of Jane Taylor, the charming author of a popular and never-tiring little book of "Original Poems for Children," that "you only knew that the stream of literature had passed over her mind by the fertility it left behind it."[3]

We have witnessed, when two distinguished lady-writers chanced to be at the same party, an unmannerly disposition to "pit them against each other"—placing them side by side, or vis-à-vis, and saying something about, "When Greek meets Greek," &c., and absolutely collecting a circle round them, to be amused or edified by the expected dialogue. This is rude and foolish.

It is not treating a talented woman with due consideration, to be active in introducing to her the silliest and flattest people in the room, because the said flats have been worked up into a desire of seeing, face to face, "a live authoress"—though in all probability they have not read one of her works.

That notorious lion-hunter, the Countess of Cork, was so candid as to say to certain celebrated writers, "I'll sit by *you* because you are famous." To a very charming American lady whom she was persuading to come to her party, she frankly added, "My dear, you really must not refuse me. Don't you know you are my decoy-duck."

There are mothers (called pattern-mothers) who uphold the theory that every thing in the world must bend to the advantage (real or supposed) of children, that is, of their own children—and who have continually on their lips the saying, "a mother's first duty is to her children." So it is, and it is her duty not to render them vain, impertinent, conceited, and obtrusive, by allowing them to suppose that they must on all occasions be brought forward; and that their mother's visiters have nothing to do but to improve and amuse *them*. Therefore a literary lady often receives a more than hint from such a mother to talk only on edifying subjects when the dear little creatures are present; and then the conversation is required to take a Penny-Magazine tone, exclusively—the darlings being, most probably, restless and impatient all the time, the girls sitting uneasily on their chairs and looking tired, and the boys suddenly bolting out of the room to get back to their sports. It is true the children will be less impatient if the visitor will trouble herself to "tell them stories" all the time; but it is rude to ask her to do so.

When directing a letter to "a woman of letters," it is not considered polite to insert the word "Authoress" after her name.

And yet we have seen this done by persons who ought to know better. If you are unacquainted with the number and street of her residence, direct to the care of her publisher; whose place you may always find, by referring to the title-page of one of her last works, and by seeing his advertisements in the newspapers. The booksellers always know where their authors are to be found. So do the printers—for their boys convey the proof-sheets.

Observe that the term "learned lady" is not correctly applied to a female, unless she has successfully cultivated what is understood to be the learning of colleges—for instance, the dead languages, &c. Unfortunately, the term is now seldom used but in derision, and to denote a woman whose studies have been entirely of the masculine order. You may speak of a well-informed, well-read, talented, intellectual, accomplished lady; but call her not *learned*, unless she is well-versed in the Greek and Latin classics, and able to discuss them from their original language. Even then, spare her the appellation of *learned*, if gentlemen are present. In the dark ages, when not every lady could read and write, the few that *were* entitled to the "benefit of clergy," frequently "drank deep in tasting the Pierian spring," and proceeded to study the learned languages with great success; for instance, Lady Jane Grey and Queen Elizabeth.[4]

In desiring the autograph of a literary lady, do not expect her to write in your album "a piece of poetry." Be satisfied with her signature only. There is a spice of meanness in requesting from her, as a gift, any portion of her stock in trade. As well might you ask Mr. Stewart, or Mr. Levy, to present you with an embroidered collar, or a pair of gloves. For the same reason, never request an artist to "draw something" in your album. It is only amateur poets, and amateur artists, that can afford to write and draw in albums. Those who make a living by their profession, have no time to spare for gratuitous performances;

and it is as wrong to ask them, as it is to invite public singers to "favour the company with a song" at private parties, where they are invited as guests. It is, however, not unusual for professional musicians to kindly and politely gratify the company by inviting themselves to sing; saying, "Perhaps you would like to hear my last song." And sometimes, if quite "in the vein," a real poet, when modestly asked for merely his signature, will voluntarily add a few lines of verse. But do not expect it.

There are pretty little books of fine paper, handsomely bound, that are used for the purpose of containing signature autographs; one on each page. A lady owning such a book, can send it to any distinguished person of whose hand-writing she wishes to possess a specimen.

When the name at the bottom of a letter is shown to you as an autograph, it is rude to take the letter into your own hand, and read the whole, or even to glance your eye over it. It is not intended that you shall see any thing but the signature.

We will now address a few words to beginners in the art of writing, with reference to their intercourse with women of well-established literary reputation. If these ladies of decided standing in the republic of letters have sufficient leisure, they will generally be very kind in assisting with their counsel a young aspirant, who shows any evidence of talent for the profession. Unluckily, too many novices in the art, mistake a mere desire to get into print, for that rarest of gifts—genius. And without genius, there is no possibility of gaining by the pen, either fame, or fortune.

Long manuscripts are frequently sent for the revisal "at leisure" of a person who has little or no leisure. Yet in the intervals of toiling for herself, she is expected to toil for some one else; probably for a stranger whom she does not know, in whom she can take no interest, and who has evidently "no writing in her soul." If, however, the modest request is kindly complied with, in all probability the corrections will only give offence, and may perhaps be crossed out before the manuscript is offered to the publisher, who very likely may reject it for want of these very corrections. We have known such incidents.

The least talented of the numerous females pretending to authorship, are generally the most conceited and the most obtrusive. They are frequently very great annoyances to women "well-up the ladder," who are expected, in many instances, not only to revise the manuscript, but immediately to find a purchaser for it—a purchaser of high rank among publishers—one who will bring it out handsomely, ensure it an immense circulation, pay promptly, and pay as much as is given to the standard authors. And besides being desired to "get it published," the reviser of the manuscript will, perhaps, be requested to correct the proofs; that is, if the literary novice should chance to know what proof-sheets are.

The work thus arrogantly thrust upon the time and attention of a deservedly-popular writer may be a book of "sweet poetry," on weak, worn-out, common-place subjects, done into feeble, halting, ill-rhyming verses, such as few read, and none remember. Or the aspirant after fame, may have chosen the easier path of prose, and produced a fiction without fancy, a novel without novelty, "a thrilling tale" that thrills nobody, a picture of fashionable life after no fashion that ever existed, or "a pathetic story of domestic life," neither pathetic nor domestic.

Yet if a practised and successful author ventures to pronounce an *unfavourable* verdict on such productions, because the writer desired her *candid* opinion, she will probably light up a flame of resentment, that may never be extinguished, and make an enemy for life; the objections being imputed to "sheer envy," and to a malignant design of "extinguishing a rising star."

A sufficient introduction to a publisher is to send him the manuscript, accompanied by a note requesting his opinion as soon as convenient. If he approves it, and believes it will be profitable, there is no doubt of his being willing to print the work. And if he thinks he shall make nothing by it, it is equally certain that he will decline the offer. It is too much to expect that he will be so regardless of his own interest as to publish a book, the sale of which will not remunerate him for the cost of paper and printing.

Ladies who live in the same house with an authoress, have opportunities enough of seeing her in the parlour, and at table; therefore they may dispense with visiting her in her own room. Spare her all interruptions of applying for the loan of books, paper, pens, ink, &c. Do not expect that, because she writes, she must necessarily keep a free circulating library, or a gratuitous stationer's shop. Supply yourself with all such conveniences from the regular sources. Buy them, and pay for them, instead of troubling one who has not time to be troubled. Above all, refrain from the meanness of asking her to lend you any book written by herself. If she volunteers the loan, then receive it thankfully; and take care to return it speedily, and in good condition. It is *her* interest, and the interest of her publishers, that a large number of copies shall be *sold*; not lent, or given away. Many persons erroneously suppose that an author has always on hand an unlimited number of her own books; or that the publisher will kindly give her as many as she can want for herself and friends. This is by no means the case. It is usual, when the first edition comes out, for the publisher to send the author half a dozen copies of the book, or a dozen, if it is a small one. After that, if she wants any more, she is expected to buy them of the bookseller. Therefore, she has none to *give away*, except to members of her own family, or to friends whose circumstances will not permit them to expend money in books, and who have an ardent love for reading without the means of gratifying it. We have known ladies, possessing diamonds and India shawls, and living in splendid houses, ask the author for the loan of a cookery-book, with the avowed purpose of "copying out the best receipts."

Apropos to cookery-books:—If you have faithfully followed a receipt, and the result is not quite satisfactory, there is nothing amiss in your acquainting the writer with that fact, provided it *is* a fact. On the contrary, you may do her a kindness, by enabling her to detect an error in the directions, and to rectify that error in a future edition.

Women often assert that the receipt was not a good one, and that upon trial it proved a failure, when, on investigation, you will find that, from false economy, some of the ingredients were left out; or the relative proportions diminished in quantity—too much of the cheapest articles being put in, and not enough of the more costly. Or else, that sufficient time and pains were not bestowed on the mixing and preparing; or that the thing was not sufficiently cooked.

By-the-bye, remember that a receipt for cookery, is not to be called a *recipe*. The word *recipe* belongs to pharmacy, and is only used with reference to medical prescriptions. The cook uses *receipts*, the apothecary *recipes*.

Whatever article you may wish to borrow from an inmate of the same house, apply first to persons whose time is of comparatively small importance to them, before you disturb and interrupt a literary lady. Do not trouble her for the loan of umbrellas, overshoes, hoods, calashes, &c., or send to her for small change.

We once lived in a house where coal-fires were scarce, and wood-fires plenty. Our own fire-arrangement was wood in a Franklin stove, and no other person in the house was the fortunate owner of a pair of bellows. Liking always to be comfortable, we had bought a pair for ourselves.

Ten times a day we were disturbed by a knock at the door,

from a coloured girl who came "a-borrowing" this implement to revive the fire of some other room. She called it by a pleasing variety of names—running through all the vowels. Sometimes she wanted the bellow*sas;* sometimes the bellow*ses*; or the bellow*sis*, the bellow*sos*, or the bellow*sus*. These frequent interruptions, with others that were similar, became a real grievance. We thought it would cost us less to present the bellows to the house, and buy another pair for ourselves. We did so—but very soon the first pair was somehow missing, and our own was again in requisition.

Since that winter we have burnt anthracite, and therefore have no bellowsas to lend.

Notes

The Travelling Tin-Man

1. Common name for The Society of Friends, a religious sect whose members were known for distinguishing themselves by plain speech and attire, as well as pacifism.
2. Prior to marriage, Quaker couples were to be approved by the Meeting, or congregation, with which they were affiliated.
3. A dried-out, hollow gourd often used as a container.

Mrs. Washington Potts

1. Mrs. Goodfellow was the proprietor of a Philadelphia cooking school that Leslie attended.
2. Pearl ash is a leavening agent obtained by leaching ashes of wood or other plants.
3. Most likely a fictional name.
4. Note in original: "Thick sour milk."
5. Arrangement of the centre-table was such an important domestic art that Leslie wrote a short story dedicated to the subject ("The Centre-Table").
6. *contre-temps*: French, an awkward or difficult situation or mishap.
7. A hat with a narrow, sometimes turned-up brim, a full crown, and usually a plume, worn by men and women, especially in sixteenth-century France.
8. "Early to bed and early to rise makes a man healthy, wealthy, and wise": old English proverb, made even more famous in America through its appearance in Benjamin Franklin's *Poor Richard's Almanac* in 1735.
9. Drusa is explaining that a jar of quinces, supposedly preserved with sugar, unfortunately has begun to ferment.

10. *Vivian Gray* is an 1827 novel by Benjamin Disraeli.
11. A Revolutionary War hero, the French Marquis de Lafayette visited the United States to much fanfare in 1824 and 1825.
12. Niccolò Paganini (1782–1840) was a prominent Italian violinist, violist, guitarist, and composer.
13. Sir Peter Paul Rubens (1577–1640) was a Flemish Baroque painter known for his Counter-Reformation altarpieces, portraits, landscapes, and scenes with mythological and allegorical subjects. Sir Joshua Reynolds (1723–1792) was known especially for his portraits and leadership of the Royal Academy, to which Eliza Leslie's brother Charles Robert was later inducted.
14. Benjamin West (1738–1820), an American painter well known for works depicting the Revolutionary War, was also celebrated in England as a member and president of the Royal Academy in London. Note in original: "The author takes this occasion to remark that the illustrious artist to whom so many of his countrymen erroneously give the title of *Sir* Benjamin West, never in reality had the compliment of knighthood conferred on him. He lived and died *Mr.* West, as is well known to all who have any acquaintance with pictures and painters."
15. Travel literature describing life in North America was quite popular in England and France. See, for example, Frances Trollope, *Domestic Manners of the Americans* (1832). Leslie was believed to be a European writer, due to her acerbic comments about Americans. See "Our Contributors," *Godey's Magazine and Lady's Book*, January 1846, 1.
16. From Thomas Gray (1716–1771), "The Descent of Odin: An Ode," lines 39–40.
17. *comme il faut*: French, literally, "as it's done"; proper.
18. The United States Hotel was the prominent Philadelphia hotel in which Eliza Leslie lived during the last decade of her life.
19. *ci-devant*: French, of former times.
20. *soi-disant*: French, self-proclaimed.

The Settlers

1. Most likely a reference either to the character Chevalier Pirouette, performed by actor John Reeve in the popular drama *Henriette the Forsaken* by John Baldwin Buckstone or to a comedic character enacted by Buckstone prior to the publication of the play in 1834. Buckstone

performed regularly, and the drama ran successfully at the Adelphi Theater in London. *Pirouette* is the French term for a whirl and a specific movement in ballet.

2. According to the *Oxford English Dictionary*, one type of girdle used in the nineteenth century was a large, heavy circular plate of iron used for cooking, also known as a griddle.
3. See chapter 2, note 14.

Eliza Farnham, or The Love Letters

1. Alexander Pope (1688–1744), "Eloisa to Abelard" (1717), line 51.
2. Hannah More (1745–1843), *Essays on Various Subjects Principally Designed for Young Ladies* (1777).
3. The periodical *The Rambler* (1750–52) was published by Samuel Johnson and included literature, essays on morality, society, politics, and religion.
4. Swiss philosopher and physician Johann Georg Zimmermann (1728–1795). His essays translated from the German, including *On Solitude*, were popular in Europe and America.
5. A popular nineteenth-century painting style imitating "Oriental" art. Thick opaque color without background and with little shading was applied to thin paper to produce flowers, birds, and the like.
6. Handbooks and instruction on letter writing were quite popular. See, for example, Eve Tavor Bannet, *Empire of Letters: Letter Manuals and Transatlantic Correspondence, 1680–1820* (New York: Cambridge University Press, 2005), and Lucille Schultz, "Letter-Writing Instruction in 19th-Century Schools in the United States," in David Barton and Nigel Hall, eds., *Letter Writing as Social Practice* (Philadelphia PA: John Benjamins, 2000). Leslie's *Ladies Guide* includes a chapter on "Letters," which discusses the topic of women addressing men.
7. Unidentified quotation. Note in original: "Centre Polo."
8. In the mid-nineteenth century Samuel Johnson's popular dictionary was abridged and reprinted for use in schools, with John Walker's pronunciation included. John Entick's and Noah Webster's dictionaries also were popular at the time.
9. Hugh Blair (1718–1800) was a Scottish rhetorician whose *Lectures on Rhetoric and Belles Lettres* (1783) influenced the teaching of speech and composition for almost a century.
10. *on-dits*: French, gossip; literally, "one says."

Mr. and Mrs. Woodbridge

1. On the cultures associated with boarding-houses, see Thomas Butler Gunn, *The Physiology of New York Boarding-Houses* (1857), edited and reprinted with an introduction by David Faflik (Piscataway NJ: Rutgers University Press, 2009). Eliza Leslie assisted in her mother's boarding house in Philadelphia, which was established after Mrs. Leslie was widowed.
2. *au fait*: French, up on the latest, or on the ball with.
3. A wide collar designed to cover and thus emphasize the shoulders' breadth while giving the waist a diminutive appearance. It could look very much like a cape.
4. Mary Julia Young, *A Summer at Brighton* (London: D. N. Shury, 1807). Thomas Skinner Surr, *A Winter in London* (London: Richard Philips, 1806). Marianne Spencer Hudson, *Almack's: A Novel in Three Volumes* (London: Saunders and Otley, 1826). Catherine Cuthbertson, *Santo Sebastiano* (London: George Robinson, 1806). These were considered "fashionable" or "silver fork" novels, also called "Regency romances." See Winifred Hughes, "Silver Fork Writers and Readers: Social Contexts of a Best Seller," *Novel: A Forum on Fiction* 25.3 (1992): 328–47.
5. *giorno felice*: Italian, happy day.
6. *sélon les régles*: French, according to the rules.
7. Various types of fabric.
8. William Cowper, *The Task* (1785), book 4, "The Winter Evening," lines 39–40.
9. The opera *La Cenerentola, ossia La bontà in trionfo*, was performed first in Rome in 1817. With music by Gioachinno Rossini and libretto by Jacopo Ferretti, the opera is known in English as *Cinderella, or Good Triumphant*, based on the fairytale.
10. *sotto voce*: Italian, whispered; literally, "under voice."
11. John Langhorne (1735–1779),"Owen of Carron" (1778), sec. 18, lines 9–12: "Oh married Love!—thy bard shall own, / Where two congenial souls unite, / Thy golden chains inlaid with down, / Thy lamp with heaven's own splendor bright."
12. *ménage*: French, household.
13. *allongement*: French, stretching; literally, "elongation."

14. Most likely from "Dabbling in the Dew," a popular English folk song that was also printed in books of nursery rhyme.

Nothing Morally Wrong

1. Many so-called utopian ideals and communities related to them appeared in mid nineteenth-century America. See Robert S. Fogarty, *Dictionary of American Communal and Utopian History* (Westport CT: Greenwood, 1980).
2. In the mid-nineteenth century many women were involved with the science of plants. See Tina Gianquitto, *Good Observers of Nature: American Women and the Scientific Study of the Natural World, 1820–1885* (Athens: University of Georgia Press, 2007).
3. Dugald Stewart (1753–1828), one of the Scottish "Common Sense" philosophers, was popular in the early Republic and antebellum America.

Seventy-Five Receipts for Pastry, Cakes, and Sweetmeats

1. The seeds, or stones, have been removed.
2. Little balls made from sugar, available in many colors and shapes, used to decorate cakes and cookies.

The Elephant

1. The engraving appeared with Leslie's original edition. Similar engravings appeared as the frontispiece and within the volume by Godfrey Charles Mundy (1804–1860), *Pen and Pencil Sketches, Being the Journal of a Tour in India*, published by John Murray (1832).

The Ladies' Guide to True Politeness and Perfect Manners

1. Note in original: "When the name of the state is short, you may give all the letters that compose it, as Maine—Ohio—Iowa—Texas—Utah."
2. *Paul Pry* (1825) was a popular comedy by John Poole with a long run at London's Haymarket Theatre and performances elsewhere throughout the nineteenth century. The title character curiously asks questions of everyone in an often obnoxious manner.
3. Jane Taylor (1783–1824) collaborated with her sister, Ann, on several collections, including *Original Poems for Infant Minds* (1804), *Poems for Children* (1811), and *Original Poetry for Young Minds* (1818).

4. The "benefit of clergy" refers to an English law that allowed clergy to be judged by different standards; thus, Leslie refers to women not being held to as high an expectation for learning. The second quotation is taken from Alexander Pope (1688–1744), *An Essay on Criticism* (1709), part 2, lines 15–18: "A little learning is a dangerous thing; / drink deep, or taste not the Pierian spring: / there shallow draughts intoxicate the brain, / and drinking largely sobers us again."

Chronology of Eliza Leslie's Published Works

All works are given in order of first known appearance in print. Refer to the selected bibliography for full publication details.

1803

The Young Ladies' Mentor, or Extracts in Prose and Verse

1827

Seventy-five Receipts for Pastry, Cakes and Sweetmeats

1828

Eugene and Lolotte: A Tale for Children

The Mirror, or Eighteen Juvenile Tales and Dialogues

1829

Stories for Adelaide: Being a Second Series of Easy Reading Lessons, with Divided Syllables

Stories for Emma: Being a Series of Easy Reading Lessons, with the Syllables Divided

The Young Americans, or Sketches of a Sea-Voyage, and a Short Visit to Europe

1830

"The Clean Face, or The Boy Washed by His Elder Sister"

"Country Lodgings in America"

"Frederick Ormsby"

"The Mysterious Picture"

"The Quilting"

"The Travelling Tin-Man: An American story"

1831

American Girl's Book

"Anthony and Clara, or The Elephant of Siam"

"Alphonsine"

"Frank Finlay: An American Tale"

History of Philadelphia: A Game for Children

"Lady Jane Grey"

"The Launch of the Frigate"

"The Log Bridge"

"Lucy Nelson, or The Boy-Girl"

"Maria Medway and her Grandmother"

"The Souvenir"

1832

"Billy Bedlow, or The Girl-Boy"
"The Cadet's Sister: A Dramatic Dialogue Founded on Fact"
Cards of Boston
Domestic French Cookery
"The Duchess and Sancho"
"Mrs. Washington Potts"
"The Revolutionary Officer"
"The Settlers"
"Susanna Meredith"
Wonderful Travels: Being the Narratives of Munchausen, Gulliver, and Sinbad

1833

Atlantic Tales, or Pictures of Youth
"The New-Year's Gifts"
Pencil Sketches
"The Quaker Girl"
"The Show Girl"

1834

"The Album: A Sketch"
"Laura Lovel"
"The Set of China: A Sketch"

1835

The Gift
"The Ladies' Ball: A Sketch"
Pencil Sketches
"The Reading Parties: A Sketch"
"That Gentleman, or Pencillings on Ship-Board"

1836

"Chase Loring: A Tale of the Revolution"
"Constance Allerton, or The Mourning Suits"
"A Dream of Songs"
The Gift
The Violet

1837

Directions for Cookery: Being a System of Art, in Its Various Branches
"The Old Farm House"
Pencil Sketches

1838

"Althea Vernon, or, The Embroidered Handkerchief"
The Gift
"Gleanings and Recollections"
"*Kitty's Relations*"
The Tell Tale, and The Week of Idleness
The Violet

1839

The Gift
"Gleanings and Recollections"
The Violet

1840

Birth Day Stories
Miss Leslie's Lady's House-Book
"Mr. Smith"

1841

"Dulcinea"
"Eliza Farnham, or The Love Letters"
The Gift
"Leonilla Lynmore"
"Mr. and Mrs. Woodbridge"
"The People That Did Not Take Boarders"

1842

"Alina Derlay"
"Barclay Compton"
"The Beaux"
"Boston Ramblings"
"The Daughters of Dr. Byles"
"The Rain King"
"Recollections of West Point"
"The Tenth Passenger"

1843

"Annetta Haverstraw"
"Eunice Rookley
The Gift
"The Kingsburys
Mrs. Washington Potts, and Mr. Smith

1844

"The Centre-Table"
"The Dampwoods"
"The Manderfields"
"The Parlours, Both, Are Occupied"
"Pencillings of Boston"

1845

"The Bloxhams and Mayfields"
"Dudley Villiers"
"Harriet Enfield"
"Niagara"
"Recollections of Mathews"
Stories for Helen
"Western New York"

1846

"The Batson Cottage"
"The Boy with an Inquiring Mind"
"Fourth of July Doings"
The Indian Meal Book
Kitty's Relations
The Lady's Receipt-Book
Leonilla Lynmore, and Mr. and Mrs. Woodbridge
"Recollections of Lisbon"
"The Watkinson Evening"
The Young Revolutionists

1847

Amelia, or, a Young Lady's Vicissitudes
"Juliet Irwin; or, the Carriage People"
"The Lady Her Own Housekeeper"
"Lydia Leeson"
"Uncle Philip"

1848

"Clementina's Portrait"
"The Guest That Was No Stranger"

1849

"The Cleybornes"
"Nothing Morally Wrong"
"Professor Nimmons"
"Timothy Pettigrew's Wife's Husband"
"The Two Weddings"

1850

"The Baymounts"
"Jernigan's Pa'"
"Williams Wells"

1851

The Dennings and Their Beaux, and Alina Derlay
The Maid of Canal Street, and The Bloxhams

1852

"Mrs. Derrington's Reception Day"
"Peter Jones"

1853

The Behaviour Book: A Manual for Ladies
Stories for Summer Days and Winter Nights

Selected Bibliography

This bibliography of Eliza Leslie's published works and the accompanying chronological index provide a solid basis for understanding the breadth of Leslie's appearance in print. The bibliography is selective rather than exhaustive, not simply by choice but by necessity. First, there is the inevitability of oversight: it is especially difficult to locate works by Leslie that were printed first in periodicals and anthologies and later reprinted in other periodicals, many of which have never been indexed or catalogued by author name. Likewise, some publishers paraphrased and cited Leslie's works in forms that only faintly resemble the original.

Additionally, several short pieces of household advice on items such as making paste and coloring flowers have been excluded. Readers should be aware that searches of the *American Periodical Series Online* will easily return some of these items, such as those in *Parley's Magazine* and *Godey's*. Others may be found in volumes noted within the bibliography but without full entries; thus, the bibliography directs readers to various points of entry for further research.

The bibliography's compilation has depended upon several texts and electronic databases, such as Lyle H. Wright's *American Fiction 1774–1850*; *WorldCat* of the Online Computer Library Center (OCLC); *Wolfpac*, the catalog of the Library Company of Philadelphia; the catalog of the American Antiquarian Society; and the *American Periodical Series Online*. As much as possible, imprints and editions have been confirmed by examination, including examination of digitized materials available through *Google Books*. The exceptions are Leslie's numerous culinary and domestic texts, due in part to the sheer quantity of varying imprints but also due to the availability of the excellent culinary bibliographies that describe these works. Researchers interested in this genre should consult William R. Cagle and Lisa Killion Stafford's *American Books on Food and Drink* and Eleanor Lowenstein and Waldo Lincoln's *Bibliography of American Cookery Books, 1742–1860*.

In cases where authorship previously has been attributed to Leslie but seems unlikely, the work has not been included. Some items catalogued as Leslie's upon examination proved not to be by "Miss [Eliza] Leslie of Philadelphia," as she generally was acknowledged on title pages. A catalog search by author for works in the British Library, for example, returns *Stray Leaves* (1866), a volume of poetry whose title page indicates one Eliza A. Leslie as its author. Yet the dedication page and some poems within the volume clearly were composed after Leslie the Philadelphian's death, and the place of publication suggests the volume was written by a British writer who had the same name but lived at a later time. Also illustrative are several short moralistic tales for children published in such anthologies as *The Drawing-Room Tales* of the 1830s. While catalogues may list E. Leslie or even Eliza Leslie as a contributing author, the title pages of these stories indicate they were written by Emma Leslie.

For each entry, subsequent imprints and editions follow in chronological order, with the title or parts of the title page repeated or added only to indicate changes. In cases where the contents differ significantly but the title does not, separate entries appear. For example, the edition of *Pencil Sketches* published in 1852 includes selections from three previous collections of *Pencil Sketches*, creating a fourth compilation entirely different from the previous three volumes. Thus, there are four entries for *Pencil Sketches*. The culinary volumes again provide an exception here, since the contents in later editions varied greatly. Researchers are advised to consult culinary bibliographies for a more detailed explanation of variations in these volumes.

To indicate when a work or part of a work later appeared with others, it may be described as either "bound with" or "collected in." "Bound with" indicates longer works by Leslie that were combined with longer works by other authors. For example, in 1833 Munroe and Francis bound Leslie's *Seventy-Five Receipts* with N. K. M. Lee's *The Cook's Own Book and Housekeeper's Register*. Yet in 1988 Hope Peek compiled *Antique American Recipes: From Eliza Leslie's Cookbooks*, which collected selections from *Seventy-Five Receipts*. Thus, "collected in" most often signifies shorter works gathered into or reprinted in an anthology, gift book, or periodical.

For anthologies and gift books whose contents are entirely Leslie's, the writings are listed generally by title, in order of appearance, in brackets but without page numbers. In some cases, such as that of the *American Girl's Book, or Occupation for Play Hours* (1831), the brevity and quantity of shorter items preclude listing them by title. When a reprint of one of these shorter works has not been located elsewhere, it is not given a separate entry by title. For example, a separate entry has not been created for "Augusta Curzon," one of the eighteen shorter works comprising *The Mirror*, because it has not been located in any other imprint. However, "The Boarding School Feast," which first was published in Leslie's *Atlantic Tales*, is given a separate entry for each of its subsequent appearances.

For periodicals and anthologies that include works by other authors, only the works by Leslie are listed, in order of appearance. There are exceptions. *Parley's Magazine*, to which Leslie was a regular contributor, also reprinted numerous paraphrases and excerpts from Leslie's previous publications, such as her *American Girl's Book*. The bibliography does not include these numerous items individually, but it does list Leslie's column "Gleanings and Recollections," which appeared in *Parley's* and refers researchers to the periodical because most of the shorter works included in it have not been located elsewhere.

The chronological index by short title provides a quick overview of the first appearance of many of Leslie's works. Thus, when a work or works were reprinted subsequently in a different format, such as *Antique American Recipes* (1988), the latter publication generally does not appear in the chronological index.

Finally, deserving more than a footnote is an acknowledgment that this bibliography was influenced significantly in style by the "Chronological Bibliography of the Works of Catharine Maria Sedgwick" by Lucinda L. Damon-Bach, who was assisted by Allison J. Roepsch and Melissa J. Homestead. See Lucinda L. Damon-Bach and Victoria Clements, eds., *Catharine Maria Sedgwick: Critical Perspectives* (Boston: Northeastern University Press, 2003: 295–313). Likewise, this volume's bibliography would not have been completed without the able assistance of Patrick S. Williams, Craig A. Meyer, Ingrid M. Bohnenkamp, Katherine Ellerbrake, Brooksie Trout, and Gordon C. Appleton Jr.

"The Album: A Sketch." *Atkinson's Saturday Evening Post*, August 16, 1834, 1.

———. *Atkinson's Casket, or Gems of Literature, Wit, and Sentiment* 9.10 (1834): 459–65.

———. *Pencil Sketches, or Outlines of Character and Manners*. 2nd series. Philadelphia: Carey, Lea, and Blanchard, 1835. 35–65.

———. *Pencil Sketches, or Ourlines of Character and Manners*. Philadelphia: A. Hart, 1852. 131–46.

"Alina Derlay, or the Two Caps: A Tale." *Godey's Lady's Book, and Ladies' American Magazine* (Aug. 1842): 88–94; (Sep. 1842): 115–21; (Oct. 1842): 194–98.

———. *The Dennings and Their Beaux, and Alina Derlay.* Philadelphia: A. Hart, 1851. 45–69.

"Alphonsine." Trans. from French by Eliza Leslie. *The Lady's Book and Magazine of Belle Lettres, Fashions, Music, &c.* (Apr. 1831): 201–16.

———. *Pencil Sketches, or Outlines of Character and Manners*. 3rd series. Philadelphia: Carey, Lea, and Blanchard, 1837. 234–83.

"Althea Vernon, or The Embroidered Handkerchief." *The Lady's Book and Magazine of Belle Lettres, Fashions Music &c.* (Jan. 1838): 28–32; (Mar. 1838): 99–105; (Apr. 1838): 170–75; (May 1838): 217–24.

———. *To Which Is Added, Henrietta Harrison, or The Blue Cotton Umbrella*. Philadelphia: Lea and Blanchard, 1838. 9–200.

Amelia, or A Young Lady's Vicissitudes: A Novel. Godey's Lady's Book (Oct. 1847): 195–203; (Nov. 1847): 257–64; (Dec. 1847): 317–25; (Jan. 1848): 25–53; (Feb. 1848): 109–15; (Jul. 1848): 37–44; (Aug. 1848): 101–8; (Sep. 1848): 158–66.

———. Philadelphia: Carey and Hart, 1848.

American Girl's Book, or Occupation for Play Hours. Boston: Munroe and Francis, 1831; 2nd ed., enlarged, 1834; 4th ed. Boston: Munroe and Francis, 1838, 1840; 14th ed., 1851; 16th ed. New York: C. S. Francis, 1859; 16th ed. New York: Allen Brothers, 1869, 1870.

———. Selections collected in *The Girl's Book of Diversions, or Occupation for Play Hours*. London: Thomas Tegg and Son, 1835; 3rd ed., 1837.

———. Bound with "Child, Lydia Maria." *The Little Girl's Own Book*. Glasgow: J. Fraser, 1843.

———. Bound with *Hints for Happy Hours, or Amusements for All Ages*. New York: C. S. Francis, 1857.

"Annetta Haverstraw: A Story." *Godey's Lady's Book, and Ladies' American Magazine* (Jan. 1843): 38–44; (Feb. 1843): 80–85; (Mar. 1843): 113–18; (Apr. 1843): 164–69; (May 1843): 241–45; (Jun. 1843): 255–61.

"Anthony and Clara, or The Elephant of Siam." *The Pearl, or Affection's Gift for 1832*. Philadelphia: Thomas T. Ash, [1831]. 102–25.

———. *Birth Day Stories*. Philadelphia: Henry F. Anners, [1840]. 24–50.

Atlantic Tales, or Pictures of Youth. Boston: Munroe and Francis, 1833; 2nd ed., 1835. ["The Boarding School Feast," "The Tell-Tale," "The Week of Idleness," "Madeline Malcolm," and "Russel and Sidney, or the Young Revolutionists: A Tale of 1777."]

———. Selections collected in *Stories for Helen*. Philadelphia: H. F. Anners, 1845.

"Barclay Compton, or The Sailor's Return: A Story." *Godey's Lady's Book, and Ladies' American Magazine* (Nov. 1842): 212–17; (Dec. 1842): 294–303."

"The Batson Cottage." *Godey's Magazine and Lady's Book* (Nov. 1846): 195–201.

———. Bound with Corbin, Austin. *Mneomi, or The Indian of the Connecticut*. Boston: Gleason's, 1847.

"The Baymounts." *Saturday Evening Post*, December 7, 1850, December 14, 1850, December 21, 1850, December 28, 1850.

"The Beaux: A Sketch." *Godey's Lady's Book, and Ladies' American Magazine* (Jan. 1842): 19–24; (Feb. 1842): 109–13; (Mar. 1842): 139–45; (Apr. 1842): 220–25; (May 1842): 259–66.

———. *The Dennings and Their Beaux, and Alina Derlay*. Philadelphia: A. Hart, 1851. 5–44.

The Behaviour Book: A Manual for Ladies. Philadelphia: W. P. Hazard, 1853, 1854; *The Ladies' Guide to True Politeness and Perfect Manners, or Miss Leslie's Behaviour Book, a Guide and Manual for Ladies*. Philadelphia: W. P. Hazard, 1855; Philadelphia: T. B. Peterson, 1859, 1864; New York: W. L. Allison, 1893; New York: Arno, 1972.

———. Selections collected in *Nineteenth-Century American Women Writers: An Anthology*. Edited by Karen Kilcup. Cambridge MA: Blackwell, 1997. 21–24.

"Billy Bedlow, or The Girl-Boy." *Juvenile Miscellany*, January 1, 1832, 274–81.

Birth Day Stories. Philadelphia: Henry F. Anners, [1840]. ["The Souvenir," "Anthony and Clara, or The Elephant of Siam," "The Show Girl," "The Log Bridge," "Frederick Ormsby," "The Launch of the Frigate," "The Cadet's Sister," "The Clean Face, or The Boy Washed by His Elder Sister."]

"The Bloxhams and Mayfields, or People of the Last Century." *Godey's Magazine and Lady's Book* (Jan. 1845): 6–11; (Feb. 1845): 50–55; (Mar. 1845): 103–8; (Apr. 1845): 149–54; (May 1845): 197–201; (Jun. 1845): 243–48.

———. *The Maid of Canal Street, and The Bloxhams*. Philadelphia: A. Hart, 1851.

"The Boarding School Feast." *Atlantic Tales, or Pictures of Youth*. Boston: Munroe and Francis, 1833; 2nd ed., 1835.

———. *Stories for Helen*. Philadelphia: H. F. Anners, 1845. 28–66.

"Boston Ramblings." *Graham's Lady's and Gentleman's Magazine* (Jul. 1842): 33–38.

"The Boy with an Inquiring Mind: A Sketch." *Godey's Magazine and Lady's Book*, January 1, 1846, 5–13.

"The Cadet's Sister: A Dramatic Dialogue Founded on Fact." *The Pearl, or Affection's Gift: A Christmas and New-Year's Present for 1833*. Philadelphia: Thomas T. Ash, [1832]. 45–66.

———. *Popular American Literature of the 19th* Century. Edited by Paul C. Gutjahr. New York: Oxford University Press, 2001. 95–104.

———. *Birth Day Stories*. Philadelphia: Henry F. Anners, [1840]. 153–78.

———. *Stories for Summer Days and Winter Nights*. Philadelphia: Henry F. Anners, 1853. 24–49.

Cards of Boston: Comprising a Variety of Facts and Descriptons Relative to that City, in Past and Present Times, So as to Form an Instructive and Amusing Game for Young People [Boston, 1832].

"The Centre-Table." *Godey's Magazine and Lady's Book* (Jul. 1844): 37–41; (Aug. 1844): 51–57; (Sep. 1844): 99–104; (Oct. 1844): 183–90.

"Chase Loring: A Tale of the Revolution." *The Rural Repository: Devoted to Polite Literature* (Aug. 1836): 41–46; (Sep. 1836): 49–52.

———. *Pencil Sketches, or Outlines of Character and Manners*. 3rd series. Philadelphia: Carey, Lea, and Blanchard, 1837. 193–233.
———. *The Young Revolutionists: Containing the Stories of Russel and Sidney and Chase Loring; Tales of the American Revolution*. New York: C. S. Francis, 1846; 2nd ed. Philadelphia: W. P. Hazard, 1853. 134–85.
"The Clean Face, or The Boy Washed by His Elder Sister." *The Pearl, or Affection's Gift for 1831*. Philadelphia: Thomas T. Ash, [1830]. 161.
———. *Affection's Gift, or A Holiday Present for 1832*. New York: J. C. Riker, [1831]. 207.
———. *The Hawthorn: A Christmas and New Year's Present for 1845*. New York: J. C. Riker, [1844]. 99.
———. *The Common School Speaker: a New Collection of Original and Selected Pieces, for Reading and Recitation*. Edited by William Fowler. New Haven CT: S. Babcock, 1844. 35.
———. *Pencil Sketches, or Outlines of Character and Manners*. 1st series. Philadelphia: Carey, Lea, and Blanchard, 1833. 271.
———. *Birth Day Stories*. Philadelphia: Henry F. Anners, [1840]. 179.
———. *Stories for Summer Days and Winter Nights*. Philadelphia: Henry F. Anners, 1853. 148.
"Clementina's Portrait: An Autobiographical Sketch." *Godey's Lady's Book* (Dec. 1848): 352–61.
"The Cleybornes." *Godey's Lady's Book* (Sep. 1849): 187–92; (Oct. 1849): 265–72; (Nov. 1849): 305–11; (Dec. 1849): 434–41.
"Constance Allerton, or The Mourning Suits: A Story of Domestic Life." In *The Token and Atlantic Souvenir: A Christmas and New Year's Present for 1836*. Edited by S. G. Goodrich. Boston: Charles Bowen, [1835]. 323–58.
———. *Atkinson's Casket, or Gems of Literature, Wit, and Sentiment* (Jan. 1836): 13–19.
———. *The Saturday Evening Post*, February 6, 1836, 1.
———. *Pencil Sketches, or Outlines of Character and Manners*. 3rd series. Philadelphia: Carey, Lea, and Blanchard, 1837. 35–68.
———. *Pencil Sketches, or Outlines of Character and Manners*. Philadelphia: A. Hart, 1852. 415–40.
"Country Lodgings in America." In *The Juvenile Forget-Me-Not: A*

Christmas and New Year's Gift, or Birthday Present for 1835. Edited by S. C. Hall. London: Ackermann, 1834. 190–212.

———. *Pencil Sketches, or Outlines of Character and Manners*. 2nd series. Philadelphia: Carey, Lea, and Blanchard, 1835. 76–92.

———. *Pencil Sketches, or Outlines of Character and Manners*. Philadelphia: A. Hart, 1852. 402–14.

"The Dampwoods: A Slight Sketch." *Godey's Magazine and Lady's Book* (Dec. 1844): 244–50.

"The Daughters of Dr. Byles: A Sketch of Reality." *Graham's Lady's and Gentleman's Magazine* (Jan. 1842): 61–66; (Feb. 1842): 114–19.

The Dennings and Their Beaux, and Alina Derlay. Philadelphia: A. Hart, 1851.

Directions for Cookery: Being a System of Art, in Its Various Branches. Philadelphia: E. L. Carey and A. Hart, 1837; 3rd ed., 1838; 4th ed., with improvements and supplementary receipts, 1838; 6th ed., with improvements and supplementary receipts, 1839; 7th ed., 1839; 8th ed., 1839; 10th ed., 1840; 11th ed., 1840; 12th ed., 1841; 13th ed., 1841; 14th ed., 1841; 15th and 16th eds., 1842; 18th ed., 1843; 20th ed., with improvements, supplementary receipts, and a new appendix, 1844; 23rd ed., with improvements, supplementary receipts, and a new appendix, 1845; 24th ed., 1846, 25th ed., 1847; 28th ed., 1847; 30th ed., 1848; 31st ed., 1848; 32nd ed., 1849; 33rd ed., 1849; 34th ed., 1849; Philadelphia: Henry C. Baird, 35th ed., 1850; 36th ed., 1850; 38th ed., 1851; 40th ed., thoroughly revised, with additions, published by Henry Carey Baird, 1851; 43rd ed., 1852; 48th ed., 1853; 49th ed., 1853; 51st ed., 1853; 52nd ed., 1854; 54th ed., 1854; 55th ed., 1855; 56th ed., 1856; 57th ed., 1856; 58th ed., 1858; 59th ed., 1861; 60th ed., 1870. *Directions for Cookery: In Its Various Branches*. New York: Clark, Austin, and Smith, 1859. Edited by Louis Szathmary, New York: Arno, 1973 [1848 edition]; rpt. Monterrey CA: Creative Cookbooks, 2001 [1848 edition]. *Miss Leslie's Directions for Cookery: An Unabridged Reprint of the 1851 Classic*. Mineola NY: Dover, 1999.

———. Bound with *The Cook's Own Book and Housekeeper's Register* and *Seventy-Five Receipts for Pastry, Cakes, and Sweetmeats*. Boston: Munroe and Francis, 1851; 3rd ed. Philadelphia: E. L. Carey and A. Hart, 1837.

———. Selections collected in *Antique American Recipes: From Eliza Leslie's Cookbooks*. Edited by Hope Peek. Mount Vernon NY: Constantia, 1988. Also collected in *Receipts: Salem, N.C., 1844–1854*. Winston-Salem NC: Domestic Skills Program, Old Salem, 1990.

Domestic French Cookery. Trans. from Sulpice Barué by Eliza Leslie. Philadelphia: Carey and Hart, 1832; 3rd ed., 1835; 4th ed., 1836; New ed., 1844, 1846; Philadelphia: Henry Carey Baird, 1855.

———. Selections collected in *Antique American Recipes: From Eliza Leslie's Cookbooks*. Edited by Hope Peek. Mount Vernon NY: Constantia, 1988.

"A Dream of Songs." *Atkinson's Casket, or Gems of Literature, Wit, and Sentiment* (Apr. 1836): 193–94.

———. Version embedded in "The Serenades." *Pencil Sketches, or Outlines of Character and Manners*, 3rd series. Philadelphia: Carey, Lea, and Blanchard, 1837. 123–32.

"The Duchess and Sancho." *The Atlantic Souvenir*. Philadelphia: Carey and Lea, 1832. 64–65.

———. *Pencil Sketches, or Outlines of Character and Manners*. 1st series. Philadelphia: Carey, Lea, and Blanchard, 1833. 270.

"Dulcinea." *The Gift: A Christmas and New Year's Present for 1842*. Philadelphia: Carey and Hart, 1841. 43.

"Dudley Villiers: A Sketch." *Godey's Magazine and Lady's Book* (Aug. 1845): 39–46.

———. *Leonilla Lynmore, and Mr. and Mrs. Woodbridge, or A Lesson for Young Wives, also, Dudley Villiers*. Philadelphia: Carey and Hart, 1847. 108–18.

"Eliza Farnham, or the Love Letters." *Godey's Lady's Book, and Ladies' American Magazine* (May 1841): 217–21; (Jun. 1841): 245–51.

"The Escorted Lady." *Pencil Sketches, or Outlines of Character and Manners*. 1st series. Philadelphia: Carey, Lea, and Blanchard, 1833. 1–33.

———. *Kitty's Relations and Other Pencil Sketches*. Philadelphia: Carey and Hart, 1847. 42–59.

Eugene and Lolotte: a Tale for Children. Trans. from the French of Madame de Genlis by Miss Leslie. Boston: Munroe and Francis, 1828.

"Eunice Rookley: A Sequel to the Story of Leonilla Lynmore." *Godey's Lady's Book, and Ladies' American Magazine* (Sep. 1843): 113–19; (Oct. 1843): 182–87; (Nov. 1843): 230–35; (Dec. 1843): 278–85."
"Fourth of July Doings: A Sketch—Founded on Fact." *Godey's Magazine and Lady's Book*, October 1, 1846, 146–53."
"Frank Finlay: An American Tale." In *The Juvenile Forget-Me-Not: A Christmas and New Year's Gift, or Birthday Present for 1832*. Edited by S. C. Hall. London: Frederick Westley and A. H. Davis, [1831]. 33–64.
———. *Pencil Sketches, or Outlines of Character and Manners*. 1st series. Philadelphia: Carey, Lea, and Blanchard, 1833. 126–44.
———. *The American Miscellany, or Popular Tales, Essays, Sketches of Character, Poetry, and Jeux d'Espirit by Transatlantic Authors*. Vol. 18. London: G. Berger, Holywell Street, Strand, 1840. 273–79.
"Frederick Ormsby." *The Pearl, or Affection's Gift for 1831*. Philadelphia: Thomas T. Ash, [1830]. 36–56.
———. *Affection's Gift, or A Holiday Present for 1832*. New York: J. C. Riker, [1831]. 187–206.
———. *Hawthorn: A Christmas and New Year's Present for 1845*. New York: J. C. Riker, [1844]. 9–27.
———. *Birth Day Stories*. Philadelphia: Henry F. Anners, [1840]. 113–36.
———. *Stories for Summer Days and Winter Nights*. Philadelphia: Henry F. Anners, [1853]. 150–73.
The Gift: A Christmas and New Year's Present. Edited by Eliza Leslie. Philadelphia: E. L. Carey and A. Hart, 1835. ["The Serenades."]
The Gift: A Christmas and New Year's Present for 1837. Edited by Eliza Leslie. Philadelphia: E. L. Carey and A. Hart, 1836. ["The Officers."]
The Gift: A Christmas and New Year's Present for 1839. Edited by Eliza Leslie. Philadelphia: E. L. Carey and A. Hart, [1838]. ["Mrs. Chaloner's Visit: A Sketch."]
The Gift: A Christmas and New Year's Present for 1840. Edited by Eliza Leslie. Philadelphia: E. L. Carey and A. Hart, [1839]. ["The French in La Mancha," "The Ghost-Book," and "Scott and Shakspeare."]
The Gift: A Christmas and New Year's Present for 1842. Edited by Eliza

Leslie. Philadelphia: Carey and Hart, 1841. ["Dulcinea," "The People That Did Not Take Boarders."]

The Gift: A Christmas and New Year's Present 1844. Philadelphia: Carey and Hart, 1843. ["Pencillings of Boston."]

The Gift: A Christmas and New Year's Present 1845. Edited by Eliza Leslie. Philadelphia: Carey and Hart, 1844.

"Gleanings and Recollections." By Miss Leslie. *Parley's Magazine* 1838. ["The Bell," 354; "Clocks" 69; "Custard," 142; "King's Evil," "Song of English History," "The Magpie," and "The Elephant," 202; "The Man with the Iron Mask," 378; "The New York Fire," 30; "English Chimney Sweepers," 291; "Lafayette's Visit to Philadelphia," 117; "Old Barbara" 238; "Punchinello" 97; "Cicerone" and "Mummies," 97; "Roses," 188.]

———. *Parley's Magazine* 1839. ["The Tame Beaver," 42–43; "The Swine General," "Monkies," and "The Plane Tree of Frauenstein."]

"The Guest That Was No Stranger." *Godey's Ladies Book* (Oct. 1848): 219–28.

"Harriet Enfield, or The Ball Dress." *Godey's Magazine and Lady's Book* (Oct. 1845): 135–43.

"Henrietta Harrison, or The Blue Cotton Umbrella: A Sketch." *Godey's Lady's Book and Magazine* (Jul. 1877): 29–37; (Aug. 1877): 143–52.

———. *Althea Vernon, or The Embroidered Handkerchief: To Which Is Added, Henrietta Harrison, or The Blue Cotton Umbrella*. Philadelphia: Lea and Blanchard, 1838. 203–76.

"The Lady Her Own Housekeeper." *Godey's Magazine and Lady's Book* (Jan. 1847): 37–43.

History of Philadelphia: A Game for Children. 60 cards, 8 x 6 cm. Philadelphia: [Thomas T. Ash], 1831 and 1872.

The Indian Meal Book: Comprising the Best Receipts for the Preparation of that Article London: Smith, Elder, 1846; 2nd ed., 1848; Philadelphia: Carey and Hart, 1847.

———. Reprinted as *Corn Meal Cookery: A Collection of Heirloom Corn Meal Recipes Dating from 1846*. Hamilton OH: Lawrence D. Burns, Simon Pure Enterprises, 1998.

———. Selections collected in *Antique American Recipes: From Eliza*

Leslie's Cookbooks. Edited by Hope Peek. Mount Vernon NY: Constantia, 1988.

"Jernigan's Pa'." *Mammoth Gazette*, January 26, 1850; February 2, 1850, 1.

"John W. Robertson, A Tale of a Cent." *Pencil Sketches, or Outlines of Character and Manners*. 2nd series. Philadelphia: Carey, Lea, and Blanchard, 1835. 201–38.

———. *Pencil Sketches, or Outlines of Character and Manners*. Philadelphia: A. Hart, 1852. 197–216.

"Juliet Irwin, or The Carriage People." *Godey's Magazine and Lady's Book* (June 1, 1847): 278–87.

"The Kingsburys: A Sketch." *Godey's Lady's Book, and Ladies' American Magazine* (Jul. 1843): 5–13."

"Kitty's Relations." *The Lady's Book and Magazine of Belle Lettres, Fashions, Music, &c.* (Oct. 1838): 180–87; (Nov. 1838): 232–37; (Dec. 1838): 241–47.

———. *Kitty's Relations and Other Pencil Sketches*. Philadelphia: Carey and Hart, 1847. 9–41.

Kitty's Relations and Other Pencil Sketches. Philadelphia: Carey and Hart, 1847. ["Kitty's Relations," "The Escorted Lady," "The People That Did Not Take Boarders," "A Pic-nic at the Sea-shore," and "The Tenth Passenger."]

"The Ladies' Ball: A Sketch." *The Saturday Evening Post*, January 24, 1835, 1.

———. *Atkinson's Casket, or Gems of Literature, Wit, and Sentiment* (Feb. 1835): 62–70.

———. *Pencil Sketches, or Outlines of Character and Manners*. 2nd series. Philadelphia: Carey, Lea, and Blanchard, 1835. 239–81.

———. *The American Miscellany, or Popular Tales, Essays, Sketches of Character, Poetry, and Jeux d'Espirit by Transatlantic Authors*. Vol. 18. London: G. Berger, Holywell Street, Strand, 1840. 237–375, 390–396.

———. *Pencil Sketches, or Outlines of Character and Manners*. Philadelphia: A. Hart, 1852. 217–39.

"Lady Jane Grey." *The Atlantic Souvenir*. Philadelphia: Carey and Lea, 1831. 84–86.

———. *The Juvenile Forget-Me-Not: A Christmas and New Year's Gift, or Birth-Day Present for 1833*. Edited by S. C. Hall London: R. Ackermann, [1832]. 210–12.

———. *Pencil Sketches, or Outlines of Character and Manners*. 1st series. Philadelphia: Carey, Lea and, Blanchard, 1833. 272–74.

The Lady's Receipt-Book: A Useful Companion for Large or Small Families; By Miss Leslie, Being a Sequel to Her Former Work on Domestic Cookery; Comprising New and Approved Directions for Preparing Soups, Fish, Meats, Vegetables, Poultry, Game, Pies, Puddings, Cakes, Confectionary, Sweetmeats, Jellies, &c. Philadelphia: Carey and Hart, 1847. *Miss Leslie's Lady's New Receipt-Book: A Useful Guide for Large or Small Families Containing Directions for Cooking, Preserving, Pickling . . .* Philadelphia: A. Hart, 1850; 3rd ed., 1851; 6th ed., enlarged; *More Receipts: By Miss Leslie, Comprising New and Approved Methods of Preparing Soups, Fish, Oysters, Terrapins, Turtle, Vegetables, Meats, Poultry, Game. . .*, Philadelphia: A. Hart, 1852; 7th ed., *New Receipts for Cooking*, Philadelphia: T. B. Peterson, [1854].

"The Launch of the Frigate." *Affection's Gift, or A Holiday Present for 1832*. New York: J. C. Riker, [1831]. 266–79.

———. *Birth Day Stories*. Philadelphia: Henry F. Anners, [1840]. 137–52.

———. *Hawthorn: A Christmas and New Year's Present for 1845*. New York: J. C. Riker, [1844]. 196–208.

———. *Stories for Summer Days and Winter Nights*. Philadelphia: Henry F. Anners, 1853. 86–101.

"Laura Lovel." *Atkinson's Saturday Evening Post*, 10 May 1834, 1; 17 May 1834, 1.

———. *Atkinson's Casket, or Gems of Literature, Wit, and Sentiment* (Jan. 1834): 193–202 [*sic* 212].

———. *Pencil Sketches, or Outlines of Character and Manners*. 2nd series. Philadelphia: Carey, Lea, and Blanchard, 1835. 125–200.

———. *Pencil Sketches, or Outlines of Character and Manners*. Philadelphia: A. Hart, 1852. 157–96.

Laura Lovel: A Sketch, for Ladies Only. Lowell MA: Franklin Bookstore, 1834.

"Leonilla Lynmore." *Godey's Lady's Book, and Ladies' American Magazine* (Jul. 184)1: 3–8; (Aug. 1841): 83–89; (Sep. 1841): 133–37; (Oct. 1841): 180–84; (Nov. 1841): 229–37; (Dec. 1841): 283–90.

———. *Leonilla Lynmore, and Mr. and Mrs. Woodbridge, or A Lesson for Young Wives, also, Dudley Villiers*. Philadelphia: Carey and Hart, 1847. 9–68.

Leonilla Lynmore, and Mr. and Mrs. Woodbridge, or A Lesson for Young Wives, also, Dudley Villiers. Philadelphia: Carey and Hart, 1847.

"The Log Bridge." *Affection's Gift, or A Holiday Present for 1832*. New York: J. C. Riker, [1831]. 254–64.

———. *Birth Day Stories*. Philadelphia: Henry F. Anners, [1840]. 100–112.

"Lucy Nelson, or The Boy-Girl." *The Juvenile Miscellany* Nov.-Dec. 1831: 149–60.

"Lydia Leeson: A Story of a Silk Dress." *Godey's Magazine and Lady's Book*, March 1, 1847, 137–45.

"Madeline Malcolm." *Atlantic Tales, or Pictures of Youth*. Boston: Munroe and Francis, 1833.

———. *Stories for Helen*. Philadelphia: H. F. Anners, 1845. 89–140.

The Maid of Canal Street, and The Bloxhams. Philadelphia: A. Hart, 1851.

"The Manderfields." *Godey's Magazine and Lady's Book* (Jan. 1844): 46–51; (Feb. 1844): 64–69; (Mar. 1844): 111–17; (Apr. 1844): 189–94; (May 1844): 237–42; (Jun. 1844): 252–60.

"Maria Medway and Her Grandmother." In *The Pearl, or Affection's Gift for 1832*. Philadelphia: Thomas T. Ash, [1831]. 178–99.

The Mirror, or Eighteen Juvenile Tales and Dialogues. By a lady of Philadelphia. Boston: Munroe and Francis, 1828. ["The Black Satin Pelisse," "The Thunder-Storm," "The Snow-Storm," "The Parrot," "Marianne Carrington," "Augusta Curzon," "The Fourth of July," "A Visit to the Sea-Shore," "The Indians," "The Dog Milo," "The Quaker Boy," "The Truant," "The Birth-Day Invitations," "The Mimic," "Dominic Morris," "Little Martenise," "The Shawl Dance," and "A Day at West-Point."]

———. Selections paraphrased in *The Little Child's Present*. Boston: Munroe and Francis, [1838–1853?].

Miss Leslie's Lady's House-Book: A Manual of Domestic Economy, Containing Approved Directions for Washing, Dress-Making, Millinery, Dyeing, Cleaning. . . . 1st, 2nd, and 3rd eds., Philadelphia: Carey and Hart, 1840; 5th ed., 1841; 7th ed., 1845; 12th, 13th, and 14th eds.,

Philadelphia: A. Hart, 1850; 18th ed., 1853; 14th ed., Philadelphia: H. C. Baird, 1850; 18th ed., 1853; 19th ed., 1855; [19th ed., enlarged] 1863; Philadelphia: Parry and McMillan, 1854.

Miss Leslie's Nursery Stories, or Tales of Truth, and Cautions for Children. London: Edward Lacey, [1830]; with fine cuts, 1848. ["The Monkey," "Little Anthony," "The Sparrow's Nest," "The Pet Calf," "Poor Crazy Samuel," "The Mischievous Boy," and "The Four Little Dogs."]

"Mr. and Mrs. Woodbridge: A Story of Domestic Life." *Godey's Lady's Book, and Ladies' American Magazine* (Jan. 1841): 2–7; (Feb. 1841): 74–79; (Mar. 1841): 109–15; (Apr. 1841): 168–75.

———. *Mr. and Mrs. Woodbridge, with Other Tales, Representing Life as It Is: And Intended to Show What It Should Be.* Providence RI: Isaac H. Cady, 1841. 13–123.

———. *Leonilla Lynmore, and Mr. and Mrs. Woodbridge, or A Lesson for Young Wives, also, Dudley Villiers.* Philadelphia: Carey and Hart, 1847. 69–107.

"Mr. Smith." *Godey's Lady's Book, and Ladies' American Magazine* (Aug. 1840): 49–61.

———. *Mrs. Washington Potts, and Mr. Smith.* Philadelphia: Lea and Blanchard, 1843. 38–63.

———. *Pencil Sketches, or Outlines of Character and Manners.* Philadelphia: A. Hart, 1852. 50–81.

———. *The Baronet's Bride, Mrs. Washington Potts, and Its Sequel Mr. Smith, Mary Powell, The Disponent, and Twenty-five Other Capital Stories.* Philadelphia: J. Van Court, 1858. 59–73.

"Mrs. Derrington's Reception Day." *The Female Prose Writers of America: With Portraits, Biographical Notices, and Specimens of Their Writings.* Edited by John S. Hart. Philadelphia: E. H. Butler, 1852. 32–48.

"Mrs. Washington Potts." *Godey's Lady's Book and Magazine* (Oct. 1832): 169–83.

———. *Atkinson's Saturday Evening Post*, November 17, 1832, 1–2.

———. *Atkinson's Casket, or Gems of Literature, Wit, and Sentiment* (Jan. 1833): 29–38.

———. *Pencil Sketches, or Outlines of Character and Manners.* 1st series. Philadelphia: Carey, Lea, and Blanchard, 1833. 162–206.

———. *The Rural Repository: Devoted to Polite Literature*, March 13, 1841, 154–58.
———. *Mrs. Washington Potts, and Mr. Smith*. Philadelphia: Lea and Blanchard, 1843. 9–37.
———. *Pencil Sketches, or Outlines of Character and Manners*. Philadelphia: A. Hart, 1852. 13–49.
———. *The Baronet's Bride, Mrs. Washington Potts, and Its Sequel Mr. Smith, Mary Powell, The Disponent, and Twenty-Five Other Capital Stories*. Philadelphia: J. Van Court, 1858. 42–58.
———. *Godey's Lady's Book* (Jan. 1865): 68–76; (Feb. 1866): 158–67.
———. *Provisions: A Reader from 19th-Century American Women*. Edited by Judith Fetterley. Bloomington: Indiana University Press, 1985. 75–104.
———. *Rediscoveries: American Short Stories by Women, 1800–1916*. Edited by Barbara H. Solomon. New York: Mentor, 1994.
Mrs. Washington Potts, and Mr. Smith. Philadelphia: Lea and Blanchard, 1843.
"The Mysterious Picture." *The Pearl, or Affection's Gift for 1831*. Philadelphia: Thomas T. Ash, [1830]. 195–209.
———. *Affection's Gift, or A Holiday Present for 1832*. New York: J. C. Riker, [1831]. 208–21.
———. *Hawthorn: A Christmas and New Year's Present for 1845*. New York: J. C. Riker, [1844]. 57–70.
"The New-Year's Gifts." *The Juvenile Forget-Me-Not: A Christmas and New Year's Gift, or Birthday Present for 1834*. Edited by S. C. Hall. London: Ackermann, [1833]. 65–97.
———. *The Violet: A Christmas and New-Year's Gift, or Birth-Day Present, 1839*. Edited by Miss Leslie. Philadelphia: E. L. Carey and A. Hart, (1838). 165–200.
"Niagara." *Godey's Magazine and Lady's Bo*, December 1, 1845, 230–38.
"Nothing Morally Wrong." *Godey's Lady's Book* (Jul. 1849): 41–48; (Aug. 1849): 136–44.
"The Officers." *The Gift: A Christmas and New Year's Present for 1837*. Edited by Eliza Leslie. Philadelphia: E. L. Carey and A. Hart, [1836]. 210–51.
———. *Pencil Sketches, or Outlines of Character and Manners*. 3rd series. Philadelphia: Carey, Lea, and Blanchard, 1837. 69–109.

———. *Pencil Sketches, or Outlines of Character and Manners*. Philadelphia: A. Hart, 1852. 266–96.

"The Old Farm House." In *The Token and Atlantic Souvenir: A Christmas and New Year's Present*, edited by S. G. Goodrich. Boston: Charles Bowen, 1837. 257–84.

———. *Pencil Sketches, or Outlines of Character and Manners*. 3rd series. Philadelphia: Carey, Lea, and Blanchard, 1837. 134–59.

———. *Pencil Sketches, or Outlines of Character and Manners*. Philadelphia: A. Hart, 1852. 314–42.

"The Parlours, Both, Are Occupied: A New Song, Dedicated to the Inmates of All Fashionable Boarding-Houses Throughout the United States." *Godey's Magazine and Lady's Book* (Feb. 1844): 100–102.

Pencil Sketches, or Outlines of Character and Manners. 1st series. Philadelphia: Carey, Lea, and Blanchard, 1833. ["The Escorted Lady," "A Pic-nic at the Sea-Shore," "The Miss Vanlears," "Country Lodgings," "Sociable Visiting," "Frank Finlay," "The Travelling Tin-Man," "Mrs. Washington Potts," "Uncle Philip," "The Revolutionary Officer," "Poland and Liberty," "The Duchess and Sancho," "The Clean Face," and "Lady Jane Grey."] [Selections collected in *Pencil Sketches* (1852).]

Pencil Sketches, or Outlines of Character and Manners. 2nd series. Philadelphia: Carey, Lea, and Blanchard, 1835. ["The Wilson House, or Village Gossip," "The Album," "The Reading Parties," "The Set of China," "Laura Lovel," "John W. Robertson: A Tale of a Cent," and "The Ladies' Ball."] [Selections collected in *Pencil Sketches* (1852).]

Pencil Sketches, or Outlines of Character and Manners. 3rd series. Philadelphia: Carey, Lea, and Blanchard, 1837. ["The Red Box, or Scenes at the General Wayne," "Constance Allerton, or The Mourning Suits," "The Officers: A Story of the Last War," "The Serenades," "The Old Farm House," "That Gentleman, or Pencillings on Ship-Board," "Chase Loring, a Story of the Revolution," and "Alphonsine."]

Pencil Sketches, or Outlines of Character and Manners. Philadelphia: A. Hart, 1852. ["Mrs. Washington Potts," "Mr. Smith," "Uncle Philip,"

"The Album," "The Set of China," "Laura Lovel," "John W. Robertson: A Tale of a Cent," "The Ladies' Ball," "The Red Box, or Scenes at the General Wayne," "The Officers: A Story of the Last War with England," "Peter Jones: A Sketch from Life," "The Serenades," "The Old Farm-House," "That Gentleman: or Pencillings on Ship-Board," "The Serenades," "Sociable Visiting," "Country Lodgings," and "Constance Allerton, or the Mourning Suits."]

"The People That Did Not Take Boarders." *The Gift: A Christmas and New Year's Present for 1842*. Philadelphia: Carey and Hart, 1841. 172–203.

———. *Kitty's Relations and Other Pencil Sketches*. Philadelphia: Carey and Hart, 1847. 60–76.

"The Pet Calf." *Stories for Adelaide: Being a Second Series of Easy Reading Lessons, with Divided Syllables*. Philadelphia: Thomas T. Ash, 1829 and 1856.

———. *Miss Leslie's Nursery Stories, or Tales of Truth, and Cautions for Children*. London: Edward Lacey, [1830]; with fine cuts, 1848.

"Pic-nic at the Sea-Shore." *Pencil Sketches, or Outlines of Character and Manners*. 1st series. Philadelphia: Carey, Lea, and Blanchard, 1833. 34–48.

———. *Kitty's Relations and Other Pencil Sketches*. Philadelphia: Carey and Hart, 1847. 77–84.

———. *Americans at Home, or Byeways, Backwoods, and Prairies*. Edited by the author of "Sam Slick." London: Hurst and Blackett, 1854. 199–222.

"Professor Nimmons: A Sketch." *Godey's Lady's Book* (May 1849): 339–45; (Jun. 1849): 405–14.

"The Quaker Girl." *The Pearl, or Affection's Gift: A Christmas and New-Year's Present for 1834*. Philadelphia: Thomas T. Ash, [1833]. 70–98.

"The Quilting." *The Pearl, or Affection's Gift for 1831*. Philadelphia: Thomas T. Ash, [1830]. 93–115.

———. *Affection's Gift, or A Holiday Present for 1832*. New York: J. C. Riker, [1831]. 232–53.

———. *The Cloak*. Edited by Mrs. [Mary Martha] Sherwood. London: William Darton and Son, 1836. 46–72.

———. *Hawthorn: A Christmas and New Year's Present for 1845*. New York: J. C. Riker, [1844]. 133–54.

———. *Americans at Home, or Byeways, Backwoods, and Prairies*. Edited by the Author of "Sam Slick." London: Hurst and Blackett, 1854. 162–68.

"The Rain King, or A Glance at the Next Century." *Godey's Lady's Book, and Ladies' American Magazine* (Jul. 1842): 7–12.

"The Reading Parties, A Sketch." *The Token and Atlantic Souvenir: A Christmas and New Year's Present*. Edited by S. G. Goodrich. Boston: Charles Bowen, 1835. 216–45.

———. *Pencil Sketches, or Outlines of Character and Manners*. 2nd series. Philadelphia: Carey, Lea, and Blanchard, 1835. 67–104.

"Recollections of Lisbon." *Godey's Magazine and Lady's Book*, February 1, 1846, 53–59.

"Recollections of Mathews: Referring Only to the First Time of His Visiting America." *Godey's Magazine and Lady's Book* (Jul. 1845): 6–13.

"Recollections of West Point." *Graham's Lady's and Gentleman's Magazine* (Apr. 1842): 205–10; (May 1842): 290–96.

"The Red Box; or Scenes at the General Wayne." *Pencil Sketches, or Outlines of Character and Manners*. 3rd series. Philadelphia: Carey, Lea, and Blanchard, 1837. 1–34.

———. *Pencil Sketches, or Outlines of Character and Manners*. Philadelphia: A. Hart, 1852. 240–65.

"The Revolutionary Officer." *The Atlantic Souvenir*. Philadelphia: Carey and Lea, 1832. 252–54.

———. *Pencil Sketches, or Outlines of Character and Manners*. 1st series. Philadelphia: Carey, Lea, and Blanchard, 1833. 267–68.

———. *The Young Revolutionists: Containing the Stories of Russel and Sidney and Chase Loring: Tales of the American Revolution*. New York: C. S. Francis, 1846; 2nd ed., Philadelphia: W. P. Hazard, 1853. 186–87.

"Russel and Sidney, or The Young Revolutionists: A Tale of 1777." *Atlantic Tales, or Pictures of Youth*. Boston: Munroe and Francis, 1833; 2nd ed., 1835.

———. *The Young Revolutionists: Containing the Stories of Russel and*

Sidney and Chase Loring: Tales of the American Revolution. New York: C. S. Francis, 1846; 2nd. ed., Philadelphia: W. P. Hazard, 1853. 5–133.

"The Salamarian Springs." *The Lady's Book* (Jul. 1839): 38–43; (Aug. 1839): 62–68.

"The Serenades." *The Lady's Book.* Vol. 10–11, n.d.

———. *The Gift: A Christmas and New Year's Present for 1836.* Edited by Eliza Leslie. Philadelphia: E. L. Carey and A. Hart, 1835. 271–92.

———. *Pencil Sketches, or Outlines of Character and Manners.* 3rd series. Philadelphia: Carey, Lea, and Blanchard, 1837. 110–33.

———. *Pencil Sketches, or Outlines of Character and Manners.* Philadelphia: A. Hart, 1852. 147–56.

———. *Cyclopaedia of Wit and Humor.* Vol. 1. Edited by Wayne E. Burton and William Evan Burton. New York: D. Appleton, 1867. 135–39, 242–51.

"The Set of China: A Sketch." *Atkinson's Casket, or Gems of Literature, Wit, and Sentiment* (Jan. 1834): 193–202 [*sic* 212].

———. *The Knickerbocker, or New-York Monthly Magazine.* Vol. 4 (Dec. 1834). New York: Clark and Edson, 434–41.

———. *Pencil Sketches, or Outlines of Character and Manners.* 2nd series. Philadelphia: Carey, Lea, and Blanchard, 1835. 105–24.

———. *Pencil Sketches, or Outlines of Character and Manners.* Philadelphia: A. Hart, 1852. 147–56.

"The Settlers." *The Juvenile Forget-Me-Not: A Christmas and New Year's Gift, or Birth-Day Present for 1833.* Edited by S. C. Hall. London: R. Ackermann, [1832]. 42–64.

Seventy-Five Receipts for Pastry, Cakes, and Sweetmeats: By a Lady of Philadelphia. Boston: Munroe and Francis, 1828; 2nd ed., 1829; 3rd ed., with an appendix, 1830; 4th ed., improved with an appendix, 1832; 7th ed., revised, with forty additional receipts, 1834; 8th ed., 1835; 9th ed., 1836; 10th ed., 1838; 11th ed., revised, 1839; 20th ed., enlarged, 1846, 1847, 1851; San Francisco: American Institute of Wine and Food, 1986; Bedford MA: Applewood, 1993, 1998.

———. Bound with Lee, N. K. M. *The Cook's Own Book and Housekeeper's Register.* Boston: Munroe and Francis, 1833, 1837, 1838, 1839, 1840, 1845, 1849, 1851, 1854. Lee, N. K. M. *The Cook's Own Book.*

New York: J. Miller, 1864; New York: O. S. Felt, 1865; New York: R. Worthington, 1885; San Francisco: Three Forks, 1977. Lee, N. K. M. *The American Family Cook Book*. Boston: Higgins, Bradley, and Dayton, 1858.

———. Partially collected in *Antique American Recipes: From Eliza Leslie's Cookbooks*. Edited by Hope Peek. Mount Vernon NY: Constantia, 1988.

———. Partially collected in *Receipts: Salem, N.C., 1844–1854*. Edited by Eliza Leslie and L. L. Senseman. Winston-Salem NC: Domestic Skills Program, Old Salem, 1990.

"The Show Girl: Founded on Fact." *The Pearl, or Affection's Gift: A Christmas and New-Year's Present for 1834*. Philadelphia: Thomas T. Ash, [1833]. 146–85.

———. *Birthday Stories: Intended as a Companion to the Youth's Keepsake.* London: William Darnton and Son, Holborn Hill, [1835]. 85–138.

———. *Birth Day Stories*. Philadelphia: Henry F. Anners, [1840]. 51–99.

———. *The Hyacinth, or Affection's Gift: A Christmas, New-Year, and Birth-Day Present for 1853*. Philadelphia: Henry F. Anners, [1852]. 115–60.

———. *Stories for Summer Days and Winter Nights*. Philadelphia: Henry F. Anners, 1853. 102–47.

"The Souvenir." *Affection's Gift, or a Holiday Present for 1832*. New York: J. C. Riker, [1831]. 53–67.

———. *Birth Day Stories*. Miss Eliza Leslie. Philadelphia: Henry F. Anners, [1840]. 5–23.

———. *Hawthorn: a Christmas and New Year's Present for 1845*. New York: J. C. Riker, [1844]. 157–71.

———. *The Hyacinth, or, Affection's Gift. A Christmas, New-Year, and Birth-Day Present for 1853*. Philadelphia: Henry F. Anners, [1852]. 13–31.

———. *Stories for Summer Days and Winter Nights*. Philadelphia: Henry F. Anners, 1853. 5–23.

Stories for Adelaide: Being a Second Series of Easy Reading Lessons, With Divided Syllables. Philadelphia: Thomas T. Ash, 1829. ["The Fawn,"

"The Monkey," "The Sun-Bonnet," "The Mischievous Boy," "The Pet Calf," "The Listener," "The Four Little Dogs," "The Young Cheat," and "The Cranberry Tarts."] *Stories for Adelaide: A Second Book for Her Little Friends.* Philadelphia: W. P. Hazard, 1856. [Selections collected in *Miss Leslie's Nursery Stories* (1830, 1848).]

Stories for Emma: Being a Series of Easy Reading Lessons, With the Syllables Divided. Boston: Munroe and Francis, 1829. ["Emily Ross," "Francis Williams," "George Wilcox," "Ellen Martin," "Gilbert Watson," "Catherine Harris," "Richard Manning," "Helen Wallis," "Adeline Woodley," "Rosa Dennison," "Lewis Jennings," "Laura Darwin," "Edward and William Jones," "Edith and Lucy Fenwick," "Felix Harvey," "Sophia Stanley," "Eleanor Weston," "Peter Warren," "Jane Somers," "Louisa Thomson," "Mary Bradstone," "Charlotte Murray," "Caroline Gordon," and "Matilda Morgan."]

Stories for Helen. Philadelphia: H. F. Anners, 1845. ["The Tell-Tale," "The Boarding School Feast," "The Week of Idleness," and "Madeline Malcolm."]

Stories for Summer Days and Winter Nights. Philadelphia: Henry F. Anners, [1853]. ["The Souvenir," "The Cadet's Sister," "Susanna Meredith, or The Village School," "The Launch of the Frigate," "The Show Girl," "The Clean Face, or The Boy Washed by His Elder Sister," and "Frederick Ormsby."]

"Susanna Meredith." *The Pearl, or Affection's Gift: A Christmas and New-Year's Present for 1833.* Philadelphia: Thomas T. Ash, [1832]. 180–211.

———. *Stories for Summer Days and Winter Nights.* Philadelphia: Henry F. Anners, 1853. 50–85.

"The Tell Tale." *Atlantic Tales, or Pictures of Youth.* Boston: Munroe and Francis, 1833; 2nd ed., 1835.

———. *The Tell Tale, and The Week of Idleness.* London: Dean and Munday, 1838, 1840.

———. *Stories for Helen.* Philadelphia: H. F. Anners, 1845. 5–27.

"The Tenth Passenger: A Sketch." *Godey's Lady's Book, and Ladies' American Magazine* (Jun. 1842): 318–26.

———. *Kitty's Relations and Other Pencil Sketches.* Philadelphia: Carey and Hart, 1847. 85–97.

"That Gentleman, or Pencillings on Ship-Board." *The Saturday Evening Post*, June 6, 1835, 1.

———. *Atkinson's Casket, or Gems of Literature, Wit, and Sentiment* (Jul. 1835): 362–70.

———. *Pencil Sketches, or Outlines of Character and Manners.* 3rd series. Philadelphia: Carey, Lea, and Blanchard, 1837. 160–92.

———. *Pencil Sketches, or Outlines of Character and Manners.* Philadelphia: A. Hart, 1852. 333–57.

"Timothy Pettigrew's Wife's Husband: A Sketch." *Godey's Lady's Book* (Feb. 1849): 112–19; (Mar. 1849): 169–76; (Apr. 1849): 269–76.

"The Travelling Tin-Man: An American Story." *The Juvenile Forget-Me-Not: A Christmas and New Year's Gift, or Birthday Present; For the Year 1831.* Edited by S. C. Hall. London: F. Westley and A. H. Davis [1830]. 51–77.

———. *Atkinson's Casket, or Gems of Literature, Wit, and Sentiment.* (Mar. 1831): 123–28.

———. *Pencil Sketches, or Outlines of Character and Manners.* 1st series. Philadelphia: Carey, Lea, and Blanchard, 1833. 145–61.

———. *Edmands's Lilliputian Quarto.* Vol 2. Boston: B. Franklin Edmands [1845]. [7]–64.

———. *Americans at Home, or Byeways, Backwoods, and Prairies.* Edited by the Author of "Sam Slick." London: Hurst and Blackett, 1854. 135–61.

———. *A Treasury of New Favourite Tales for Young People.* Edited by Mary Howitt. Illustrated by Palmer and Coleman. London: James Hogg and Sons, 1861. 177–93.

———. *My First Cruise.* Edited by William Henry Giles. London: Cassell, Petter, and Galphin, 1866, 1868.

———. *The Little Trapper and Other Stories.* Edited by W. Heard Hillyard. Philadelphia: J. E. Potter, 1866, 1867, 1868.

"The Two Weddings: A Sketch." *Godey's Lady's Book* (Jan. 1849): 53–60.

———. *New Monthly Belle Assemblée: A Magazine of Literature and Fashion, Under the Immediate Patronage of Her Royal Highness the Duchess of Kent* (Jan.-Jun. 1851): 43–48.

"Uncle Philip." *Pencil Sketches, or Outlines of Character and Manners.* 1st series. Philadelphia: Carey, Lea, and Blanchard, 1833. 207–66.

———. *Godey's Magazine and Lady's Book* (Jul. 1847): 37–44; (Aug. 1847): 77–83; (Sep. 1847): 110–19.

———. *Pencil Sketches, or Outlines of Character and Manners.* Philadelphia: A. Hart, 1852. 82–130.

The Violet: A Christmas and New-Year's Gift, or Birth-Day Present, 1837. Philadelphia: E. L. Carey and A. Hart, 1836. ["Introductory Dialogue," "The Phials (from the French)," "Emma and Her Brothers," "The Dove (from the French)," and "Viola."]

The Violet: A Christmas and New-Year's Gift, or Birth-Day Present, 1839. Philadelphia: E. L. Carey and A. Hart, [1838]. ["Snow-Balling, or, The Christmas Dollar," "The New-Year's Gifts," and "Lauretta's Fawn."]

The Violet: A Christmas and New-Year's Gift, or Birth-Day Present, 1840. Philadelphia: E. L. Carey and A. Hart, [1839]. ["Dick Davis."]

"The Watkinson Evening." *Godey's Magazine and Lady's Book*, December 1, 1846, 265–72.

———. *The Best American Humorous Short Stories.* Edited by Alexander Jessup. New York: Modern Library, 1920. 34–51.

"The Week of Idleness." *Atlantic Tales, or Pictures of Youth.* Boston: Munroe and Francis, 1833; 2nd ed., 1835.

———. *The Tell Tale, and The Week of Idleness.* London: Dean and Munday, 1838 and 1840.

———. *Stories for Helen.* Philadelphia: H. F. Anners, 1845. 67–97.

"Western New York: A Slight Sketch." *Godey's Magazine and Lady's Book*, November 1, 1845, 185–91.

"William Wells." *The Juvenile Forget-Me-Not: A Christmas and New Year's Present.* Philadelphia: Henry F. Anners, 1850.

Wonderful Travels: Being the Narratives of Munchausen, Gulliver, and Sinbad. Boston: Munroe and Francis, 1832. ["Travels of Baron Munchausen," "Gulliver's Voyage to Lilliput," "Gulliver's Voyage or Brobdignag," and "The Seven Voyages of Sinbad the Sailor."]

The Young Americans, or Sketches of a Sea-Voyage, and a Short Visit to Europe. Boston: Munroe and Francis, 1829.

The Young Ladies' Mentor, or Extracts In Prose And Verse For The Promotion Of Virtue and Morality. Philadelphia: Jacob Johnson, Thomas, and Manning, 1803.

The Young Revolutionists: Containing the Stories of Russel and Sidney and Chase Loring; Tales of the American Revolution. New York: C. S. Francis, 1846; 2nd ed., Philadelphia: W. P. Hazard, 1853.

In the Legacies of Nineteenth-Century American Women Writers series

The Hermaphrodite
By Julia Ward Howe
Edited and with an introduction by Gary Williams

In the "Stranger People's" Country
By Mary Noailles Murfree
Edited and with an introduction by Marjorie Pryse

Two Men
By Elizabeth Stoddard
Edited and with an introduction by Jennifer Putzi

Emily Hamilton and Other Writings
By Sukey Vickery
Edited and with an introduction by Scott Slawinski

Nature's Aristocracy: A Plea for the Oppressed
By Jennie Collins
Edited and with an introduction by Judith A. Ranta

Selected Writings of Victoria Woodhull: Suffrage, Free Love, and Eugenics
By Victoria C. Woodhull
Edited and with an introduction by Cari Carpenter

Christine: Or Woman's Trials and Triumphs
By Laura Curtis Bullard
Edited and with an introduction by Denise M. Kohn

Observations on the Real Rights of Women and Other Writings
By Hannah Mather Crocker
Edited and with an introduction by Constance J. Post

Selections from Eliza Leslie
Eliza Leslie
Edited and with an introduction by Etta M. Madden

To order or obtain more information on these or other University of Nebraska Press titles, visit www.nebraskapress.unl.edu.

www.ingramcontent.com/pod-product-compliance
Lightning Source LLC
Chambersburg PA
CBHW031933110726
47902CB00001B/152

* 9 7 8 0 8 0 3 2 3 2 9 5 2 *